Homoerotic
Narrative
in the
Literature
of Ancient
Israel

JACOB'S WOUND

Theodore W. Jennings Jr.

continuum

NEW YORK • LONDON

Unless otherwise indicated, Scripture quotations are from the New Revised Standard Version of the Bible, copyright 1989 by the Division of Christian Education of the National Council of the Churches of Christ in the USA; used by permission; all rights reserved. Quotations marked KJV are from the King James Version; NASB, from the New American Standard Bible; NIV, from the New International Version; RSV, from the Revised Standard Version; LXX, from the Septuagint, a Greek text of the OT; MT, from the Masoretic Text of the Hebrew Bible.

T & T Clark International
Madison Square Park, 15 East 26th Street, New York, NY 10010

T & T Clark International
The Tower Building, 11 York Road, London SE1 7NX

T & T Clark International is a Continuum imprint.

Cover art: *Jacob and the Angel*, by Jacob Epstein, courtesy of Tate Gallery, London/Art Resource, New York.

Cover and interior design by Corey Kent

Library of Congress Cataloging-in-Publication Data

Jennings, Theodore W.
    Jacob's wound : homoerotic narrative in the literature of ancient Israel / Theodore W. Jennings Jr.
        p. cm.
    Includes bibliographical references and index.
    ISBN 0-8264-1712-4 (pbk.)
    1. Homosexuality in the Bible. 2. Bible. O.T.—Gay interpretations. I. Title.
    BS1186.5.J46 2005
    221.6'086'64—dc22
                                            2004029022

Printed in the United States of America

05 06 07 08 09 10   10 9 8 7 6 5 4 3 2 1

FOR THE FACULTY
of the Chicago Theological Seminary,
in grateful appreciation
for their learning, their commitment, and their friendship

Contents

Preface

THE LAD IN THE HOSPITAL seemed to know that he was dying of what had only recently been identified as AIDS. And to the ailments that wracked his slender body was added the terrible fear that God hated him because he was gay—a fear provoked by the way the Bible had been used as a club to batter people into submission to reigning cultural values. He was the first of many whom I would know in that condition in California in the late 1980s. Beyond the proverbial cup of cold water, there was nothing I could do to relieve his physical suffering. But I determined that I would do what I could to relieve the wholly unwarranted spiritual agony that afflicted him and so many others. From that encounter grew the seeds of the wider project of which this volume is a portion. The Bible seemed to me to be too wonderful and important a treasure for it to be used as a weapon of mass destruction against the vulnerable and defenseless.

When I returned to Chicago Theological Seminary in 1991 as a professor of theology, I also began to develop seminars in the area of gay studies with the support of my colleagues. When the young man who had accompanied us to Chicago also died of AIDS, the faculty and trustees began a scholarship fund in his honor. Since then, several more colleagues who share the commitment to antihomophobic labor have joined me. Of the faculty members who have joined in this work, I am especially indebted to my colleague Ken Stone, whose vast knowledge of biblical scholarship and of queer studies has been generously deployed in careful, critical, and insightful reading of my attempts to make fresh sense of the Hebrew Bible. A portion of this text was earlier published in his book *Queer Commentary and the Hebrew Bible* (Sheffield Academic Press, 2001), and I am grateful for permission to use some of that material here.

I extend thanks to the students who have participated over the years in seminars on homosexuality and hermeneutics, whose questions and concerns have been a constant provocation to greater clarity and intellectual daring. Wil Brant and Kunitoshi Sakai have not only been students in some of my seminars; they have also served as research assistants, without whose work my own labors would have been considerably less fruitful.

I am particularly grateful to Henry Carrington of Continuum, who has shown such great interest in and support for this project, and to all those at Continuum who have had a hand in the production of this book. Ryan Masteller has kept this project moving with remarkable efficiency. The copyeditor, David Garber, has been extraordinarily attentive both to the manuscript and to the Bible. This is a better book because of his herculean labor.

In spite of the controversy stirred by my earlier work in rereading the Bible from a gay-affirmative perspective, the faculty, students, administration, and trustees have been unflinching in their support of the freedom of academic inquiry and of our shared commitments to justice and mercy. It is an honor to be a part of such a community.

Introduction

EVERYONE WHO HAS ATTEMPTED TO READ the Old Testament (OT) or Hebrew Bible (MT) knows that its stories are filled with an unabashed eroticism. This is especially evident to those who undertake in adolescence to read straight through the Bible, or at least its stories. Nor has this been lost on the dream merchants of Hollywood, who have cranked out endless epics on David and Bathsheba or Samson and Delilah, although other tales from the Hebrew Bible appear to be too much even for Hollywood. The tales of women who use sex to get what they need from men—Tamar and Judah, Ruth and Boaz, Rahab and the Hebrew spies, or Esther—may still be too subversive for popular culture. And tales of incest between father and daughter (Lot) or brother and sister (Amnon and Tamar) are even more "controversial." Even tales of adultery popularized by Hollywood are too much for many people who prefer to remain ignorant about practices of polygamy and concubinage and even the romanticism of the Song of Songs. Nevertheless, even the more or less casual reader of the Scriptures of Israel should know that these texts are replete with frank and multiple accounts of the place of eroticism in human life. What has been virtually missing from this recognition of the eroticism of Hebrew narrative, however, is an engagement with the homoerotic elements of these sagas.

The very suggestion that there may be homoeroticism in Hebrew narrative, in the OT, may seem odd, given the all too common supposition that the religion and culture of ancient Israel resolutely opposed same-sex relationships of an erotic nature. This is due to the way in which the apparent prohibition of homosexuality in Leviticus and the story of Sodom from Genesis have been made to speak for the whole Hebrew Bible. The oddity of this situation has not been lost on some interpreters who have recognized that the story of Sodom tells us no more about attitudes toward what we call homosexuality than the story of the rape of Dinah tells us about attitudes toward heterosexuality. They also see that the legal codes of Israel contain a number of elements that homophobic interpreters have no intention of applying to themselves, such as not mixing types of cloth in the same outfit, or canceling all debts every fifty years.

This book, however, does not begin by trying to deal with these dubious texts. For too long they have occupied center stage in the debate about what the Bible says about homosexuality. This is a dreary debate that is largely beside the point.

It is beside the point because a focus on these well-chewed scraps has diverted attention from what I suggest is a whole feast of homoerotic material in the Hebrew Bible. That is, I show that the well-known eroticism of the Hebrew Bible is not confined to heterosexuality but also includes an astonishing diversity of material that lends itself to homoerotic interpretation.

There is nothing in this that should be too surprising. Homoeroticism is ubiquitous in human cultural experience. Hence, a library of texts as frank about human eroticism as the OT might be expected to offer a full range of sexually suggestive material—if it were not for the prejudice that nothing of the kind could be here since we all know, without having read or considered, that this should be impossible for a culture presumed to be homophobic.

The supposition that Hebrew Bible texts are uniformly opposed to same-sex sexual practice, and indeed express a horror of this as "abomination," has been justification for the supposition that it is homophobic. To this has been added the supposition that the OT, whatever its deviations from Victorian morality, nevertheless uniformly promotes heterosexuality (heteronormativity). So commonplace have these assumptions become that they are regularly asserted without argument both by homophobic readers and by those who seek to develop a counterhomophobic or "gay-affirmative" stance. Whether from the side of the religious right or from that of "gay rights," the uniform chorus is that the Bible, especially the Hebrew

Bible, promotes heterosexuality and is aghast at the very possibility of homosexuality. If, instead of simply assuming this to be true, we suspend this pre-
supposition and inquire of the texts what might appear if we looked at them
with fresh eyes, then new possibilities of reading and interpreting emerge.

Because the presumption of heteronormativity has been so universal in
the reading of the Hebrew Bible, my own reading has the character of
attempting to construct what Mieke Bal calls a countercoherence.[1] Though
she develops this idea of countercoherence in connection with a feminist
project of rereading biblical narrative, especially the book of Judges, I do this
in connection with a queer[2] perspective, one that seeks for traces of homoeroticism in the narrative. I acknowledge that the sorts of readings I undertake are the result of an engagement with the text, an interrogation of the
text, collaboration with the text. What "appears" through this reading is
importantly determined by the questions I ask, the interests I bring, the passion of my own interest in contesting homophobia and heteronormativity.
Without this passion the texts could not respond as they do. This would be
true of any reading of texts. Whether we are reading them with questions
about a doctrine of God or for evidence of liturgical practices, the questions
we bring to the text help to shape what we discover. In this sense there is no
purely objective or disinterested reading.

Yet it is not the case that I imagine I have simply imposed this perspective on the text in such a way as to render the text a mute object or a blank
slate upon which to project my own concerns and interests. I do try to
attend to the texts as closely as possible. This often means that I examine
elements of the text that from a different perspective are merely puzzling.
Why does Saul accuse Jonathan of uncovering his own mother's nakedness?
Why is Michal (David's wife) so enraged by David's dance? Why do boy-
companions so often accompany warriors? Why does the lad sneeze when
Elijah stretches out on his body? Why does Saul fall into a naked swoon
when he comes into contact with Samuel's dancing associates? Why is
Joseph dressed in a girl's outfit? Why do prophets talk about Israel, and
Judah, as if he (or they) were female? Why is YHWH[3] sometimes repre-
sented by an ephod? These are only a few of the questions that many
commentators find merely puzzling, yet are, I hope, accounted for by the

---

1. Mieke Bal, *Death and Dissymmetry: The Politics of Coherence in the Book of Judges* (Chicago: University of
Chicago Press, 1988).

2. In contemporary parlance the term "queer" serves to designate multiple sexualities, practices, and identities that diverge from the norm of conventional heterosexuality. Thus it includes lesbian, gay, transgendered, and
bisexual perspectives and practices.

3. Throughout this book I alternate between "YHWH" and "Adonai" as ways of designating the divine character in the narrative. I choose not to pronounce YHWH as "Yahweh" in order to honor the Jewish convention
of not pronouncing tetragrammaton.

homoerotic interpretations that I offer here, interpretations that are curious about and attentive to traces of homoeroticism in the text or between the lines of the text.

At the same time, I hope that the interpretations of the narratives and narrative-like texts that I propose do not ignore important aspects of the narratives. That is, I also argue that the countercoherence produced by this reading is actually more coherent than that generated by readings simply supposing that Israel's literature is without homoerotic elements or aspects. Some of the readings here proposed may seem quirky (somewhat queer) in the sense that they are different from what one has been led to expect from these texts. Nevertheless, they do not depend on amputating elements of the texts in order to make them fit some procrustean bed of preconceived ideology or theology.

What this reading strategy does ask of the reader, however, is to set aside preconceived notions about the Hebrew Bible, especially its presumed homophobia, and to look with different eyes at the material, to engage it with different questions.

In this process an indispensable help may be found in the advances in what was called gay and lesbian studies and is now more often called queer studies. One of the most important results of these still nascent approaches is the way they help us to see in diverse cultures and eras a multiplicity of constructions of same-sex desire and practice. Historical retrievals of what has been "hidden from history" as well as studies of other contemporary cultures have enabled us to begin to glimpse the astonishing variety of ways in which sexual desire and practice are organized, institutionalized, and so on. Indeed, so varied are these that the very categories of homosexuality or heterosexuality are called into question because these categories seem to suppose that there is some underlying essential homosexuality that is variously expressed or suppressed. It is increasingly likely that there is rather a multiplicity of relationships and practices that may come together to form, for example, modern Western homosexuality, or something like classical Greek pederasty, or a variety of other possible patterns, institutions, and so on. The "unity" of some set of practices is, therefore, at least partially a product of the sort of questions we ask or the interests we bring to the study. What is most important for the purposes of this study is the contribution of these (historical, anthropological, literary) approaches to the study of sexual practices in enabling us to be more attentive to traces of same-sex desire and practice even when these are detected in cultures far different from our own.

This attentiveness to multiplicity in the possible forms of articulation of same-sex desire and practice comes to expression in this study through the identification of three main styles of same-sex relationships that are explored in these pages.[4] None of these is identical with or even closely parallel to what in our culture is generally assumed about "homosexuality." Nor are they identical to the institutions of pederasty as these are becoming clearer to us from the study of Greek or even Roman antiquity. Nevertheless, they are forms of same-sex relationships that have cognates in the field of queer studies.

In part 1, I examine saga materials associated with David. It is no innovation to detect, at least in the relationship between David and Jonathan, the outline of a remarkable love story between two men. What becomes clear, however, is that the tale is far more complex than this: it also involves Saul and is set within a context of a warrior society, which takes for granted that male heroes are accompanied by younger or lower-status males. Thus, the complex erotic connections between David and Saul and David and Jonathan play out against the backdrop of a representation of what Halperin called "heroes and their pals." This pattern is recognizable as a context for same-sex erotic attachment and practice.

The second type of same-sex relationship explored here is both more diffuse and less direct in terms of evidence or trace. It has to do with what may be called a shamanistic form of eroticism, in which the sacral power of the holy man is also both a product of same-sex relationship and expressed through same-sex practice. Here I deal not only with Samuel and Saul but also with Elijah and Elisha, as well as the rather controversial groups known as the *bene-hanebi'im* (sons of the prophets) and the *qedeshim* (sometimes called "temple/cultic prostitutes"). These are not warriors but persons whose sacral power is also erotic power that may find expression in erotic practices with persons of the same sex.

The third type explored here has to do with what we now call transgendered persons, especially males, and their erotic relationships to (other) males. Here I explore first the transgendering of Israel by several of the prophets who use this device to explore the adultery and promiscuity that they attribute to Israel. But following the lead of this interpretive framework, I also explore the story of Joseph.

---

4. In attending to multiple forms of male same-sex practices and relationships, none of which may be readily identified with contemporary urban gay male identities, I hope to avoid some of the pitfalls in the "history of homosexuality" indicated by David M. Halperin in *How to Do the History of Homosexuality* (Chicago: University of Chicago Press, 2002), 104–37.

In addition to seeking to identify these three types of same-sex eroticism
in the Hebrew Bible, I also explore the way in which each of these implicates the character of Israel's divinity in the same-sex relationships. Some
years ago H. Eilberg-Schwartz suggested that the relationship between a
male divinity and his male admirers or devotees was fraught with homoerotic overtones.[5] He used a Freudian template in which the latent or
suppressed homoeroticism of the relationship of the (young) male to his
father served as an interpretive framework. In this way Eilberg-Schwartz
explored indications of the fascination with the divine "phallus" inscribed
in the texts of the Hebrew Bible, most particularly in the relationship
between Moses and YHWH (following up on Freud's privileging of this
relationship in *Moses and Monotheism*).[6]

The approach I use here, while indebted to Eilberg-Schwartz for his
provocative general thesis, is not governed by a Freudian perspective, nor
does it deal with the intriguing aspects of the relationship between YHWH
and Moses. Instead of a Freudian perspective, I make more use of cross-
cultural and historical investigations that have emerged in gay and queer
studies. Save for some of the material in part 3, I deal with narratives that are
not touched on by Eilberg-Schwartz. Yet despite these differences, I do find
that homoeroticism in Hebrew narrative is heavily determined by the role
of YHWH in these narratives.

Thus, in the case of the warrior love explored in part 1, the primary
warrior and the one whose erotic attachments and exploits are most in
view is precisely the character whose name is, variously, YHWH or Adonai.
Indeed, it is precisely by trying to see what is going on between David and
his mortal lovers in connection with what is going on between David
and his divine lover that both are importantly illuminated. Of course,
here as in subsequent readings I am not talking about "God" as such but
about a character in the narrative. This character is depicted as an unpredictable and dangerous warrior and as involved with human companions in
a variety of ways, including erotic ways (just as the human characters are
related to one another in a variety of ways, including erotic ways).

In the second type that I discuss, this relationship to a divine erotic force
is brought to expression in the way of designating the type: YHWH's male
groupies. For what they have in common is the way they may be understood
as possessed by and as transmitting in some way the divine erotic potency.

In the third type it is YHWH himself who is represented as the one
who transgenders Israel and who violently accuses this male of sexual

5. H. Eilberg-Schwartz, *God's Phallus and Other Problems for Men and Monotheism* (Boston: Beacon, 1994).
6. S. Freud, *Moses and Monotheism* (trans. K. Jones; New York: Knopf, 1939).

unfaithfulness, threatens and permits extreme punishment, and seeks to woo this male (dressed in metaphorical drag) back into faithful relationship. In the sagas of Israel, I suggest that Israel himself may be the one who transvests, and perhaps transgenders, Joseph, and that this story may also illumine something of the way in which transgendering could be understood as a way of representing Israel's experience as a client-state of imperial societies.

Thus, in each of these types of same-sex relationship/practice, I attempt to attend to the complex interplay between human characters and the divine character who comes to expression alongside them.

One of the things that becomes clear through this process is that the prohibition of certain forms of male same-sex relationships and/or practices in Leviticus is anomalous relative to the rather frank portrayal of these dynamics in the narrative materials of the Hebrew Bible. It is also clear that the prohibition may in part be explained not only by the variety of ways in which same-sex practices are found in Israel's literature, but also and more particularly by the way in which homoeroticism is at work in the relationship to Israel's God.

Although this study is indebted to forms of reading that have been pioneered by feminist scholars, it concentrates on relations among males. To a large degree this is a consequence both of the androcentric character of many of these narratives and of the interest in seeing how the relationship between a male divinity and his male adherents affects the forms of homoeroticism treated here. However, I also argue that something like a homoerotic relationship finds one of its clearest expressions in the story of Ruth and Naomi, and that there are other traces of female homoeroticism in these texts. I hope that those with keener eyes than mine will further explore these texts with those concerns in mind.

❝❝❝❝❝❝❝ PART ONE

The Love of Heroes

IN THE FIRST PART of this study, we turn primarily to the sagas that recount the heroic exploits of David. It is here that we first encounter a form of homoeroticism that plays an important role in the literature of Israel. Earlier scholars and readers of the Bible have noticed the homo-erotic character of the relationship between David and Jonathan. In this study we widen this focus to include a number of other relationships featured in this narrative. In the course of doing so, we find that the relationship between David and Jonathan is but an example of a wider phenomenon in these stories, all of which bear traces of the importance of homoerotic attachment among their male characters.

In the first chapter I investigate the narrative frame-work within which these relationships are played out. It is the framework of heroes and their boy-companions. This sort of relationship is seen to be characteristic of the tale of heroes that we encounter here. At this level there is nothing that seems to compel an erotic interpretation of these relationships. Whether readers sense the erotic potential of young men with younger companions in adventure largely depends on how they understand or experience similar situations in their own or other peoples' cultures. In this connection we also encounter the narrative character of YHWH and see that he too has younger male companions and that these seem to be selected to a significant degree on account of their notable beauty. A consideration of what we learn from YHWH's selection of his own "armor-bearers" sheds important light on the social phenomenon that the narrative suggests for other characters.

Against this backdrop we turn to a consideration of the men who loved David and the tangle of conflicting loyalties that this provokes. Here we'll attend not only to David's relationship with Jonathan but also to his relationship with Saul, who had first chosen David to be his armor-bearer. As we examine both of these relationships, the erotic character comes more into focus.

In chapter 3 we turn to the relationship between David and YHWH to see how strong currents of erotic attachment propel this relationship. Here we see that David's apprenticeship in being the beloved of older and more powerful males serves to illumine crucial features of his relationship to YHWH. It is therefore in this connection that we explore the erotic potency of YHWH as the primary character in these sagas.

In chapter 4 we consider what it might mean to see YHWH as a male lover of human males. This inevitably raises questions about how this picture of Israel's divinity relates to the depictions of the gods of the Greeks as interested in erotic adventures with young human males. But it also raises a number of questions about the role of eroticism in faith, and especially the role that homoeroticism may play in the formation of biblical faith.

1. Warrior Love

I BEGIN WITH SOME REMARKS about the cultural ambience of the saga concerning David. In general, it appears to be a saga written for men. It is a story for warriors and, especially, leaders of warriors. The male world is preeminently a world of battle and of court intrigue among warriors. In these stories of men constantly on the march, in a raid or skirmish, or at camp, women seldom appear.[1] Instead, the men, especially the dominant war leaders, always appear with their youthful boy-companions. One of the characteristic features of the culture of this warrior elite of Israel, especially as depicted in 1 Samuel, is that the primary companions of adult and young-adult warriors are younger or lower-status males. A quick review of the evidence demonstrates that this pairing of heroes with boy-companions is a significant feature of this saga material.

Heroes and Their Youthful Companions

Saul is presented to us initially as "a handsome young man" (1 Sam 9:2).[2] When we come to actually hear about this young man, he is accompanied

---

1. In 1 Sam 21:5 the absence of women in stories of men at war is made explicit: David avows that "women have been kept from us as always when I go on an expedition." Texts that indicate similar but by no means identical considerations include Deut 24:5 and 2 Sam 11:11.

2. Unless otherwise specified or altered for emphasis, quotations are from the NRSV.

3

by a youth with whom he goes in search of his father's donkeys. The adventures of Saul and the youth lead to Saul's encounter with the venerable Samuel, who will make him king of Israel. The handsome young man and his younger companion in adventure serve as a relational paradigm that will be played out in a variety of relationships. Examples include those between Jonathan and his armor-bearer, between Saul and David (who becomes Saul's armor-bearer), between David and Jonathan (David will briefly appear also as Jonathan's choice for armor-bearer). In all cases the hero is accompanied or partnered by a younger male companion.

In the first instance (the case of Saul and his youth) we seem to be dealing with a relationship between older and younger adolescents. Saul is sent by his father to take one of the "boys" or "lads" with him to find strayed donkeys (9:3). It is of some interest that we are several times reminded of the presence of the younger companion in the course of this journey (9:5, 7, 8, 22, 27; 10:14). The lad only disappears from the story with the coronation of Saul.

Indeed, we may say that the lad serves the pivotal function in the story. For it is the boy who persuades Saul to inquire of the seer (who turns out to be Samuel) concerning the location of the donkeys and overcomes the difficulty in this encounter by producing the coin with which they approach the seer for advice (9:8). In spite of this, Samuel (and later Saul) exclude the lad from knowledge of Saul's royal destiny. In becoming king, Saul puts away his first youthful companion.

In this first episode Saul is not a warrior. Thus, his young companion is not an armor-bearer but one of the cowboys, or donkey-boys, from the modest "ranch" of Saul's father, Kish. He is certainly no mute slave, but a true companion who manages to find a way to rescue the enterprise from failure and so to save the reputation of his older, handsome companion.

Almost immediately we are introduced to Jonathan. In the meantime Saul has defeated the Ammonites (11:11). Subsequently, Jonathan will fight the battles. The first of these encounters is the battle at the pass of Michmash (ch. 14).

Here we are introduced to Jonathan and the "young man who carried his armor" (14:1). It is clear from the narrative that the armor-bearer is not simply a servant but a companion in the battle (14:6–7, 12–14). Between them they manage to kill about twenty Philistines of the garrison, provoking a general panic. Taking advantage of the panic (although acting with extraordinary caution), Saul finally commits his men to the battle. "So the LORD gave Israel the victory that day" (14:23).

It is clear that Jonathan, like his father before him, has a young comrade with whom he undertakes the adventure that earns him praise. Because now we have to do with the adventures of warriors, the comrade is no longer a donkey-herder but an armor-bearer. Yet the structure is similar. In both cases we have an apparently younger companion of somewhat lower status who nevertheless is a full partner in the adventures of the hero and who shares in the remembered glory of the hero. If the companion were only incidental either to the action or to the hero, we would expect subsequent retelling to have erased the companion from memory. That this has not occurred suggests that the companion is a necessary part of the saga. Under what conditions might this be so? Certainly, a pattern is emerging in which it is expected that the youthful hero be accompanied by a faithful sidekick who, while younger and of lesser status, is nevertheless essential to the story. The social context within which these stories of heroic adventure are told seems to require this form of homosociality.

Subsequently, in a section of the story we will consider again, David is chosen, at least in part for his beauty, to be Saul's boy-companion and armor-bearer (16:21–22). Even after David and Jonathan become friends, Jonathan is accompanied by a boy-companion (ch. 20). In the final battle Saul, who has lost David as his boy-companion, has with him another armor-bearer, who refuses to help the king commit suicide when the latter is desperately wounded. But when Saul performs the deed for himself, the armor-bearer does, in grief, fall upon his own sword (31:3–6; 1 Chron 10:4–5). Indeed, this story echoes the first appearance of an armor-bearer in the saga material, in Judg 9 in the account of Abimelech's death. The relation most closely parallels that of Saul and his last armor-bearer, for Abimelech also begs his armor-bearer to slay him lest he die of the mortal blow caused by a woman crushing his skull with a millstone. The "young man who carried his armor" in that case does comply with the last wish of his war-chief hero (9:54).

If a youthful companion regularly accompanies the warrior-hero, we should observe that it is only of David that we never hear that he has taken such a young companion for himself.

Are we to read this saga as entailing an erotic attachment between the heroes and their younger male companions? The saga itself does not directly speak of this. In order to flesh this out, we would have to ask whether homosocial relationships between older and younger adolescents engaged in adventure may be thought to have an erotic and even an overtly sexual component. Here the answer we give would depend on at least two factors.

The first has to do with what we suppose to be the case between older and younger adolescent male adventurers where women are absent. This may depend on one's particular view of psychodynamics. Do we regard such relationships to be characterized by an erotic component? And do we suppose that such relationships may include sexual practice?

In this latter connection another consideration comes into play: the cultural expectations or potentialities with respect to such relationships. Certainly, we know of cultures within which it would be expected as a matter of course that such a relationship should find sexual expression. We also know of cultures in which sexual practice under such circumstances while not infrequent would be nevertheless interdicted. To which cultural sphere does the story of Saul, Jonathan, and David correspond?

To a certain extent the answer one gives will depend upon the experience of the reader. Those who have had sexual experience under such circumstances or who are familiar with persons or cultures that take such experience for granted will be inclined to read the story as inclusive of sexual potentiality. Those inclined to regard this as unthinkable will not notice the possibilities of such a reading or will even be outraged by its suggestion.

In my view there is nothing in the heroic saga material of Israel (Judges–2 Samuel) that precludes erotic or even sexual readings. It appears to me that a rather matter-of-fact attitude toward this would be most likely. If there were anxiety about this, it would scarcely be necessary to outfit Saul with such a companion or to give the lad such an important role.

The stories we have thus far considered do not thematize the emotional attachment between the hero and his companion. They merely exhibit a structure that appears to have similarities to relational structures among young warriors, which are familiar from other societies, many of which accept and expect the relationship to find sexual expression.

Is that what is happening here? We cannot say for sure without a detailed consideration of the relationships that are foregrounded in the narrative; those between David and his lovers: Saul, Jonathan, and YHWH. Before we turn to that consideration, however, we need to look at additional evidence in the text for the relationship between warriors and their companions. This will come from a consideration of the relation of YHWH to his "armor-bearers" or lower-status companions.

YHWH as War Chief

We may gain further clarity about the conventions that govern the relationship between warriors and their youthful companions by attending to the way in which YHWH is characterized in the saga.

Within this context YHWH is the preeminent warrior-chieftain. The entire saga depends on the way in which YHWH is being displaced as the immediate warrior-chief of Israel through the demand of the people for a "king," for a war leader who has the characteristics of the leaders of other nations (1 Sam 8:7). Indeed, YHWH himself interprets the desire of the Israelites for a warrior-chief (king) to be a rejection of himself as their warrior-chief: "They have rejected me from being king over them" (8:7). The writer and reader/hearer of this saga regard YHWH as acting in accordance with the warrior code. Thus, he is often harsh, insisting on blind obedience and utter loyalty, capricious, capable of apparent pettiness and clever strategy.

How does this warrior-chieftain choose his youthful companions? In fact, the structure of the saga depends on the choices that *this* warrior-chief makes concerning who will be his youthful companion and armor-carrier. He chooses two. First is Saul, and then, when Saul has displeased him, he chooses David. Insofar as we can discern the motive for the choices, it is the astonishing physical beauty of the young men. This is always the first characteristic mentioned in the text. Thus, when we are first introduced to Saul, we are told:

> There was a man of Benjamin. . . . He had a son whose name was Saul, a handsome young man. There was not a man among the people of Israel more handsome than he; he stood head and shoulders above everyone else. (9:1–2)

Saul thus has two related qualifications: his beauty and his imposing height.

The remarking upon the beauty of a male protagonist is something found in biblical literature only in two places outside the saga of David. The first is in the story of Joseph, where it serves as the explanation of Potiphar's wife's infatuation with Joseph:

> Now Joseph was handsome and good-looking. And after a time his master's wife cast her eyes on Joseph and said, "Lie with me." (Gen 39:6–7)

The story of the attempted seduction occupies the entire chapter, results in Joseph's being imprisoned, and leads to the interpretation of dreams, which launches Joseph's career and thus is the hinge of the entire saga.

The only other text, apart from the David saga, in which male beauty is remarked upon in a protagonist is in the erotic poems of the Song of Songs. Hence, the presentation of male beauty is offered to the eroticizing gaze. In two instances outside the David saga, this gaze is the gaze of women, but in the David saga it is the gaze of (male) warrior-chieftains (YHWH, Saul, and Jonathan).[3]

In the selection of David to replace Saul, seven sons of Jesse pass before Samuel. None of them is appropriate to YHWH, however, who disregards the height of Eliab (the height of Saul had apparently played a role in his earlier selection). YHWH claims that he does not look on outward appearances but at the heart (will) of the person (1 Sam 16:7). However, when the last of Jesse's sons comes into the room, we are told:

> Now he was ruddy, and had beautiful eyes, and was handsome. The LORD said [to Samuel], "Rise and anoint him; for this is the one." (16:12)

Thus, the selection of David as the boy-companion of the main warrior-chief, while it departs from the standards of beauty set by Saul, appears nonetheless to begin with his remarkable beauty.[4] The choice is never made on the basis of prior prowess. The first thing we know about Saul and David is their beauty. Hence, this certainly tells us that the hearers/readers of this saga expect male beauty to be the initial criterion for the selection of youthful companions. To be sure, other attributes are expected to follow: both Saul and David demonstrate bravery and boldness, as does Jonathan's anonymous boy-companion. Absolute loyalty appears also to be essential, and we see how this is depicted in the apparent trustworthiness of Jonathan's companion in his assignations with David or in the final loyalty of Saul's last armor-bearer. This loyalty comes to most dramatic expression in the steadfast refusal of David to harm the man whose boy-companion he had once been, even when Saul tries by every available means to kill David.[5]

---

3. Indirect evidence for this relationship between male beauty and the desire of other males comes from one of the Servant Songs of Isaiah. The astonishing thing about the one in whom YHWH delights here is precisely that, from the standpoint of the powerful males (kings) of the earth, this servant has "nothing in his appearance that we should desire him" (Isa 53:2). Somewhat more ambiguous in this regard is the presumed attraction of a (transgendered) Israel for the masculine youthful beauty of Assyrian cavalry officers (Ezek 23:23).

4. Roland Boer in *Knockin' on Heaven's Door: The Bible and Popular Culture* (London: Routledge, 1999) observes, in an intriguing paragraph devoted to this topic, that "one of the relationships that is most often neglected in readings of these chapters is that between YHWH and David" (29). He also suggests that "YHWH responds apparently to his appearance" (ibid.). A much more detailed analysis of other aspects of the relationship between David and YHWH will occupy us in a subsequent chapter.

5. The reason David himself gives is that Saul has been chosen by YHWH as his "anointed," that is, as YHWH's companion or armor-bearer (1 Sam 24:6, 10).

There appear to be two exceptions to this indication of male beauty as motivating YHWH's selection of a male companion in the latter part of David's story concerning his reign as king. Two of David's sons are said to be beautiful, yet they do not become the "chosen" of YHWH. In 2 Samuel we are told of the remarkable beauty of David's third son, Absalom:

> Now in all Israel there was no one to be praised so much for his beauty as Absalom; from the sole of his foot to the crown of his head there was no blemish in him. (2 Sam 14:25)

And at the end of David's story, we are told of the beauty of his fourth son, Adonijah:

> He was also a very handsome man, and he was born next after Absalom. (1 Kgs 1:6)

Do these instances of male beauty contradict the interpretation of male beauty as signaling YHWH's choice of companion?

As it turns out, in both cases, what is going on is that the beauty of the younger male serves as an explanation for what indeed appears to be YHWH's choice of them over the aging David.

In the case of Absalom, what is prepared for by the remark concerning his beauty is that all Israel comes to suppose that he is indeed YHWH's chosen. Thus, there ensues a full-scale uprising against David, which results in David's flight from Jerusalem into the wilderness and nearly results in his death and capture. Moreover, it appears that the people of Israel are not in error in supposing that YHWH has chosen the beautiful young Absalom. After all, Absalom is the instrument to fulfill YHWH's punishment of David for the death of Uriah, which had been arranged to cover up Bathsheba's pregnancy resulting from David's seduction (rape) and adultery (2 Sam 11). In response to that crime, YHWH had assured David that there would be severe internal strife in his household (12:11). Absalom is the instrument for the accomplishment of that curse and is to that extent actually chosen by YHWH.

In the case of Adonijah, his beauty is cited (together with his seniority as next after Absalom) as the plausible ground for his determination to be king in place of the now elderly and frail David. Adonijah's credentials for being chosen by YHWH seem to come down to his beauty (no other exploits of his are recounted), and this, indeed, seems enough to persuade both the high priest Abiathar and David's longtime general Joab.

As it turns out, Adonijah is accepted by the most influential in Israel as the next king, but by a quick preemptive strike instigated by Bathsheba (with the collusion of Nathan), Solomon is anointed first.

At first these cases appear to be exceptions to the use of male beauty as signaling the choice of someone to be YHWH's boy-companion. But we instead find that this is precisely what makes it plausible to suppose, as Israel does, that YHWH has chosen them over his earlier but now aging favorite, David. As it turns out, YHWH, who had spurned his first companion, Saul, in order to select David, has in the meantime himself learned the virtue of loyalty and remains loyal to David to the end.

In this same saga, four times we are told of the beauty of female characters. In at least three of the four cases, what such beauty signals is overpowering physical attraction. It is the beauty of Bathsheba that provokes David to lose his head over her (2 Sam 11:3). It is the beauty of Tamar, sister of Absalom, that drives Amnon, David's first son, to be so overcome with lust that he rapes her (ch. 13). It is the beauty of Abishag that leads to her selection to "warm the bed" of the dying David (1 Kgs 1:1–4). The only exception (with no mention of erotic attraction) appears to be the case of Tamar the daughter of Absalom (14:27), but her named beauty may well be a displacement from Absalom's sister of the same name. Thus, the connection between beauty and presumed erotic attachment applies equally to male and to female characters. But whether it is the male or the female who is beautiful in this saga, it is a male character who notices (or is expected to notice) and is drawn to (or is expected to be drawn to) the beautiful one.

Given this rather cursory overview, we may identify certain characteristics of the relationship between the hero and his armor-bearer. First, as the name suggests, the armor-bearer is the constant companion of the hero or warrior. While we often glimpse him in battle alongside the hero, he must be present away from battle if he is to carry the arms or armor that, in battle, would be worn or employed by the warrior himself. Hence, we can gather that he is expected to be the constant companion of the warrior.

Further, the youth is distinguished by an absolute loyalty to the warrior-hero. In two cases, that of Saul and that of Abimelech, this loyalty is demonstrated by a determination not to outlive the hero. From the youth's perspective, the relationship is one of loyalty to the death.

This is, however, not necessarily true of the warrior's relation to the youth. Saul's sidekick disappears from the narrative only later to be replaced by David, who is in turn replaced by at least one other (the one who dies at Saul's side). The same appears to be true of Jonathan as well, who selects David to be his armor-bearer in place of (or alongside) the one with whom he had gained glory in the battle of Michmash. Even as the relation with David deepens in intensity, Jonathan has another armor-bearer whom he can trust absolutely in the conspiracy to protect David from the wrath of Saul. YHWH too selects at least two such companions: Saul and David.

We may hazard here an analogy with marriage in that the husband/ warrior may have more than one youth/wife, while the youth/wife may have only one hero/husband. Indeed, the theme of Saul's jealousy when his own son seems to supplant him as the lover of David provides one of the main driving plots of the narrative (see ch. 2).

This analogy is in important respects misleading, however, since the youth is not in other respects "feminized."[6] In these narratives the youth is regularly noticed for his boldness and bravery, sharing in the dangers and the adventures of the warrior; indeed, sometimes outshining the hero in these masculine qualities. Moreover, if David is illustrative, the beloved youth may also exercise the functions of a husband to a wife without severing the relation to his warrior-hero.

Nevertheless, the youth, we have seen, is selected, as are female consorts, at least to a significant degree because of his beauty, a beauty that awakens the desire and favor of the lover/hero.

The sort of homoerotic attachments we encounter in this text have some points of contact with what we find in other warrior cultures. In Greek terms, the appropriate analogy is not so much Athenian pederasty but the attachments of male lovers that appear characteristic of Sparta[7] or the famous band of lovers at Thebes.[8] Something similar appears in accounts of pre-Christian northern European warriors[9] and may even lie behind some of the homoerotic attachments of early feudal Europe.[10] One of the most elaborately documented examples of homoeroticism in warrior cultures is found in Tokugawa (period of) Japan, in accounts of the relationships between samurai and their boy-companions.[11] In most of these cases both lover and beloved are warriors or warriors in training. The beloved is thus not a "kept boy" but a partner in adventure, distinguished by

---

6. Given the remarkable exploits of Deborah and Jael (Judg 5–6), one should, however, exercise great caution in trying to identify what would count as "feminization."

7. See, for example, Plutarch's *Life of Lycurgus.*

8. See Plutarch's *Life of Pelopidas.*

9. For an overview, see David F. Greenberg, *The Construction of Homosexuality* (Chicago: University of Chicago Press, 1988), 111.

10. Ibid., 242–49.

11. See Ihara Saikaku, *The Great Mirror of Male Love* (trans. Paul G. Schalow; Stanford, CA: Stanford University Press, 1990), a seventeenth-century Japanese writer who composes his book as a collection of forty short stories. The first twenty deal with erotic attachments between Samurai and their boy-companions. For a discussion of a number of texts relating to this theme, see Gary Leupp, *Male Colors: The Construction of Homosexuality in Tokugawa Japan* (Berkeley: University of California Press, 1995).

his beauty, boldness, and loyalty. The context of these relationships means that the beloved need not be assimilated to the heterosexual model and is thus less likely to be "feminized" than appears to be the case in more sedentary homoerotic cultures.

Thus far we have seen that the depiction of YHWH in this narrative places him within a context in which relationships between warriors and their younger companions appear to have a homoerotic character that is determined, in part, by considerations of the physical beauty of the younger companion. Hence, the relation appears to be one mediated by some sort of homoerotic desire or that at least presupposes some of the features of homoerotic desire. But this suggestion remains somewhat abstract without attention to some of the episodes within which the relation among the characters is played out. We will therefore turn to an examination of the relationships depicted between David and Saul and David and Jonathan before turning again to the role of the character named YHWH in the saga.

The culture for which these stories are written is one that thinks of itself as a warrior culture or as formed by those traditions. In this culture adult males of high status select beautiful youths to be their constant companions. We know of other warrior societies in which this pederastic structure includes homoeroticism as a matter of course, including sexual relations. This is well documented, for example, in the samurai culture of Japan, and it appears to be a strong contributing factor to the development of pederastic culture among the males (who formed the citizen's militia) of Athens. It is also well attested of the most famous love affair of late antiquity, that of Hadrian and Antinous.[12] Is Israel an exception to the homoerotic character of these bonds or to the acceptance of a sexual mediation to this relationship? A closer look at the stories of our main characters will help to clarify the situation.

---

12. See Greenberg, *Construction*, 110–16, for additional references to "warrior-love." David M. Halperin's "Heroes and Their Pals," in his *One Hundred Years of Homosexuality* (New York: Routledge, 1990), 75–87, contains insightful discussion as well.

2. Love Triangle

DAVID'S HUMAN LOVERS

IN THIS CHAPTER we turn to the scrutiny of two intertwined relationships that serve as the emotional hinge of that part of 1 Samuel in which David plays a role. His relationships to Saul and Jonathan are placed within the pattern that we have noticed of warriors and their boy-companions—what Halperin calls "heroes and their pals."[1] But these two relationships do not simply stand alongside one another. For Saul and Jonathan are father and son and are rivals from the beginning not only for the loyalty of the men of Israel but also for the affections of the youth who will one day be king in their stead. The stories we read are therefore characterized not only by emotional depth but also by psychological complexity. It is, perhaps, the first great love triangle in Western literature.

Saul and David

I will first discuss the relationship between Saul and David. While the homoerotic character of the attachment between David and Jonathan has often been pointed out, it is quite rare to find recognition of this dynamic

---

1. David M. Halperin, "Heroes and Their Pals," in his *One Hundred Years of Homosexuality* (New York: Routledge, 1990), 75–87.

in the relationship between David and Saul.[2] Yet this is by far the more complex and in many ways more interesting of these relationships.

How does Saul come to take up with David? As will happen again, we are given two quite different explanations for the fateful relationship that comes to unite them.[3] Both accounts seem to take for granted the fact that David has already been chosen to replace Saul after Saul has managed to displease God by not completely exterminating the Amalekites. In fact, Saul seems to have spared only the king, the best of the sheep and cattle, and other valuable property (1 Sam 15).

God, in his persona as fierce warrior-chieftain, was sorry that he had chosen Saul and resolved to choose another. When we come to the actual selection, however, we are reminded that the initially apparent criterion is extraordinary beauty (16:12). How is David to be brought to the attention of the once-beautiful youth, now headstrong king, he is to replace?

We have two accounts of the way in which David comes to Saul's attention. In the first Saul is said to have an evil spirit that torments him. He needs someone to soothe him in the moments of madness, and it appears that music has this capacity. Saul's servants, probably terrified of their master's strange fits of madness and melancholy, advise him that there is a certain (young) man known for his skill in playing the lyre and "of good presence (16:18)." Saul sends to Jesse for this prodigy, who comes to enter Saul's service:

> Saul loved him greatly, and he became his armor-bearer. Saul sent to Jesse, saying, "Let David remain in my service, for he has found favor in my sight." And whenever the evil spirit from God came upon Saul, David took the lyre and played it with his hand, and Saul would be relieved and feel better, and the evil spirit would depart from him. (16:21–23)

Thus, YHWH has contrived to smuggle David into Saul's service by sending an evil spirit that only David can cure. David thus becomes indispensable to the mad king and not only is his companion on the field (as armor-bearer) but also is constantly at his side even at home, soothing his jangled nerves as if he were a favorite wife or concubine.

In the second account (simply joined to the first), Saul is at war with a Philistine band whose secret weapon is a giant named Goliath. David (not

---

2. The most compelling attempt at such an interpretation of this relationship is in André Gide's play *Saül* (written, 1896; first published, 1903), in *My Theater* (trans. Jackson Matthews; New York: Knopf, 1951).

3. Because of a consistent pattern of seemingly divergent perspectives in the story, scholars have identified at least two sources for the saga. In this reading of the saga, we will keep attention focused on the saga, as thus compiled rather than attempting to sort out the details of the history of its compilation.

yet in Saul's service) comes to bring food to his older brothers, who are in the militia. In this account David is a mere boy (17:33). Here David has no previous experience with battle, although in the earlier account he was called "a man of valor, a warrior" (16:18); but he has taken on lions and bears in his duties as a shepherd-boy. He is apparently slight of stature, or at least no match for the armor of Israel's king. In the course of the ensuing adventure, we are again informed that David is too young and pretty for the taste of the Philistine warrior:

> When the Philistine looked and saw David, he disdained him, for he was only a youth, ruddy and handsome in appearance. (17:42)

The Philistine sees only another "pretty boy," a chief's "boy-toy," perhaps, but not someone to be taken seriously as a warrior. He was wrong! The pretty boy does away with the great warrior-giant and is immediately taken into service by the king (18:2).

This story is linked with the previous one of David the musician by an episode in which Saul, again attacked by madness, seeks to pin David to the wall with a spear cast. But David somehow eludes the royal assassin (18:10–11).

Just as two accounts tell how David comes to be loved by Saul, so also two accounts tell how it is that the relationship sours, at least from Saul's point of view, almost from the beginning. From 18:10 to 26:25 the story is driven by Saul's attempts to murder David.

What is the basis of this unrelenting enmity? Again we have two explanations. The first is that David comes to have great success as a warrior in Saul's service. Thus, the people all love David (18:16).[4] Saul becomes jealous of his popularity. This is given a certain degree of plausibility within the story line that has David come into Saul's service as a young adult known for his musicianship. But it is hard to fathom from the narrative line that has David come as a mere boy or stripling who is despised by the Philistine both for his youth and his prettiness.

There is another ground for Saul's jealousy that is far more plausible within this other narrative line. It is that just as the old king is taking David on as his boy-companion, there appears a rival for the affections of this

---

4. For reflections on how another famous "beloved" is also a favorite of the people, see Allan Bloom's reflections on Alcibiades in "The Ladder of Love," in *Plato's "Symposium"* (trans. S. Benardete; commentaries by A. Bloom and S. Benardete; Chicago: University of Chicago Press, 2001), 113–14. In this connection, as Bloom points out, "The Lover cannot love the people. But the beloved can enjoy the admiration of the people" (113). This observation could be transposed exactly onto the story of Saul and David.

pretty youth: Saul's own young-adult son, Jonathan! Jonathan is himself already a proven warrior and, as the king's eldest son, the one who is likely to be his father's heir, perhaps even king after him (20:31). Within this narrative line Jonathan is older and more experienced than the stripling whose beauty has been so often remarked upon, whose adolescent braggadocio has been heard, and whose boldness has just been witnessed.

> When David had finished speaking to Saul, the soul of Jonathan was bound to the soul of David, and Jonathan loved him as his own soul. Saul took him that day and would not let him return to his father's house. Then Jonathan made a covenant with David, because he loved him as his own soul. Jonathan stripped himself of the robe that he was wearing, and gave it to David, and his armor, and even his sword and his bow and his belt. (18:1–4)

Saul and Jonathan thus become competitors for the same boy-companion, the same prospective armor-bearer. We are not yet told of the response of David to this extravagant wooing. For now, David remains in the service of the older man, who had chosen him first. But it is clear that Jonathan is eventually to be the more successful suitor. Indeed, as so often happens with jealousy, Saul drives David to the protective arms of his younger rival by his mad attempts on David's life.

Before going into the story of David and Jonathan, it is well to attend a bit to Saul's jealousy and to see how it betrays itself as having an erotic ground.

Well after David and Jonathan have become fast friends, Saul realizes that he has lost out in this competition. He has in fact lost David, whom he has driven away by his murderous jealousy. Saul also seems to have lost the loyalty of his son, who not only has apparently won David's affection but has also become David's protector (thus also supplanting Saul's role). The description of his reaction is as follows:

> Then Saul's anger was kindled against Jonathan. He said to him, "You son of a perverse, rebellious woman! Do I not know that you have chosen the son of Jesse to your own shame, and to the shame of your mother's nakedness? For as long as the son of Jesse lives upon the earth, neither you nor your kingdom shall be established" . . . Jonathan rose from the table in fierce anger and ate no food on the second day of the month, for he was grieved for David, and because his father had disgraced him. (20:30–31, 34)

What is the character of the disgrace into which Saul has cast Jonathan? There is, of course, the public tirade of the king. But within the king's tirade there is a remarkable phrase:

> Do I not know that you have chosen the son of Jesse to your own shame, and to the shame of your mother's nakedness?

The shame here has to do at least in part with the way in which Jonathan's alliance with David will mean that David comes nearer the throne, and that somehow this will mean that Jonathan will lose the throne. It is never explained how it is that this friendship will produce that effect save that Jonathan is so smitten with David that he could refuse him nothing, even preeminence in the kingdom. But the most remarkable phrase here is that Jonathan's relationship with David is somehow to "the shame of your mother's nakedness." The exposure of someone's nakedness is regularly an expression that designates the consequence of a sexual act. Here, for example, are some of the words of Leviticus:

> You shall not uncover the nakedness of your father, which is the nakedness of your mother; she is your mother, you shall not uncover her nakedness. You shall not uncover the nakedness of your father's wife; it is the nakedness of your father. (Lev 18:7–8)

This continues for several verses of forbidden sexual relations, a theme picked up again in Lev 20 with similar terminology. In general, person A uncovers the nakedness of person B by having sexual relations with person X. How are we to understand Saul's charge against Jonathan? In Leviticus, one uncovers one's mother's nakedness by uncovering "the nakedness of your father." But Jonathan has certainly not done this directly. Somehow, his relationship with David uncovers Saul's nakedness, which thereby uncovers Jonathan's mother's nakedness. How could this be so? As far as I can see, the best explanation is that in having an erotic/sexual relationship with David, Jonathan has had a relationship with someone who has had sexual relations with his father, and thus he has exposed his father's nakedness. In thus indirectly exposing his father's nakedness, Jonathan has exposed the nakedness of someone else with whom his father has had sexual relations: Saul's wife, Jonathan's mother. Intimacy with David exposes the nakedness of David's first lover (Saul) and thus of that sexual partner of Saul's who is also Jonathan's mother.

What is significant is that Saul's outburst does not make sense if only the relationship between David and Jonathan is sexually mediated. Rather, the relationship between Saul and David must also have been sexual if this chain of exposing nakedness is to work. Otherwise, Jonathan might expose David's nakedness but not his father's, and so not his mother's either.

I am not claiming that this is mathematically conclusive evidence of a sexual mediation of the relationship between Saul and David or Jonathan and David. But it is certainly as strong an indication as we are likely to get in a narrative that does not indulge in quasi-pornographic description.

The "disgrace" of Jonathan lies not only in the public dressing-down he has received but in the way in which the private sexuality of two persons has been exposed to public view and made to seem both tawdry and somehow treasonous. Of course, the mad king has only succeeded in exposing himself, especially his own mad jealousy. In disgracing himself in this way, he has also disgraced his son and heir.

Certainly the erotic character of the relationship between the aging king and the beautiful boy with its likely sexual mediation goes far in helping to explain the extravagance of Saul's jealousy. In his madness he can even lash out at his heir, but this would ultimately be suicidal. Thus, he can only dispose of the one who has been seduced away from himself and driven into the arms of Jonathan.

Before seeing how the structure we have identified here applies to the situation of David, it is also important to get a view of Saul's relation to Jonathan. It quickly becomes apparent that Jonathan has become a rival of Saul for the affection and loyalty of the people, especially the militia, of which Saul is the war-chief (king). Jonathan's daring raid, accompanied by his own boy-companion, stands in contrast to the indecisiveness of Saul, who awaits the outcome before joining forces with Jonathan (1 Sam 14:16–20). In the ensuing episode Jonathan seems disposed to take the welfare of the members of the militia into account, while Saul imposes an arbitrary and seemingly self-defeating vow of fasting upon the fighting troops (14:24). Jonathan's inadvertent disobedience of Saul's vow leads Saul to the point of willingly sacrificing his own son to the exigencies of his arbitrary and rash decision (14:44).

Saul is prevented from carrying out his sacrifice of Jonathan by the threatened mutiny of the whole militia, which rises up in indignant defense of Jonathan in spite of the fact that Jonathan has not defended or excused himself, but simply pointed out the senselessness of Saul's policy. Here Jonathan is no mere son; he is clearly a rival. It is to him that the troops are loyal despite the position of Saul. It is clear that Saul's position at the head of the militia depends on not coming into opposition to Jonathan.

In the course of the story, David will replace Jonathan as the rival for the affection of the militia and the people of Israel. Moreover, he will replace Jonathan as the object of Saul's murderous intent. This displacement onto David of both popular adulation and Saul's jealous rage sets the context for another conflict between Saul and Jonathan, the rivalry for David's affection. It also helps to explain why it is that instead of getting rid of the rival (Jonathan), Saul must seek to eliminate David. For it has already been made clear that Saul cannot attack Jonathan without destroying his own position as war-chief.

David Saves Saul

The action of 1 Sam 18–30 is largely taken up by the accounts of Saul's murderous rage directed against David, his former boy-toy. We have seen that this rage may be understood as driven by a strong undertow of sexual jealousy. The specifically sexual character of this relationship is pointed to by Saul's outburst against his own son (and rival for the affections of David). In it, the uncovering of the nakedness of Jonathan's mother (and Saul's wife) points to the sexual character of the relationship between David and Saul and between David and Jonathan. But the stories that explicate the jealous rage of Saul contain two episodes that may further underline the sexual charge in the relationship between David and Saul. They also may direct us toward a clarification of David's character as beloved, a theme of momentous consequences for the narrative as a whole.[5]

The crucial episodes in this respect are those in which David, rather ostentatiously, makes clear that he could eliminate the threat posed by the rage of his jealous lover, yet ultimately refuses to do so. The episodes of 1 Sam 24 and 26 dramatically exhibit this theme. I will "read" these narratives as they relate to the hypothesis that the relationship between Saul and David is erotically determined. On this basis it will also be possible to explore something of the strange character of David's returned love for Saul.

Two stories deal with how David comes into Saul's court, and there are two explanations of how Saul comes to be enraged with David. Similarly, there are two stories that have as their theme David's refusal to assassinate his tormentor. Both of these stories have a rather similar structure. In both,

---

5. Indeed, the Hebrew name David may be construed as "beloved" since the consonants are the same.

Saul is in relentless pursuit of David. In both cases he is closing in because David has been betrayed by people who know where he and his outlaw raiders are hiding. In both cases David and his band are camped in the wilderness, where Saul closes in on them with his army.

David and his band are vastly outnumbered by the approaching royal forces, which in both cases number "three thousand chosen men of Israel" (24:2; 26:2). Yet in each case Saul is ironically placed in a position of great vulnerability. In the stories David initially takes advantage of this vulnerability in such a way as to publicly demonstrate that Saul's life is really in his hands. Yet in both cases David forgoes the chance to actually kill his former lover. The result of this forbearance in both cases appears at first to be the repentance of Saul and his apparent determination to relent in his obsessive pursuit of David. Yet in both cases this resolve appears unreliable and short-lived. The presumed reconciliation is depicted as false, and the enmity continues unabated.

These two tales have a remarkably similar structure. They seem indeed to be almost the same story. The similarity of structure suggests a set piece or subgenre in a tale of adventure, where the loyalty of the subordinate partner among the adventurers is cast in doubt and subsequently proved to be genuine. As a bare form the stories would seem to reach their natural climax in the repentance of the one who had doubted the loyalty of the other. In 24:17 Saul avers:

> You are more righteous than I; for you have repaid me good, whereas I have repaid you evil. Today you have explained how you have dealt well with me, in that you did not kill me when the LORD put me into your hands. For who has ever found an enemy, and sent the enemy safely away? So may the LORD reward you with good for what you have done to me this day.

And at the conclusion of the second episode, Saul says:

> I have done wrong; come back, my son David, for I will never harm you again, because my life was precious in your sight today; I have been a fool, and have made a great mistake. (26:21)

The stories continue with answering words of David and again of Saul, in which it would appear that the pact of trust between them is restored. The genre of the stories would seem to require this reconciliation, or at least the apparently amicable separation with which the episodes close: "So David went his way, and Saul returned to his place" (26:25; see 24:22). The wider narrative frame within which these stories occur, however, makes clear that the reconciliation is not genuine and that Saul's enmity continues. Thus, it would seem that a tale of reconciliation, of trust doubted, demonstrated, and confirmed, has been adapted to the quite different purposes of the narrator of the relationship between Saul and David. That is, the kind of tale we are looking at probably functions normally to develop the theme of reconciliation, but has been rather brusquely inserted into a larger narrative in which true reconciliation is impossible. The result of this insertion and adaptation is to underline the loyalty of David and the irrational character of Saul's murderous rage.

Despite the similarity of these episodes, however, there are remarkable differences between them that can perhaps be best brought out by beginning with the, in many ways, simpler and more straightforward of the two stories, the last told. This episode most straightforwardly exhibits the theme of reconciliation between rival warlords or between a warrior-chieftain and his former lieutenant.

In the episode of chapter 26 (the wilderness of Ziph), David spies out the place where Saul and his army are encamped and enters the camp accompanied by one of his lieutenants (Abishai) while Saul is asleep (with Abner!) and surrounded by his sleeping army. However, David makes clear to Abishai that he has no intention of harming Saul: "Do not destroy him; for who can raise his hand against the LORD's anointed, and be guiltless?" (26:9). Thus, the story absolves David of any intent to commit lèse-majesté. Instead, David takes trophies (a spear and a water jar) to demonstrate that he did in fact have it in his power to attack Saul but forbore. To be sure, the trophies may be somewhat overdetermined. After all, the water jar is what makes life in the wilderness possible. But even more, the spear has been the instrument of Saul's phallic aggression, twice against David (18:10–11) and then against Jonathan (20:33) when the latter took David's part. And the dramatic function of the spear continues as David first displays it (26:16) and then has it returned to Saul (26:22).

In spite of the rather telling detail of the spear and its various uses in the wider narrative, the story seems to conclude in a rather conventional way with a declaration of mutual reconciliation and covenant.

In contrast, the first episode (in the wilderness of Engedi) seems far more intimate and emotionally charged. Here David does not go out into the public space of the plain. Instead, Saul inadvertently enters into the intimate space of the cave where David is holed up. On the plain Saul is surrounded by the masculine space of a war camp, whereas here he enters into the womblike feminine space of the cave.

This difference is further underlined by the mode of Saul's resultant vulnerability. On the plain he is simply asleep with his general and his soldiers. In the cave we have the rather graphic and probably scatologically humorous detail that he goes there to squat in order to defecate in privacy. This at least seems to be the plain meaning of the assertion that he was postured so as "to cover his feet," a phrase translated "to relieve himself." (In the squatting position of defecation, the robe "covers the feet.") It is difficult to believe that this part of the story would be told with a straight face or without the accompanying guffaws of the amused audience.

While the unwary Saul is in this posture, David alone approaches him. Later, on the plain, David will be accompanied by one of his men, but here the encounter is private as befits the "privy." Moreover, David's motive for thus approaching Saul is ambiguous. He has been egged on by his men, who have seen Saul squatting. Yet David, after cutting off a piece of the latter's robe, is stricken with conscience and reproves his men (after the fact) for the thought of killing Saul (24:6). This contrasts with the more deliberate determination not to kill Saul, as announced in the episode on the plain (26:9–11). That David was first egged on by his men and later scolds them suggests that the sneaking up on Saul as he is thus exposed is a kind of prank prior to the actual killing of Saul. In this story, then, it is the exposure of his former lover's vulnerability that persuades David not to kill him. In the second story David clearly has no such intention to kill Saul and from the beginning seeks only to get a trophy to demonstrate his loyalty to Saul.

The rather Rabelasian ribaldry of this first episode is rather quickly altered into what seem like set speeches between David and Saul in the aftermath. However, the mood of intimacy in fact continues into the tone of the story's denouement. First, we are told that David was "stricken to the heart because he had cut off a corner of Saul's cloak" (24:5). This seems to be a rather extreme reaction unless what is at stake is the quasi-sexual exposure of his former lover. There is no such reaction of David to the escapade on the plain. In both cases David calls Saul "my lord" (24:8, 10; 26:17) after the fact while displaying the trophy, but here in the first episode he also calls Saul "my father" (24:11).[6] In both episodes Saul repents of his attack on David, but in the episode following the encounter in the cave, we are told that Saul wept. This first episode is told in such a way as to convey far more emotional charge in the relation between David and Saul than the rather more formal character of the second story. The emotional overtones of this

---

6. The question of the function of the term "father" to indicate a sexually charged relation will be explored in a subsequent chapter concerning the prophets. See also H. Eilberg-Schwartz, *God's Phallus and Other Problems for Men and Monotheism* (Boston: Beacon, 1994).

telling seem consistent with the intimacy of the encounter and again recall the physical intimacy of the relationship that lies at the basis of the episode.

As these comparisons demonstrate, the first episode (in the cave) is remarkably intimate and seems to have a certain erotic charge. The second has a somewhat more formal character like the relationship between a vassal and a lord, a commander and a lieutenant. Precisely in this contrast we are led to see in the first a more graphic depiction of the personal relationship between a lover and his beloved.

Indeed, so intimate and erotically charged is this episode that one could imagine it being adaptable to telling the story of a husband who is persuaded of the unfaithfulness of his wife. It is she who would have the opportunity of getting close to him (in the house or palace) when he is in his "privy chamber," perhaps even to murder him in his vulnerability. But instead she snips off a piece of his robe to display as proof of her loyalty. The emotional charge of her being stricken at heart and his weeping would fit well in such a context; far better perhaps than in the context of dueling warrior-chiefs. The point of this is not to say that one or even both of the characters are actually "feminized" in this episode but to suggest the parallel to more familiar scenes of erotic intimacy.

Given what we have seen of the erotic power of the relationship between Saul and David, we can say that the erotic intimacy of this tale of failed reconciliation fits extraordinarily well into the overall picture of a love relationship gone sour.

The present sequencing of these two episodes not only casts the differences between them into bold relief (thereby allowing us to detect more easily the erotic character of the first); it also serves to suggest the growing distance between David and Saul. The more formal relation of vassal and lord displaces the intimate relation of disaffected lovers, thereby charting the course of the deteriorating relationship. Yet in spite of the deterioration in the relationship, it is clear that David remains doggedly loyal to the man who had first chosen him as his favorite. As we shall see, this steadfast loyalty of David to Saul will serve as a template for David's loyalty to Jonathan and later even to Adonai.

The last episode of David's sparing of Saul's life brings the narrative of Saul's pursuit of David to a close. The estranged lovers will not meet again. But this is because David removes himself from the sphere of Saul's influence by hiring himself out to Israel's traditional enemies, the Philistines.

Now this is an extraordinary step, for it brings David into the position of an enemy of Israel. The narrator will go to great lengths to mitigate this strange apparent betrayal of those he will subsequently lead as war-chief and king, but the implications of the alliance between David and Achish are close to the surface. In David's speech protesting his loyalty to Saul in the last episode, he had said: "If it is mortals [who have stirred you up against me], may they be cursed before the LORD, for they have driven me out today from my share in the heritage of the LORD, saying, 'Go, serve other gods'" (26:19). The setting out from the land of Israel, the moving into the land of the Philistines, and the alliance with Achish—all seem precisely to have placed David in the position of serving other gods.

The narrator, however, insists that David, whatever cultic obligations he may have had to fulfill in his new home, managed to avoid raiding the settlements of his former countrymen. However, he manages to keep his new king in the dark by claiming that it is Israelite settlements that he has raided. Since David takes the precaution of leaving no survivors, the ruse works.

Yet it is only by apparent chance that David avoids the final fatal encounter with Saul and Jonathan on Mount Gilboa. It is not David's new "top" (King Achish) who suspects his loyalty, but only the other Philistine commanders, who insist that David not accompany them on what will turn out to be the final battle against Saul. In contrast, his new benefactor takes David's loyalty to be absolute. Achish has said to David, "I will make you my bodyguard for life" (28:2), granting him, as it were, the place of permanent armor-bearer. When the other commanders reject David's help in the battle of Gilboa, Achish says: "You are as blameless in my sight as an angel [messenger] of God" (29:9). The Philistine commander's trust in David stands in strong contrast to the jealous fury of Saul. In this respect we may even find David's apparent willingness to engage in the final campaign against Saul understandable; has he at last found a lover whose love is reliable?

Despite the near escape from the final confrontation, the narrative does serve to underline David's loyalty to the older and stronger men who adopt him as their favorite. In this sense David is portrayed as what we might call the ideal "bottom"—one whose love is utterly steadfast even when sorely tested.

In these final episodes concerning David's relationship to Saul, we thus have a further piece of evidence underlining the erotic, indeed sexual, character of the relationship. We also have a strong indication of the role that David plays in relation to his lovers as one who is astonishingly loyal to the older and more powerful males who make him their favorite. Both of these features will play an important role in the further tales of David's erotic attachments to males.

Jonathan and David

Although the erotic character of the relationship between David and Saul is seldom if ever noticed, the erotic character of the relationship between David and Jonathan has been the subject of gay friendly interpretation, especially by Tom Horner.[7] Accordingly, a more summary treatment of this topic can be offered here. We have given attention to the culture in which warrior-chiefs select for themselves beautiful, bold, and loyal boy-companions, and to the erotic character of the doomed bond between the aging king and the boy David. Both of these add greater credence to the homophilic interpretation of one of the most striking love stories of ancient literature.

As we have noticed, the attraction of Jonathan to David begins almost immediately as Saul is delighting in his new companion. This attraction is given extravagant expression. In the first place it appears to be love at first sight. We are told: "When David had finished speaking to Saul, the soul of Jonathan was bound to the soul of David" (1 Sam 18:1). Is it something David has said? Not likely. For what David has said to Saul is "I am the son of your servant Jesse the Bethlehemite" (17:58). It is not something David has said. Instead, the reader's gaze has twice been directed to David's extraordinary beauty.

Not only does Jonathan love David at first sight; he also loves him "as his own soul" (18:1). As Bloom points out, the only reference to friendship in the law codes of the Hebrew Bible also uses the simile of the friend being "as your own soul" (Deut 13:6 RSV), but the code does not seem to regard friendship in an especially favorable light.[8] "Soul" (*nephesh*) here and in Hebrew literature generally has no specifically religious connotation. It means that by virtue of which we take in air, water, and food. It is the principle of need and desire that is life itself. It is the expression of fundamental yearning.[9] And this yearning for the beautiful beloved is given extravagant expression:

> Jonathan stripped himself of the robe that he was wearing, and gave it to David, and his armor, and even his sword and his bow and his belt. (18:4)

Here Jonathan entrusts David with the weapons that signal his own pre-eminence. He makes David his own armor-bearer despite the fact that Saul has already chosen David for this role (16:21).

---

7. Tom Horner, *Jonathan Loved David* (Philadelphia: Westminster, 1978), 26–39.

8. Bloom, in "Ladder of Love," 63.

9. See Hans Walter Wolff, *The Anthropology of the Old Testament* (trans. M. Kohl; Philadelphia: Fortress, 1974). The discussion of *nephesh* is entitled "Needy Man" (10–25).

We are thus clearly in a situation of dangerous rivalry between father and son for the same object of desire.

Subsequently, it is reported, "All Israel and Judah loved David; for it was he who marched out and came in leading them" (18:16). David appears to have moved into Jonathan's role as the one loved by the people, and more especially by the militia of Israel and Judah. And Saul, who had been ready to sacrifice his own son but was prevented by the loyalty of the people to Jonathan, now turns his rage against David.

David's first advocate and protector is Michal, Jonathan's sister. First we are told: "Now Saul's daughter Michal loved David" (18:20).

Saul tries to turn this love into a trap for David by sending him on an apparently suicidal mission, which involves the collection of foreskins from the penises of slain Philistines. David not only accepts this strange challenge but also manages to exceed the conditions set by Saul. In consequence, David is given Michal as a wife (18:27).

Now Saul attempts to enlist Jonathan in a plot to murder David.

Saul spoke with his son Jonathan and with all his servants about killing David. But Saul's son Jonathan took great delight in David. (19:1)

Jonathan rescues David and temporarily reconciles Saul (19:7). This has served, however, to make clear that Jonathan as well has taken David's part. This is but a foretaste of the great conflict to follow.

But first it is Michal's turn to rescue David from an assassination plot and to reconcile Saul (19:11–17). In this rescue of David we have a concrete demonstration of Michal's earlier reported love of David (18:20, 28). This love could have been the hinge of the plot, but it is instead only a paradigm for a greater love. It will be Michal's brother Jonathan who supplants her as the lover and protector of David.

There follows an entire chapter (20) devoted to Jonathan's love for David. David tells Jonathan that Saul will kill David and that Saul is hiding this from Jonathan because "your father knows very well that I have found favor in your eyes" (20:3 NIV). The critical question, though, is how to know if Saul really is planning to assassinate David. Jonathan replied to David, "Come, let us go out into the field" (20:11). He then proposes:

"May the LORD be with you, as he has been with my father. If I am still alive, show me the faithful love of the LORD; but if I die, never cut off your faithful love from my house. . . ." Thus Jonathan made a covenant with the house of David, saying, "May the LORD seek out the enemies of David." Jonathan made David swear again by his love for him; for he loved him as he loved his own life. (20:13–17)

They work out a signal involving the shooting of arrows and the words that Jonathan will say to his "boy."

When Saul hears that David is not at court because Jonathan has given him permission to leave, Saul becomes enraged:

> Then Saul's anger was kindled against Jonathan. He said to him, "You son of a perverse, rebellious woman! Do I not know that you have chosen the son of Jesse to your own shame, and to the shame of your mother's nakedness? For as long as the son of Jesse lives upon the earth, neither you nor your kingdom shall be established". . . Jonathan rose from the table in fierce anger and ate no food on the second day of the month, for he was grieved for David, and because his father had disgraced him. (20:30–31, 34)

This outburst on the part of Saul demonstrates that the relationship between Saul and David as well as that between Jonathan and David may be construed as involving sexual intimacy. If Saul has sought to expose Jonathan's sexual relationship with David, he has done so only by exposing the sexual character of his own relationship with David.

In any case, Jonathan now knows that his father's rage is implacable. Saul is enraged at Jonathan but has already learned that he cannot dispose of his son without losing control of the militia. Thus, the rage is directed against David. Here the motive appears even more clearly to be sexual jealousy.

Jonathan goes with his lad to engage in the mime that would let David know the situation. But this is apparently unsatisfactory to Jonathan, so he sends the boy away on a pretext in order to speak to David, who has been hiding in the field.

> As soon as the boy had gone, David rose from beside the stone heap and prostrated himself with his face to the ground. He bowed three times, and they kissed each other, and wept with each other; David wept the more. Then Jonathan said to David, "Go in peace, since both of us have sworn in the name of the LORD, saying, 'The LORD shall be between me and you, and between my descendants and your descendants, forever.'" (20:41–42)

In this incident David is still the social inferior of Jonathan. His prostration makes this clear. But now David's love is in the process of being transferred from Saul to Jonathan. Saul's jealousy has driven him into Jonathan's arms.

There follows the incident of David and the holy bread, which will later be cited by Jesus to justify his own disregard for religious taboos (21:3–6; Mark 2:25–26). The priest inquires whether David and his men have kept themselves unpolluted by abstaining from sex with women (while on campaign; 21:4). David replies in the affirmative and receives the bread.

David now becomes a bandit leader:

> Everyone who was in distress, and everyone who was in debt, and everyone who was discontented gathered to him; and he became captain over them. (22:2)

In retaliation, Saul slays the priests who had aided David (22:11–19). In the process he exclaims:

> No one discloses to me when my son makes a league with the son of Jesse, none of you is sorry for me or discloses to me that my son has stirred up my servant against me. (22:8)

It is clear that in Saul's view it is Jonathan who has seduced David from Saul. This in fact corresponds to what we have seen in the unfolding of the narrative. For Jonathan loved David at first sight, just as David was being taken into Saul's service. But what Saul does not see is the way in which he himself has abetted this seduction through his own jealousy.

Subsequently, David and Jonathan contrive to meet again:

> Saul's son Jonathan set out and came to David at Horesh; there he strengthened his hand through the LORD. He said to him, "Do not be afraid; for the hand of my father Saul shall not find you; you shall be king over Israel, and I shall be second to [beside] you; my father Saul also knows that this is so." Then the two of them made a covenant before the LORD. (23:16–18)

It is unclear whether Jonathan is saying that he will be second in command or that he will be coruler with David. If it is the first, then Jonathan's love is such that he is prepared to completely surrender his own preeminence for the sake of the beloved. In the second possibility we are offered a glimpse of the abolition of male rivalry on the basis of love. In this way the

two may constitute cocommand of the militia and so of Israel. The homoerotic bond thus appears to subvert the whole hierarchical order in which
such relationships are otherwise inscribed. As in the Greek saga of Harmod-
ius and Aristogiton, the homoerotic bond overthrows tyranny and does so
in principle.[10]

David and Jonathan will not meet again. But already the love that unites
them has replaced that of Michal for David in its demonstrativeness and
depth. Here it must be clear that the love and loyalty that bind David and
Jonathan are by no means a mere "alliance" to gain political advantage.
Jonathan continues to serve Saul and to fight beside him and indeed to die
beside him. David refuses to lift his hand against Saul in spite of extraordinary provocations. Hence, the love and loyalty that bind David and
Jonathan appear to be entirely personal in nature, an expression of their love
but not an alliance of political conspirators.[11]

In time the love of Jonathan and David becomes the very paradigm for
all love, even the conjugal love it replaces. Thus, in this love Aelred of
Rievault can see a pattern to be emulated not only for same-sex friends but
also for a man and a woman who seek to love one another as equals.[12]

Aftermath: Grief and Loyalty

The jealousy of Saul has the result first of driving David into the arms of
Jonathan and then of depriving both lovers of the presence of David.
David continues to demonstrate his loyalty to Saul by refusing to take the
latter's life on two separate occasions, but this does not assuage the jealous fury of Saul. In consequence, David and his band hire themselves
out to a group allied with the Philistines, the very enemy that David had
successfully fought in earlier episodes. In preparation for a major battle
against the Israelites, David and his men appear ready to join forces with
the Philistines. They are prevented from doing so by the suspicion of the
Philistine war leaders, who fear that David may turn against them in the
midst of battle as he has turned against his own people in allying himself
with Achish. As a result, David is not present at the final great battle in
which the Philistines finally overwhelm the forces of Israel and in which
Saul and Jonathan are slain.

---

10. This point is made in the speech of Pausanius in Plato's *Symposium* 182d.

11. This point has been well made by Gary David Comstock in his *Gay Theology without Apology* (Cleveland:
Pilgrim, 1993), in which he also develops the theme of Jonathan as unconventional nurturer (79–90).

12. See Aelred of Rievaulx, *Spiritual Friendship* (trans. M. Laker; Kalamazoo, MI: Cistercian Publications,
1974), 115–17; idem, *Mirror of Charity* (trans. E. Connor; Kalamazoo, MI: Cistercian Publications, 1990),
268–70.

First Samuel ends with one account of these deaths; 2 Samuel begins
with a somewhat different account. It is in response to this latter account
that David's grief is exhibited:

> Then David took hold of his clothes and tore them; and all the men who
> were with him did the same. They mourned and wept, and fasted until
> evening for Saul and for his son Jonathan, and for the army of the LORD and
> for the house of Israel, because they had fallen by the sword. (2 Sam 1:11–12)

Then follows David's lament for the militia, for Saul and Jonathan as
heroes, "Saul and Jonathan, beloved and lovely!" (2 Sam 1:23). Next the epic
lament changes to a far more personal tone, in which David's "I" appears:

> How the mighty have fallen
>   in the midst of the battle!
>
> Jonathan lies slain upon your high places.
>   I am distressed for you, my brother Jonathan;
> greatly beloved were you to me;
>   your love to me was wonderful,
>   passing the love of women. (1:25–26)

The poem clearly places the love of Jonathan and the love of women in
the same register; they are comparable. And within this register, the love of
Jonathan is greater. Now in what register do we meet both the love of
women and the love of Jonathan? Is it the love of friends? Is it that Jonathan
will be a better friend than, say, Michal or Abigail? Is it the love of alliance
formation? But women do not make alliances. What then? The love of
women is the sphere of the erotic, and the love of Jonathan is placed here in
this sphere in order to be compared not as apples to oranges but as apples to
apples: the greater and the less.

It is not only that the grief of David serves to illuminate the depth of his
relationship with Saul and especially with Jonathan, but also that David's
subsequent behavior demonstrates his enduring loyalty to the men who
had loved him.

One possible opportunity for the demonstration of this loyalty is
Jonathan's sister and Saul's daughter Michal, who had been given him as a
wife and who had demonstrated her love for David in an initial rescue of
David from Saul's murderous wrath. In the meantime Saul has wedded her
to another man. After Saul's death David again acquires Michal as a wife.

But she later rebukes him for the extravagance of his dancing naked before the ark of YHWH (2 Sam 6:14–23).[13] David is angry with her, and we are told that she "had no child to the day of her death" (6:23). But if Michal does not measure up to Jonathan in being a fit object for David's demonstration of love, who will?

We recall that Michal's love for David had earlier been supplanted by Jonathan's love. He displaces Michal as David's protector and thus demonstrates his love for David. Now once again, Jonathan will replace Michal, this time through the person of his surviving son.

The opportunity for the demonstration of this loyalty is provided by the survival of Jonathan's son and Saul's grandson:

> David asked, "Is there still anyone left of the house of Saul to whom I may show kindness for Jonathan's sake?" (9:1)

Earlier the reader had been introduced to this character:

> Saul's son Jonathan had a son who was crippled in his feet. He was five years old when the news about Saul and Jonathan came from Jezreel. His nurse picked him up and fled; and, in her haste to flee, it happened that he fell and became lame. His name was Mephibosheth. (4:4)

David sends for the crippled son of his former lover (and grandson of the first lover). When he arrives, David says:

> Do not be afraid, for I will show you kindness for the sake of your father Jonathan; I will restore to you all the land of your grandfather Saul, and you yourself shall eat at my table always. (9:7)

The result is that Mephibosheth "ate at David's table, like one of the king's sons" (9:11). The initial tale ends with an assurance: "Mephibosheth lived in Jerusalem, for he always ate at the king's table. Now he was lame in both his feet" (9:13).

To this point David's loyalty to Jonathan is demonstrated by taking Mephibosheth as virtually his own son. This is not the end of the story, however. Much later we are told that a certain Ziba, whose household were servants of Jonathan and then of Mephibosheth, tells David of Mephibosheth's apparent disloyalty (16:1–4), with the result that Ziba is

---

13. This will be considered at greater length in the next chapter.

made owner of the lands of Saul-Jonathan-Mephibosheth. David's decision is later altered when David meets Mephibosheth (19:24–30). Here he is "grandson of Saul" rather than son of Jonathan. David divides the property between Ziba and Mephibosheth, but the latter says he doesn't want any; he is only glad that David has returned safely.

This is not yet the end of the story. Toward the end of the account of David's reign, we read of a three-year famine in the land. The famine was attributed (by YHWH) to the bloodguilt of Saul in having put the Gibeonites to death (21:1). In order to atone for this bloodguilt and so remove the famine from the land of Israel, David offers to give them whatever they choose. They demand the death of seven of Saul's "sons." David manages to find seven, two of whom are sons by Saul's concubine Rizpah, and five who are grandsons by Saul's daughter Merab. In doing this David passes over the most obvious choice of Mephibosheth (or Merib-baal, as he is now known; NRSV note): "But the king spared Mephibosheth, the son of Saul's son Jonathan, because of the oath of the LORD that was between them, between David and Jonathan son of Saul" (21:7).

In this way the house of Saul is reduced to the line of Jonathan. When in the end David has to choose between Saul and Jonathan, it is Jonathan who is chosen, in a loyalty that lasts to the end of David's days.

This last action in fulfillment of the covenant with Jonathan only makes all the more clear that the covenant between them has nothing to do with political advantage. It is a covenant of mutual love that David fulfills to the end of his days. Forever he remains the man who was loved by and who loved Jonathan.

By means of the relationship with Jonathan's son, we are reminded throughout 2 Samuel of David's love for Jonathan (and Saul). The extraordinary passion demonstrated in David's grief is no passing fancy. It entails a lifelong commitment on David's part to honoring the memory of the two men who had loved him and especially the memory of Jonathan. If it turns out that this cannot be done through the conjugal relationship with Jonathan's sister, then it will be done through the development of a paternal bond with the son of Jonathan. Once again, the love of Jonathan replaces that of Michal and so, concretely, surpasses that of women.

Summary and Conclusion

We may now summarize the results of this homoerotic reading of the saga and draw a few conclusions.

We have seen that the warrior culture represented in, and reproduced by, the saga is characterized by significant relationships between warriors and their boy-companions. These are, in general, the most significant relationships represented in the narrative, far exceeding in importance the relationships with women.

This framework even determines (and is in return illuminated by) the behavior of YHWH, who is cast as the preeminent war-chief (king) of Israel's militia. YHWH, in accordance with the expectations of the readers of this saga, appears to regard physical beauty as a primary criterion for the selection of a boy-companion/armor-bearer. In biblical literature male beauty is regularly associated with erotic attachment. Here it is accompanied by bravery and loyalty as criteria for the prolongation of the relationship. These criteria are perfectly consistent with what we know of idealized cross-generational eroticism in warrior and other cultures.

Against this backdrop the narrative develops the love triangle of Saul, David, and Jonathan with dramatic power and psychological depth. David's relationship with Jonathan is no freestanding anomaly but operates within a supportive cultural context. It is no simple idealized friendship but a relationship fraught with themes of seduction, jealousy, conflicts of loyalty, doomed choices, and tragic consequences. Here we are dealing with no platonic friendship but with all the elements of passionate romance.

In this story David is the beloved youth of two powerful warriors who are rivals not only for his affection but also for the admiration and loyalty of the militia and people as a whole. And these are not mere rivals but also father and son, anticipating a kind of rivalry that will dog David in his later life, especially in relation to his son Absalom.

The jealousy of Saul is by no means based on illusion. For Jonathan is, from the beginning, engaged in the seduction of David, claiming for himself the armor-bearer whom Saul had chosen. Saul's jealousy has a powerful tragic dimension. Since it cannot avenge itself directly against the seducer (son), it turns against the beloved youth. But this means that it only succeeds in inexorably driving the beloved into the arms of the rival. (On the political level, similarly, it drives David away from being the champion of Israel and into alliance with Israel's greatest foe, the Philistines.)

In the end David finds a way to maintain his loyalty to his first lover without relinquishing his growing attachment to Jonathan. But this resolution is possible only after the death of both rivals at the hands of David's temporary allies. The resolution is thus expressed conclusively in David's grief and his loyalty to Jonathan's son (and Saul's grandson). Even on this level it is clear that David's love for Jonathan supplants the conjugal relationship with Michal.

The point of this brief rehearsal is to show that understanding these relationships as erotic in character makes the saga far more intelligible than readings that deny this dimension of the text.

Moreover, it enables us to incorporate elements of the story that must otherwise be explained away or passed over in silence; elements such as these: the overdetermined character of Saul's rage at David, the role of male beauty in narratives written for a male readership, and so on. Above all, we are able to account for the sexual innuendo in Saul's tirade at Jonathan, the accusation of exposing his mother's nakedness.

Thus, a gay-affirmative reading of the text does not do violence to the text and even enables us to gain a greater appreciation for the moral ambiguity and psychological complexity of the narrative. It helps us take into account prominent features of the text that must otherwise be ignored or explained away. If this reading of the narrative is accepted, then a number of interesting conclusions follow.

We deal first with what may be gleaned from the narrative concerning the homoerotic relationships that it depicts.

We first recognize that homoerotic relationships within the world of the text are by no means exclusive of heterosexual relationships. Thus, there is a profound difference between the way in which homoerotic relationships were represented in antiquity and the way in which they have commonly been represented in the late modern period.

In the contemporary construction of "homosexuality," it may seem implausible that one whose early first loves were other males should go on to be the husband and lover of many women. But for the ancients (and even the Elizabethans) there was no conflict at all in these different roles. Indeed, the literature abounds with the supposition that men who have sexual relationships with other males (whether younger or not) also fulfill their roles as lovers of women and as fathers of progeny. Not only so, but it is often enough also assumed that those especially given to the love of youths (as the ancients thought of this) were themselves "oversexed." That a man was the seducer or lover of many women only made it more rather than less likely that he would also have lovers of the same sex. Certainly, the story of David anticipates this classical profile.

There is the exception that David himself is not said to take on younger lovers, younger boy-companions. After being the beloved first of Saul and then of Jonathan (and finally, as we shall see, of YHWH), David's love life, insofar as it is noticed by the narrator, is directed to women. He remains loyal to the two men who loved him, and to the one of the two that he is said actually to have loved. Perhaps the death especially of Jonathan has closed off the possibility of loving again in that way.

We may also notice that the overarching structure of homoerotic relationships appears in this narrative to approximate the pederastic structure of cross-generational (and cross-class) eroticism of much of classical antiquity. Within this context David is always the beloved of an older lover rather than the lover of a boy-companion. In classical Greek terms David is always the *eromenos* (beloved youth) rather than the *erastēs* (older lover). He is always a beloved youth, the object of adult male desire (whether of YHWH, Saul, or Jonathan), responsive to the love of others rather than the initiator of that love. As such, David is, in modern gay parlance, a "bottom" rather than a "top." Nor is this incompatible with his subsequent role as husband, father, war leader, and king. Nearly a millennium after David it would be reported of Julius Caesar, another conqueror and founder of empire, that "he was every man's wife and every woman's husband."[14]

We may observe, however, that within this apparently pederastic structure, there is, as it were, another structure struggling to be born. It is the love of comrades or of putative equals.

David's relationship with Saul conforms clearly to the structure of cross-generational and cross-class relationships. The case of David and Jonathan is, however, more complex. The story presupposes that Jonathan is both older than David and, as putative heir to the throne, David's social superior. Jonathan's love for David seeks to abolish this hierarchical structure and indeed to overturn it. Saul certainly sees this implication in the relationship, and Jonathan appears ready to surrender his own social preeminence in favor of David on the basis of the bond of love, which grows between them.[15]

This equalizing force of love is anticipated in other barely glimpsed relationships in the narrative. For not only are the boy-companions of Saul and Jonathan younger social inferiors of the warriors; they are also full partners in the adventures of the respective heroes. In this saga, the love of men for one another tends to subvert the very hierarchical conventions within which that love is first articulated. Thus it is that later readers could understand the love of Jonathan and David as an anticipation of the mutual love of life partners, which comes to characterize ideals of both same-sex friendship and cross-sex marriage. This is not to say that this saga successfully undermines hierarchy. The structure of patriarchy remains firmly in

14. On Julius Caesar, see Suetonius, *The Twelve Caesars* ß52. The definitive study of attitudes toward sexual roles in Greece is K. J. Dover, *Greek Homosexuality* (New York: Vintage, 1978).
15. This is true whether Jonathan is suggesting coleadership of Israel or placing David alone on the throne.

place. But the story does provide a glimpse of relationships that some later readers, including Aelred, could develop into a paradigm of mutuality that would even undermine the patriarchal and hierarchical structuring of heterosexual relationships.

The erotic character of the relationships portrayed in this narrative has been occluded by the supposition that Israelite culture itself could not possibly have countenanced, still less celebrated, homoerotic relationships. For many years it has been customary to suppose that Israel was distinguished by the absence of homoerotic culture, and indeed it often has been supposed to be the fountainhead of homophobia. The examination of the tale of David and his lovers may serve to counter this impression. But there is considerably more to this story, as we shall see. For David's human lovers perish on the field of battle. But the warrior-chief who first loved him has not finished with him yet. It is to that story that we next turn.

3. *YHWH as* Erastēs

IN THE ANALYSIS of the erotic character of the relationships depicted in the narrative, we had occasion to refer to the love of YHWH for Saul and David. It is appropriate to return to that theme here at the end of our reflections on the saga.

Some may be offended that YHWH's love would be understood erotically. But biblical writers had no such compunction. Whether Israel (Ephraim) was figured as a maid or a youth, Hosea, Jeremiah, and Ezekiel did not shrink from images of wooing, courtship, jealousy, and adultery in characterizing that relationship.

Thus, in a narrative concerned with homoerotic love, it is scarcely surprising that YHWH should be cast as a lover—this time of men. And it is also here that the theological profundity of the narrative begins to come into view.

Two vied for David's love: Saul and Jonathan. But the conflict between them ultimately means that David is excluded from the company of either. The father and son rivals die together, and David goes on to fulfill his obligations as king and as producer of sons. That story has its own remarkable drama and pathos. But the story of David's lovers is not quite finished. For it was YHWH who loved him first and first set his eye upon him. And when the story ends, it will be clear that somehow YHWH has preserved his beloved for himself. It is a mellower YHWH at the end of the story than at

the beginning. No longer casting away a beloved like Saul on a whim, he
perseveres in love of David despite extraordinary provocations: the seduction/
rape of Bathsheba, the murder of Uriah, the imposition of a census. But the
David who could dance uncovered before the ark in the presence of
YHWH (2 Sam 6:20) is not cast away by the one who loved him first. Into
death and beyond, he remains the man whom YHWH loves. And in the
process the ancient desert-warrior God becomes somehow more humane,
more trustworthy, more forgiving. YHWH himself is learning to love. That
is the story to which we now turn.

We recall that David first seems to be chosen by YHWH on account of
his extraordinary beauty. In this way the selection of David to be YHWH's
young companion both conforms to and casts light upon the pattern of
warriors and their boy-companions that we examined earlier. At the end of
that discussion, we were left with the question of whether those relationships should be understood as homoerotic. The subsequent elaboration of
the relationship between David and the men who loved him has served to
greatly strengthen the case for a homoerotic interpretation of those relationships. Now we look more closely at the relationship between YHWH
and David to determine how far such a homoerotic reading of the text
sheds light also upon that relationship.

Fancy Dancer

In order to "flesh out" the erotic character of the relationship between
David and YHWH, we turn to one of the most remarkable episodes in the
account of this relationship: that of David's shameless cavorting before
Adonai and the ark as a "fancy dancer."[1]

The story of David's curious relationship with the ark of the "LORD of
hosts" occupies the whole of 2 Sam 6.[2] But we will first concentrate our
attention on the episode of 6:14–16 and its aftermath.

> David danced before the LORD with all his might; David was girded with a
> linen ephod. So David and all the house of Israel brought up the ark of the
> LORD with shouting, and with the sound of the trumpet.

1. With apologies, and a salute, to Patricia Nell Warren, *The Fancy Dancer* (New York: William Morrow, 1976).

2. I am indebted to the careful reading of this story and the one that follows (2 Sam 7) provided by J. P.
Fokkelman in his magisterial multivolume work; see *Throne and City* (vol. 3 of *Narrative Art and Poetry in the
Books of Samuel*; Assen, Netherlands: Van Gorcum, 1990). He recognizes the highly personal character of the
depicted roles of David and YHWH, stating that "what meets the eye is that the king and God are on an equal
footing" (181). This is made most clear by the move from titles such as king and God to the proper names
David and YHWH.

> As the ark of the LORD came into the city of David, Michal daughter of
> Saul looked out of the window, and saw King David leaping and dancing
> before the LORD; and she despised him in her heart. (6:14–16)

When the king has acted as priest to bless the people, he comes home,
where his enraged wife Michal meets him:

> But Michal the daughter of Saul came out to meet David, and said, "How
> the king of Israel honored himself today, uncovering himself today before
> the eyes of his servants' maids, as any vulgar fellow might shamelessly
> uncover himself!" David said to Michal, "It was before [in front of] the
> LORD, who chose me in place of your father and all his household, to
> appoint me as prince over Israel, the people of the LORD, that I have danced
> [cavorted] before the LORD. I will make myself yet more contemptible than
> this, and I will be abased in my own eyes; but by the maids of whom you
> have spoken, by them I shall be held in honor." And Michal the daughter of
> Saul had no child to the day of her death. (6:20–23)

What are we to make of David's near-naked self-display before the
physical presence of Adonai? Why is he dancing and cavorting? Why is he
uncovered or naked? And why is Michal so enraged?

The significance of Michal's reaction and David's response in 2 Samuel
is underscored by the omission of this interaction from the priestly retelling
of this story of David and the ark in 1 Chron 15. The Chronicler lives in a
significantly different cultural and historical context, writing, it is supposed,
several centuries after the composition of Samuel and in a society in which
priests rather than warriors have the leading role. We may briefly observe
some of the other differences between these accounts before returning to
the interaction between David and Michal.

In the priestly story the Levites play a major role and David appears as
their patron. It is because the priests were not in charge of the ark, for
example, that YHWH "burst out [forth]" onto Uzzah to deadly effect
(1 Chron 15:13).[3] David is said to be wearing a robe (15:27) in addition to
the ephod, which is thus converted from an undergarment to an outer garment rather like a vestment. Although 1 Chron 15:29 closely parallels 2
Sam 6:16, it omits the salient feature that David's dancing and cavorting was
"before YHWH," thereby making it seem to be simply a quasi-liturgical act

---

3. Unfortunately, at this point Fokkelman permits his own reading to be influenced by the Chronicler;
ibid., 189.

in company with the priests. Thus, the highly personal character of David's dancing is greatly reduced. He is leaping and dancing, but fully clothed, accompanied by priests and not "before the LORD."

As a consequence, Michal's earlier-expressed disgust at David's act (still retained by the Chronicler) can no longer have any sense. For David is simply doing what the Levites do. The specific erotic charge of the story has been expunged. There is no claim that David has disgraced himself in the eyes of women or that David's dance is a response to YHWH's having chosen him over YHWH's first "beloved" Saul.

The Chronicler's act of cleaning up this story tells us what to look for in the saga of 2 Samuel.[4] And we shall see that this is most telling with respect to the Chronicler's complete omission of Michal's remonstration against David and his reply. The account of 1 Chronicles serves as a reverse highlighting of the salient details for our focus.

Michal is David's wife. But she is also, as the text reminds us, the daughter of Saul, who had been David's first (human) lover. Moreover, she is the sister of David's last and most intimate (human) lover, Jonathan. Saul has rather begrudgingly given her to David as a trophy wife. And her love for David had been demonstrated by rescuing David from a jealous Saul's enraged attempt to assassinate David. Yet her role as David's protector has been taken by her own brother Jonathan, who has supplanted both Saul and Michal as David's chief lover. Perhaps it is only for Jonathan's sake that David has reclaimed her as a wife (2 Sam 3:12–16). Nevertheless, to the public she is especially known as Saul's daughter (as the narrator reminds us twice in the story) and thus as establishing a certain connection to Israel's first king.

To be sure, Michal casts her scorn as a reminder of David's royal station, a station that she perhaps believes that she ensures. In any case, his behavior seems to her to threaten his royal dignity and thus also her royal station.

But here is the rub. Michal has played second fiddle to David's erotic relationships with Saul and Jonathan. Now both are dead. But instead of having David at last for herself, she has lost him to another even more powerful male before whom he shamelessly disports himself where everyone can see. David now has another male lover with whom

---

4. That the Chronicler regularly cleans up the David saga is apparent, for example, in the elimination of the whole David and Bathsheba story and the resultant trouble in David's household with respect to Absalom. In this case it is the erotic or sexual life of David that is "cleaned up." This even goes so far as to expunge Bathsheba from the role of mother of Solomon, who simply becomes one of the sons "born in Jerusalem" (1 Chron 3:5). Is it coincidence that the priestly class responsible for the Chronicles is also the class that finds both adultery and (certain forms of) same-sex sexual practice to be abominable (Lev 18 and 20)?

she can never hope to compete. Her man, the king, is the shameless boy-toy of Adonai.[5]

Michal's outburst tells us a good deal about what David is doing here.[6] In her view he is dancing naked in front of the ark. Twice she emphasizes the claim that David has "exposed himself": "uncovering himself . . . as any vulgar fellow might shamelessly uncover himself!" This emphasis on David's having exposed himself in his dancing is, of course, what the Chronicler cannot permit us to see. That is why the Chronicler has clad David in a robe as well as the ephod that appears in 2 Sam 6:14 (on which, see below).

David's uncovering of himself is further "exposed" as that which might excite the interest and perhaps fascinated amusement of the girls of the town. Michal's explanation of her despising of David exposes to the reader's eye the display of David's nakedness.

Moreover, David's reply that the girls of the town will honor him rather than despise him for this display suggests, given what we know of David's kingly promiscuity, that his genitals are especially in view here. This is reinforced by the narrator's suggestion that Michal will remain childless after her outburst. What she has seen and despised will not be at her service to make her a mother. Michal has drawn our attention to David's nakedness and particularly to his genitals, more especially, his penis. This is what Michal (and the narrator) has caused the reader to glimpse in his shameless cavorting.

David replies that the maids will not despise him but honor him, perhaps in spite, perhaps because, of what they have seen. But does it not seem

---

5. Fokkelman, *Throne and City*, 199, also notices, though he does not develop, the aspect of sexuality evident in Michal's tirade: "Michal . . . insinuates that his religious surrender to God is something quite different. . . . We onlookers can take the clause to be a poorly-disguised sign of sexual jealousy." D. N. Fewell and D. M. Gunn, *Gender, Power, and Promise* (Nashville: Abingdon, 1993), 154, also declare: "There is a sexual dimension to her scorn." But they do not take this any further in reading the relationship between David and YHWH.

6. Michal's remonstration with David also opens up the possibility of a reading quite different from the one I am undertaking. For her point of view brings into question the entire phallocentric world that is on display in the queer reading I am attempting. Reread through her eyes, the homoeroticism of this phallocentric world is at the same time rather misogynist in the way it operates with respect to women in general and in particular in relation to her. As Fokkelman (*Throne and City*) points out, her love for David has been deflected in the meantime to a man who in fact loved her (Paltiel; 1 Sam 25:44; 2 Sam 3:15–16). Then, for reasons of state, she has been taken back by David, whom she had loved in her youth (1 Sam 18) but who does not seem to love her any more now than before (Fokkelman does not observe the displacement I have suggested by Jonathan). A feminist reading taking Michal as a point of departure would be a necessary complement to the homoerotic reading I am suggesting and is pursued by the reflections of Fewell and Gunn, *Gender*, 153–55; and by J. C. Exum, *Fragmented Women: Feminist (Sub)versions of Biblical Narratives* (Valley Forge, PA: Trinity Press International, 1993). At the same time, the retrograde "classism" of her remonstration itself (with its reference to slaves, female slaves, and riffraff) suggests the importance of a class critique of her position. The complementarity of, and tensions among, queer, feminist, and class readings that I am suggesting emphasizes the importance of multiple perspectives and thus the nonabsoluteness of the homoerotic interpretation I am proposing.

that more is going on here? For David is not dancing to impress the girls of the town. He is, as he says, dancing before YHWH. Moreover, he is not ashamed to be doing so.

Now why does David have to uncover himself in order to dance before Adonai? Surely this is not what any worshipper of the Lord does in "liturgical dance."[7] Why this shameless display of the nude body?

We recall that the Lord has chosen his young male companions at least in significant part because of their physical beauty. It was this that seemed to motivate Adonai's favor, to awaken his desire and confirm his selection first of Saul and then of David. And now in the physical presence of Adonai (the ark), David displays his body to the one who first desired him for his beauty.

Now we may ask ourselves why David is thus displaying the desired body before the great lover. The idea of erotic dance, exhibiting the body of the one who wishes to be or is desired, is well known in the literature of antiquity. To be sure, it is almost always the female who displays herself in this way, seeking to arouse the interest, the desire, the infatuation of the powerful male observer. Perhaps the most famous biblical example of this sort of behavior is the erotic dance of Salome, whose nakedness is both veiled and revealed in the dance of the seven veils. In her case she was seeking (at her mother's behest) to inflame the passion of the king in order to secure his favor and so his compliance in the plot to assassinate John the baptizer (Mark 2:17–29; Josephus, *Ant.* 18.5.4).

Is something like that going on here? Surely things are more complex, for in any case it is a male rather than a female who is cavorting in erotic self-display before a more powerful male. Is David seeking to rekindle the old flame?

It may be. But another dimension of this rather astonishing display comes to light when we consider the part of the narrative that leads up to this episode.

In the preceding narrative David had consulted Adonai as his war-chief. And the result of this had been such destruction of the Philistines that David calls YHWH the one who "has burst forth . . . like a bursting flood" (2 Sam 5:20).

In consequence of this "flood burst," David resolves to bring the ark to his town. This procession starts out with David and the men dancing before the Lord. But an untoward accident occurs. When the oxen pulling the cart on which the ark is perched stumble, the ark starts to fall. One of the

---

7. In 6:5, 15, we are told that "all the house of Israel" were dancing and celebrating the arrival of the ark. This might be regarded as a sort of "liturgy." But only of David do we have reported the notorious ephod and the remarkable reaction of Michal that suggests David's (virtual) nudity.

men, Uzzah, reaches out to brace it, and YHWH "bursts out" again (6:7–8), this time killing the one who had inadvertently touched Adonai's physical embodiment.

David is furious with his ferocious lover and decides to leave the ark where it is. He returns to Jerusalem in a sulk and lets Adonai stew out on the farm, presumably to recover from this testosteronic tantrum. Three months later David hears that the place where Adonai's ark has been left is flourishing. The juxtaposition of a deadly "bursting forth" with the unexpected bestowal of fertility and prosperity reads rather like a phallic fantasy, and we will have to return to this dimension later.

There are many ways to read this, but it looks as though what has happened is that David's sulky withdrawal has taught Adonai a lesson.[8] For instead of bursting forth in murderous rage, the ark gives bounty and blessing. It is then that David goes to fetch the ark, bring it to where he lives, and dance naked before it.

The cavorting of David, then, is not so much seductive entreaty to re-kindle an old flame but a kind of reward for Adonai's good behavior. Now that he is tamed, the love between them can be consummated. And indeed, in the ensuing narrative Adonai will basically wed himself to David (2 Sam 7).

Another detail in this episode may serve to substantiate this reading. It concerns the act of cavorting. While dancing before the Lord is sometimes spoken of in certain "liturgical" contexts (and this is surely what the Chronicler intends the reader to see), the text associates it with a term that seems to refer to cavorting, disporting, gamboling.[9] This is certainly not a liturgical dance, at least not in any ordinary sense.

We again meet with the image in one of the songs of Isaiah (13:1–22). The song/oracle has to do, we are told, with the destruction of Babylon. The picture of devastation coming to the apex of culture and civilization is remarkable. Its climaxing feature is that nothing remotely domestic or civilized will take refuge in its ruins: not nomads, not sheep—only the wildest of beasts. Prowling its ruins are hyenas and jackals, howling creatures. And there "goat-demons will dance [cavort]" (v. 21). Goat-demons? What is it

---

8. Most readers interpret this story as a reminder of YHWH's sovereignty as one whom David cannot simply bring to the city at will. But this traditional reading strikes me as partial at best, wrongheaded at worst. After all, YHWH can't transport his own ark to Jerusalem. He (with the ark) has been abandoned on the farm of Obed-edom, turned over to foreigners. (Obed-edom means "servant of Edom" and thus refers to rivals of Israel whether or not within a territory "ruled" from Jerusalem.) If he doesn't show that he can be depended on, that is where he stays. Indeed, given the earlier history of the ark and its ill effects on Philistines and Israelites alike, it is clear that the One to whom it belongs is in great need of learning a bit of self-discipline if he hopes to be given a central place in the life of his people.

9. Fokkelman, *Throne and City*, 196, reads the description of David's dancing as follows: "Pointing to the hands and feet of David, the participles are a merismus for the ruler in a total movement which stands for total surrender."

that is cavorting in this wildest and most uncivilized of places? Goat-demons. Another oracle of Isaiah to similar effect (Isa 34) has jackals and other fauna inhabiting the ruins of a former citadel of civilization together with Lilith (the storm demon) and the same goat-demons: cavorting and howling goat-demons in places of wildest devastation (34:13–14).

Here I believe we must think of the satyr figures that also inhabit the ancient Greek and Roman *imaginarium*. Their goatlike legs and cavorting habits image forth a wild and untamed eroticism. They are the contrary of culture and its "discontents." They are, if you like, unrepressed id.

This appears to comport as well with another appearance of these satyrs/goat-demons. In the instructions for offering sacrifices found in Lev 17, we are told that Moses is to tell Aaron to carefully dash all the blood of the sacrifice on the altar and to burn all the fat from the meat as a pleasing odor to the Lord (17:6). The purpose is "so that they may no longer offer their sacrifices for goat-demons, to whom they prostitute themselves" (17:7). Presumably, fat and blood are either offerings to goat-demons or regarded as intoxicating the people into prostituting themselves with the goat-demons. To be sure, "prostituting oneself" may be largely metaphorical in the sense of turning to other gods. But it does also suggest offering one-self promiscuously to service others sexually—precisely the sort of behavior a priest might suspect of those who cavort with satyrs (2 Chron 11:15).

I am not going to suggest that David is worshipping a goat demon or is himself transposed into one. Nevertheless, shepherds worshipped satyrs, who carried pipes and lyres for music and dancing, and David has been a shepherd and has also carried a lyre for making music in the fields. What this chain of associations does suggest, however, is the shamelessly erotic character of the cavorting that the narrator ascribes to David and of which his royal wife accuses him.

David's reply to his wife's accusation is rather extraordinary. In the first place, he underscores that the one whose gaze he sought in his dance was the Lord. It was YHWH he sought to entertain or delight with his cavorting.

He further explains that the motive for doing so has to do with the fact that this YHWH has chosen him. It is because YHWH is his lover, the one who has picked him above all others, that David directs his cavorting to his gaze. Moreover, David does not resist pointing out that YHWH's choice of him occurred despite the fact that YHWH had previously chosen another as his favorite and companion. That other, of course, was Saul, Michal's father. In spite of YHWH's previously having favored Saul, he has subsequently chosen David. It appears that David is rather flaunting his being beloved over Saul.

Only then does David admit that his shameless cavorting before YHWH might possibly be regarded as shameless. "I will make myself yet more contemptible than this, and I will be abased in my own eyes." How, we may wonder, does David intend to be even more shameless than he has already been in his naked cavorting before his great lover?

The KJV speaks of David "playing" before YHWH, but David seems to be saying that this is only "foreplay." He intends to "go all the way." We shall have to see whether or in what way this suggested consummation will be the subject of narration. But first we must pursue another clue in the text concerning an ephod and its relation to the ark.

Excursus: The Ark and the Ephod

And now let us examine the ephod (2 Sam 6:14). In Michal's view, David might as well have been completely naked in his satyrlike cavorting. But we are told he was wearing a linen ephod, apparently a short linen apron that covers the genitals (while at the same time perhaps calling attention to them and so exposing them).[10]

But while David's ephod may both reveal and conceal his genitals, as I have suggested, we are led in an interesting direction if we pursue another ephod—not one that belongs to David but one that belongs to Adonai.

We encounter a narrative concerning the divine ephod in Judg 8, where one is made of gold by Gideon and placed in his town of Ophrah. The priestly editor sniffs that "all Israel prostituted themselves to it there, and it became a snare to Gideon and to his family" (8:27). Notwithstanding the priestly displeasure, it appears that the Lord was not in the least offended by Israel "prostituting" themselves with this ephod, for "the land had rest forty years in the days of Gideon" (8:28).

We should not, however, overlook that the promiscuous sexuality hinted at in the term "prostituted themselves" is also attributed to the relation of Israel to the "goat-demons," whose cavorting has resembled the capering of

---

10. The question of the character of an ephod is rather mysterious. While the Hebrew Bible and the English translation use the term "ephod," we shall see that there is considerable confusion about whether it is an undergarment or an overgarment, a covering of the chest or a covering of the groin. This confusion is expressed in the Septuagint where a different term is often used for the priestly garment, reserving "ephod" (transliterated from Hebrew) for the fetishlike object in Judges and 1 Samuel. When Exod 28:6–14 describes the priestly vestments of Aaron, the LXX uses the term *epōmida* to translate the Hebrew word *'ephod* and speaks of it as having shoulder-pieces/straps. Thus, we seem to have a progression from ephod as an undergarment covering the loins (David's dance), to an outer garment (Chronicles), to a garment that is worn over the chest or shoulders (Exodus) rather than below or at the waist. It is only the first meaning that we can use to make sense of the fetish object sometimes confused with the ark.

David before the Lord. Here it is not the ark but the ephod that draws the apparently shameful behavior of Israelite males.

The Lord's ephod shows up again in another strange story later in Judges in which a young man named Micah makes an image for the Lord out of silver that he had previously stolen from his mother. This image, we are told, has the form of an "ephod and teraphim" (17:5).[11] In a story that occupies Judg 18, the Danites conspire to take possession of Micah's metal ephod (and the young Levite he had conscripted to replace his son as priest for the shrine of the ephod). By means of the stolen ephod, the Danites are successful in their attempt to take over the land of a quiet and unsuspecting people. There "they maintained as their own Micah's idol that he had made, as long as the house of God was at Shiloh" (18:31).

The point of alluding to this strange tale is once again to notice that the Lord's ephod is a potent representation of the Lord. It seems to represent the phallic prowess and potency of God and indeed brings success and bounty to those who possess it. It masks and reveals, represents and embodies the phallic power of the Lord.

This focus on YHWH's loincloth or whatever it is has a remarkable appearance in one of the symbolic actions of the prophet Jeremiah (13:1–11).[12] He is told to take his own loincloth, with which his loins are covered, and hide it in the cleft of a rock by the river. When he is told to recover it, he discovers, unsurprisingly, that it is spoiled. Now what YHWH says is that just as this loincloth clings to the loins of the wearer, so also should Judah cling to the loins of YHWH (13:11). But what clings to YHWH's loins (Judah/Jerusalem) has been ruined and so should be thrown away. From this image I wish particularly to emphasize the image of clinging, the intimacy between the loins (genitals) and the loincloth. Thus, Judah should cling to that to which YHWH's loincloth clings—his phallus.

The ephod, we have noticed, is ambiguous: it both hides and focuses attention on the genitals of the wearer. Here we may think of something like a loincloth or breechcloth, a G-string or jockstrap. Such a piece of apparel may serve to decently cover as well as indecently draw attention to the male genitalia. In the case of YHWH's "jockstrap," what happens when it serves not as a piece of apparel but as an item that represents its wearer? In

---

11. One may guess that the teraphim is what an ephod covers. At any rate the teraphim may be supposed to have something of a phallic shape since it serves to substitute more or less convincingly for the body of a man (when covered). This is part of the ruse used by Michal to help David escape from Saul (1 Sam 19:13, 16 NRSV n). The shape suggested is long and cylindrical. And it has a head to which goats' hair (!) may be affixed to complete the ruse. Hence, it is a herm.

12. The term used here is different from "ephod," but I am contending that it has a similar function, similar at least to the ephod worn by David in his dance.

other words, what happens when it becomes a fetish? When as such it is cast in hard and shiny metal like the ephods made by Gideon or Micah? How does the carrying around of a large metallic jockstrap represent YHWH?

Now imagine that this object is adored, and the men of Israel are said to prostitute themselves to it. One consults it to derive battle plans for defeating more-powerful foes. The Lord's ephod is a potent fetish of the divine phallus.

God's ephod, as it happens, plays an important role in the David saga as well. It first appears in a battle scene, where it is carried by the great-grandson of Eli (1 Sam 14:3). It is the ephod associated with Shiloh, but it is now carried into battle with the same hope that it will not only represent but also somehow *be* the potency of the Lord on the side of the outnumbered Israelites. Yet a few verses later we are told that it is "the ark of God" that is carried by the Israelites into battle (14:18).[13]

This conflation of ark and ephod is not without significance. Much later, when a jealous Saul hounds David, Abiathar brings the ephod of God to David, who enters into conversation with it about how to escape the threat of Saul (23:6, 9–12). In dire straits again for the same cause, David again calls Abiathar to bring the ephod so he can talk with it (30:7–8). Later, David will engage in precisely the same behavior, sitting before the ark in order to have conversation with the Lord.

What I want to suggest is that the ark and the ephod have the same function. They make physically present the hypermasculine presence of the Lord. They both disguise and disclose the phallic potency of Adonai. The function of the ark as phallic representation of the divine has already been at work in the story of the ark that lends to YHWH the nickname *Perez* ("Bursting Out Against"; 2 Sam 6:8; cf. 5:20). The ark before which David dances is the sheathed phallus of his lover.

That the ark functions as an ephod or phallic sheath is further illustrated in the earlier history of the ark. We recall that in 1 Samuel the ark, rather than protecting Israel against their enemies as expected, has actually been captured by the Philistines. There is a great deal that is intriguing about the history of the ark among the Philistines that would reward a queer reading. Yet the episode that most dramatically substantiates the view that the ark embodies the phallic potency of YHWH is that concerning YHWH in the house of Dagon. The Philistines transport the ark to their city of Ashdod, the setting for this curious episode:

---

13. The LXX corrects the reference to the ark here to a more consistent "ephod."

Then the Philistines took the ark of God and brought it into the house of
Dagon and placed it beside Dagon. When the people of Ashdod rose early
the next day, there was Dagon, fallen on his face to the ground before the
ark of the LORD. So they took Dagon and put him back in his place. But
when they rose early on the next morning, Dagon had fallen on his face to
the ground before the ark of the LORD, and the head of Dagon and both his
hands were lying cut off upon the threshold; only the trunk of Dagon was
left to him. (1 Sam 5:2–4)

The ark has been placed in the house or sanctuary of a fertility god of
the Philistines as a trophy of their victory and a sign of the humiliation of
YHWH. But instead of the submission of YHWH to Dagon, we have the
representation of Dagon's submission to YHWH: he is facedown on the
ground. The first such occasion might be read as the voluntary submission
of Dagon to YHWH, and thus perhaps as a cultic act of prostration. But the
second occasion makes it clear that Dagon's submission is not voluntary but
is accomplished with great violence, resulting in his dismemberment.

What is the character of this forced submission that the ark exacts of
Dagon? It seems quite likely that the narrative represents Dagon as having
been raped by the ark. Indeed, in this saga material we already have the
association of rape and dismemberment in the accounts that end the book
of Judges, concerning the Levite's concubine. Thus, the god of phallic
power, instead of dominating YHWH, has himself been dominated: forced
into head-down submission to the violent potency of the ark.

The theme of phallic assault may actually continue in the tale of
YHWH's strange sojourn (as the ark) among the Philistines. Following the
assault upon Dagon at Ashdod, we also hear: "The hand of the LORD was
heavy upon the people of Ashdod, and he terrified and struck them with
tumors" (5:6). The tumors here are regarded by several commentators as
hemorrhoids,[14] which in this context would mean that the people are
struck with the mark of anal rape. The similarity of what is happening to
the people and what had been done to Dagon is in fact underlined in the
text: "His hand is heavy on us and on our god Dagon" (5:7). When the ark
is then moved to Gath, a similar attack of YHWH upon the people occurs.
"The hand of the LORD was against the city, causing a very great panic; he

14. Peter Ackroyd, *The First Book of Samuel* (Cambridge: Cambridge University Press, 1971), proposes that
the affliction of boils or tumors that scourges the Philistines in the subsequent episodes may also be understood
as hemorrhoids! He writes: "The Hebrew text itself offers an alternative at certain points in the narrative, the
latter word being thought improper for public reading." E. Fox confirms this in comments with his translation
of the books of Samuel, *Give Us a King!* (New York: Schocken Books, 1999), 24: "The written text has 'hemorrhoids'; scribal tradition has substituted 'tumors' here."

struck the inhabitants of the city, both young and old, so that tumors [hemorrhoids] broke out on them" (5:9). Subsequently, the same is said to occur in Ekron (5:11–12).

When the Philistines decide to rid themselves of their perilous trophy, they send the ark of YHWH back toward Israel, laden with five gold hemorrhoids as a sign of their submission to Adonai (although not to Israel). The sending of five together with naming the five cities/lords of the Philistines (6:17) suggests that the narrative may have been abbreviated. Instead of three episodes of the outbreak of the potency of the LORD upon the Philistines, there may have been five such outbursts. Thus, the population of each of the five cities experienced the phallic assault of YHWH upon them, an assault that is somehow connected to the ark as the sign and seat of that potency. That YHWH afflicts the Philistines, both young and old (1 Sam 5:9; cf. Gen 19:4), with the mark of anal rape gives added emphasis to their seers' warnings about YHWH making "fools [sport] of them" (1 Sam 6:6).

This is a tale that "makes sense" in a narrative world in which the domination of aliens is regularly represented as enacted through forcible gang rape. This is the world within which the story of Sodom (Gen 19) is possible as well as that of the account of the crime of the Benjaminites in Judg 19. The idea of phallic aggression as manifestation of male dominance is well known in the ancient world (as it is in contemporary prisons and ethnic warfare). Indeed, it is not unknown to occur among the gods, as the Egyptian tale of Seth and Horus makes clear. In that tale too, Seth seeks to demonstrate his dominance of Horus through anal rape and nearly succeeds, save for a trick played by Horus. His defense includes dismemberment (his own hand, which had caught the semen), and he winds up getting his semen into Seth, who then appears to be feminized (made pregnant indeed) by Horus.[15]

I am not suggesting that this tale licenses male homosexual rape as an expression of dominance. Even in the tale of YHWH and Dagon, we see that there is a significant role reversal. The ark of the alien and vulnerable YHWH is presumably in Dagon's house in order to be submissive to Dagon. Instead of submitting to Dagon's phallic superiority, however, it is Dagon who must forcibly submit.

---

15. See E. F. Wente, trans. (from the Chester Beatty I Papyrus), "The Contendings of Horus and Seth," in *The Literature of Ancient Egypt: An Anthology* (ed. W. K. Simpson; New Haven: Yale University Press, 1973), 108–26. See also Joseph Kaster, ed., *The Literature and Mythology of Ancient Egypt* (London: Penguin, 1968), 246–53. References to this story in studies of "homosexuality" normally fail to report that the victim of anal rape here actually comes out on top. Even more rare is the recognition of the bawdy character of the tale, which seems to spoof the gods.

However, those who use the story of Sodom to condemn what two millennia later would be called "sodomy"[16] should reflect on the curious story of Dagon's forced submission. Is the Lord also a "sodomite"?

This brief excursion into the earlier history of the ark serves to make clear that it is to be understood, like the ephod, as the physical embodiment of YHWH's phallic potency.

That then sheds light on what has brought David to dance before the Lord and to dance in just this way (2 Sam 6). The Lord, we recall, has burst forth on David's enemies, like a torrential stream (ch. 5). But the Lord's potency also has burst forth on the innocent Uzzah (6:7–8). Now David's sulk had brought his unpredictable lover to a kind of contrition, and so the cavorting and (almost) naked beloved (David) welcomes the Lord/ark/ephod. The phallus is friendly, and so one may caper before it in welcome and perhaps even prepare oneself to be more shameless.

In the homoerotically suffused relationship between David and YHWH, the maleness of both characters seems essential. Both have "ephods." For each, the ephod serves both to conceal and expose: David's ephod, Adonai's ark (posing as an ephod, or is it the other way around?). David's maleness is coyly draped in linen. Adonai's is impressively sheathed in the ark. One is lover, the other beloved. But it is the lover, the *erastēs*, who has had to learn to behave himself if he is to be near his beloved, trusted by his beloved, ecstatically welcomed by the beloved. For if in this tale Adonai is the top and David (as usual) plays the role of the bottom, it is by no means the case that the top is always in control or that the bottom is simply dominated. This is not, after all, rape; it is love.

Holy Union?

The sixth chapter of 2 Samuel ends with David's indication that if Michal thinks he has thus far been shameless with YHWH, it is his intention to be even more shameless. This assertion is counterposed by the narrator's suggestion that David's relation with Michal will not be consummated. What this strange juxtaposition leads us to expect is that the relation between David and YHWH, in contrast to that between David and Michal, *will* be consummated. And the register within which we are to expect the consummation is specifically erotic, even sexual.

Now it is the case that this consummation will not be narrated in specifically sexual terms. But this is not because the sexual consummation of a

---

16. For the development of the idea of sodomy, see Mark D. Jordan, *The Invention of Sodomy in Christian Theology* (Chicago: University of Chicago Press, 1997).

relationship between YHWH and his beloved is necessarily unthinkable. The theme of the (sexual) consummation of the relationship between YHWH and his beloved is by no means alien to the literature of Israel.

The prophet Jeremiah, who speaks both in celebration of and in dismay at the intimacy of YHWH's relationship to himself as prophet, does in fact use the image of sexual seduction and even rape to complain of the way in which YHWH has treated him (Jer 20:7). And later, Ezekiel will use the image of YHWH's sexual consummation of his betrothal to Israel in a remarkable passage of almost pornographic character (Ezek 16, esp. v. 8; cf. Ruth 3). In the case of Ezekiel, the image will depend upon a transgendering of Israel into a lovely female in order to make the sexual imagery work. But there is no suggestion of Jeremiah's having been transgendered (although the Lord forbids him to have a wife and children perhaps as a sign of coming judgment; Jer 16:2).[17]

Moreover, that the divine being may be thought of as capable of a sexual consummation of relationship lies behind the notion of the relationship between Mary and God in Luke's account of the conception of Jesus (1:35). Since being "overshadow[ed]" by "the power of the Most High" results in conception (itself about the only public demonstration of sexual consummation of male-female relationships available), one must reckon with the possibility of imagining something like sexual consummation as the essential basis for Luke's narrative. Thus, readers who make something of the narrative concerning the "virgin birth" of Jesus should not be surprised that YHWH may be depicted in other contexts as sexually consummating a relationship.

The narrative of 2 Sam 7 will not provide a quasi-pornographic description of consummation of the homoerotically charged relationship between YHWH and David. But in important respects it does depend upon the suggestion of such a consummation. The narrative, in fact, has something of the function I have ascribed to an ephod. It both conceals and so draws attention to such a consummation.

The entirety of chapter 7 concerns this consummation or what takes the place of sexual consummation. The story begins with a kind of attempted role reversal. David proposes to build his lover a house of cedar like the one in which he lives. Building a house for a conjugal partner and/or the partner's divinity is something that will get Solomon into trouble later (1 Kgs 11).

---

17. That Jeremiah is not transgendered by the sexual aggressiveness of YHWH may be due to the way in which YHWH is figured in the discourse of Jeremiah not as a husband but as a warrior (Jer 20:11–12).

On one level of meaning, this building of a house seems a "reward" for YHWH. It is also a kind of domestication. In any case, it may also be a reversal in that it is the act of a husband for a wife. This apparent reversal of roles appears as something of a continuation of the way in which David has apparently caused YHWH to behave himself by leaving the ark temporarily in the territory of an alien after the outburst against Uzzah.

The provision of a house for YHWH wins the initial approval of Nathan; however, in the night YHWH accosts the prophet with a message for David. The dream-vision is at least double in character (2 Sam 7:5–17). It begins with a reminder that YHWH has been quite content to live as a warrior in a tent, as he has moved about with his people. YHWH will not live in a house, at least not while David is alive. He will maintain his freedom, living as a warrior in a camp.

Thus, YHWH corrects Nathan, who had agreed to David's original impulse, and provides an alternative: YHWH is the one who will "make [David] a house," not the other way around (7:11, 16). This negotiation of roles is quite intriguing to behold. It is affectionate, at least on the surface. But it is also declaring just who is the top here and who the bottom, who is the lover and who the beloved.[18]

To make this clear, YHWH reminds David, through Nathan's oneiric seance, that it is he, YHWH, who has the initiative in the relationship. He took David from the field, from following sheep, and made him a prince. Hence, it is not for David to take YHWH from the field (tent); instead, YHWH has already done this for David. Moreover, he has been steadfast in being with David wherever he goes. YHWH has been with David as the (divine) warrior who has defeated David's enemies (let's be clear who is the warrior and who the armor-bearer).

This discourse is both stern and affectionate. Throughout, YHWH refers to David as "my servant," a term otherwise used by YHWH of Abraham and of Moses.[19] It reasserts the role of YHWH as the initiating subject and as the loving possessor of David. YHWH is gently reminding David that he does not have to be the active subject but may rely confidently on YHWH to carry this role in their relationship.

This reminder of the dynamics in the relationship between hero and armor-bearer also brings to mind one of the features of this relation I have previously identified: the freedom of the warrior to choose one or more successive armor-bearers.

---

18. Fokkelman, *Throne and City*, 211, remarks: "David is merely to take up the position of receiver."

19. Ibid., also observing that the term "sounds intimate" (214) and remarking upon "the highly personal tone" of the discourse (215).

David has already invoked this possibility in his reply to Michal to the effect that though YHWH has first chosen Saul, he has subsequently chosen David to replace Saul as his favorite (6:21). This recollection is a double-edged sword since it both places David above Saul and also suggests the tenuousness of YHWH's selection of favored companion. At the very brink of consummation, a nagging doubt rises to the surface. Is this also why David wanted to house/domesticate YHWH? To make sure of the faithfulness of his rather unpredictable lover?

In any case, YHWH, while refusing the gift (bribe) of a cedar house, does confront this doubt, bringing it into the open and seeking to dispel it. He promises that he will not take his steadfast love (*khesed*) from David as he has earlier done with Saul (7:15). YHWH is promising lifetime faithfulness, binding himself to David always. It is something like a marriage vow, or at least as we now say, a holy union.

Now the specific form of this faithfulness, this steadfast love of YHWH for David, will take a rather surprising form. It will have to do with YHWH's relationship with David's offspring, with David's son. YHWH promises, "I will be a father to him, and he shall be a son to me" (7:14).

It is significantly not the case that YHWH is or will be a father to David. The model of homoerotic relationship that we are displaying here is quite different from what Eilberg-Schwartz sees between Moses and God or Israel and God.[20] The erotic character of the relationship to David is explained not in terms of a paternal relation between David and YHWH but in terms of a paternal relation between YHWH and David's son.

Put perhaps too briefly, David's son will have two fathers: David and YHWH. This calls to mind the way in which in contemporary society the "normalcy" of same-sex relations is offered to view in grammar school: "Solomon has two daddies."

What is particularly striking here is that the relationship YHWH proposes concerning David's son is the sort of relationship that David adopts for Jonathan's son Mephibosheth. Indeed, this latter relationship seems to bracket the whole episode. We first meet with Jonathan's crippled son in 2 Sam 4:4, and David's quasi-adoption of Mephibosheth comes in the narrative of chapter 9. Indeed, the relation between David and Mephibosheth continues far into the narrative, with 19:24–30 seeming to reach a certain conclusion in 21:7.

What is striking is that the erotic and perhaps sexual relation between David and Jonathan has taken the form of a relationship between David

---

20. H. Eilberg-Schwartz, *God's Phallus and Other Problems for Men and Monotheism* (Boston: Beacon, 1994).

and Jonathan's son after Jonathan's death. This is precisely what YHWH suggests concerning his relationship with David's (yet unborn) son after David's death.[21]

The relationship thus between human males parallels and interacts with the erotics of the relationship between David and YHWH. We therefore have to explore the intertwining of these erotic relationships.

First, however, we must turn to David's response to the avowal or betrothal proposed by YHWH.

David responds with alacrity. Immediately he places himself "before the LORD"—in the same relation as in his wild dance. Here the posture is not one of dancing but one of sitting before the Lord, before the ark. Now all is decorous and in a certain way ceremonial, although by no means cultic in character. David immediately presents himself before his lover in his lover's tent.

His reply indicates that he is more than content to be the beloved rather than the lover. There is no attempt to return to the earlier plan. Rather, the words of David are of total consent.

Given YHWH's earlier ways of behaving, what may be most remarkable is that this consent has not been produced by YHWH's fearsome power but by his offering and assurance of "steadfast love."

David picks up the term that YHWH has used ("my servant") and in speaking to YHWH repeatedly calls himself "your servant." This is counterposed to the appellation of his lover as "my lord" (Hebrew: *adonay*).[22] This is not the first time the reader of the Samuel saga will have encountered such terminology. "Your servant" is precisely what David calls himself in relation to his human lover Jonathan at the point of greatest narrated intimacy between them (1 Sam 20:7–8). The narrative has thus prepared for this terminology, to be read not only as the words of vows of love between two males but also as pointing to a love that lasts beyond death. If the love of David and Jonathan prefigures that of David and YHWH in terms of faithfulness and intimacy, what transpires in the speech of David to YHWH is an intensification of what had transpired between himself and Jonathan.

The relationship between David and YHWH is thus consummated in a kind of "marriage" that borrows its terms from the homoerotically charged relationship of David and Jonathan. Whatever it is that David had in mind about being even more shameless has been covered by this avowal of

---

21. Actually, the narrative has already mentioned Solomon as one of the sons born in Jerusalem (2 Sam 5:14) in advance of not only the relation with the ark but also the account of David's affair with Bathsheba.

22. Fokkelman, *Throne and City*, 237, observes that the word used here (*adonay*, "my lord") is unique to Samuel, but this must be a mistake.

steadfast love and its unconditional acceptance by David. This relationship will certainly cover David not so much with shame as with honor. For the relationship that YHWH initiates and consummates with David is not simply a private matter between these two principals; it is also one that implicates and in a way includes the whole of Israel.

What is perhaps most striking about the narrative we have been examining is not the homoeroticism it exhibits but the transformation that it portrays in the character of YHWH. In the early stages of this narrative, YHWH was characterized by an almost uncontrolled phallic aggression. At the beginning of 1 Samuel he was certainly rather undependable and, indeed, arbitrary. It is there that he abandons his own people in their need and yet proceeds symbolically to rape not only the god Dagon but also Dagon's people, the Philistines. Even when he is returned to Israel, he strikes out against his own people when their prying eyes seem to invade the "privates" of the ark (1 Sam 6:19 NRSV n).

In the ensuing narrative he chooses Saul as his companion but is ready to abandon him almost at once in favor of the beautiful David. Now one of the most notable characteristics of David in relation to his human lovers is an abiding loyalty. His love is indeed steadfast love not only toward Jonathan but also toward Saul. It is this that seems somehow to "win over" YHWH. This does not occur without certain setbacks along the way. In the episode with Uzzah, YHWH seems to be up to his old tricks of breaking out in testosteronic rage against his own people. But David's fury and sulk bring Adonai around, and he is welcomed with the wild abandon of his beloved. And when David almost forgets himself and appears ready to change roles, YHWH woos him back to being the beloved through the promise of fidelity to David and to his house.

The story of this relationship does not end here. David and YHWH do not live happily ever after. The marriage they have contracted will be a remarkably stormy one, characterized not only by David's high-handedness with respect to Bathsheba and her husband, Uriah, and its sorry aftermath in David's own "house" (2 Sam 11–12). YHWH will even seem to turn against David and his own people, tempting David to conduct a census that will be punished by plague (ch. 24). In spite of all the outrages and provocations, however, YHWH will not withdraw his steadfast love from David, nor will David ever finally rebel against his lover. The relationship may grow cold or distant, but it will not be repudiated by either of them. In order to see more clearly how this is true, we turn to the texts that exhibit the complex continuation of the relationship.

Marriage?

The consummation of the relationship between Adonai and David in the establishment of a kind of holy union between them is by no means the end of the story of the romance between David and YHWH. Hebrew narrative is generally not addicted to the they-all-lived-happily-ever-after form of fairy-tale narrative. On the contrary, the tales seem pervaded often with a sternly realistic or even tragic tone. And this is also true of the relationship between David and YHWH.

Two episodes call for some attention here if we are to understand the complexity of this relationship. Only after considering these episodes, which cast a subdued and even somber light on the union of David and Adonai, will we be able to consider the extraordinarily positive light in which this relationship came to be viewed in subsequent generations.

The first of these episodes concerns the occurrence of a famine that besets the land for three years (2 Sam 21), and the last concerns the coming of a plague (ch. 24). As so often true even today, the occurrence of a "natural" disaster is regarded as an "act of God." Yet this is complicated in the narrative by the fact of the special relationship between David and YHWH. This element transforms these stories from simple accounts of disaster averted by turning to YHWH into stories of a deeply personal character, implicating the relationship between lovers. They are tales of love grown cold, and of the way in which characters in lifelong relationship grow weary of one another, perhaps cruel to one another, yet without completely losing track of the vows that bind them together.

Famine, 2 Samuel 21

In the first story the persistence of the famine for three years is what appears to drive David to "inquire of the LORD." We are not told how this "inquiry" happens; whether it is by turning again to the ark, before which David had pledged his troth, or by means of the ephod, which earlier, as we have seen, substituted for the ark, or by some other means. In any case, he receives the answer that "there is bloodguilt on Saul and on his house" (2 Sam 21:1). In this case YHWH does not tell David what to do but instead simply indicates where the problem lies. It is left to David to figure out the remedy. A curious feature of this story is that the narrative has not prepared for it. Accordingly, here we are given only a brief indication of what Saul has done that has brought upon him this bloodguilt. In his zeal for his own people, we are told, he tried to massacre the Gibeonites (remnants of the Amorites; v. 2) in spite of the fact that they had been sworn to protection by the people of Israel. As we know from many stories, oaths taken before YHWH seem to have a life and power all their own, whether the oath has been taken at YHWH's behest or has simply been "volunteered."[23]

In order to expunge the bloodguilt, it is necessary to seek a way to make recompense to the Gibeonites. This can be done, not by a transaction between David and YHWH, but by an agreement between David and the aggrieved party. What the latter propose is indeed severe: "Let seven of [Saul's] sons be handed over to us, and we will impale them before the LORD at Gibeon on the mountain of the LORD" (v. 6).

In connection with David's love for Jonathan, we have already observed that David manages to save Jonathan's son from this fate.[24] He finds two sons of Saul and Rizpah, and five of Saul's grandsons, born to his daughter Merab. These seven he hands over to the Gibeonites, who do as they had proposed. They impale them and leave the bodies exposed upon the mountain of the Lord (v. 9).

However, this payment of the bloodguilt incurred by Saul's violation of the vow to protect the Gibeonites does not itself end the famine. The point of the story is thus not the necessity of keeping vows made to YHWH and the consequences of not doing so. Nor is it the importance of restitution in restoring a kind of justice from which might flow the favor of YHWH. If these had been the primary goals of the narration, we would hear that the famine was ended. Instead, we have only set up the action that will indeed bring it to an end.

The action of the narrative now shifts to Rizpah, the mother of two of Saul's sons. Indeed, her action is the dramatic hinge of this episode's narration. She went to the place where her sons have been executed, "took sackcloth, and spread it on a rock for herself, from the beginning of harvest until rain fell on them from the heavens; she did not allow the birds of the air to come on the bodies by day, or the wild animals by night" (v. 10). The duration of this grisly vigil appears to last several months, attesting to her extraordinary strength of character and her maternal loyalty to her sons.[25]

This extraordinary act of steadfast maternal love makes a belated but powerful impression upon David, who after all had some responsibility for the fate of the Saulides. This mother's deep love apparently reminds him of his own love for Saul and Jonathan, and so he determines to rescue their remains from the hands of those who have stolen their bodies from the

---

23. See the story of Jephthah and his daughter (Judg 11), discussed in chapter 11.
24. We may also recognize that Mephibosheth serves double duty since David has also promised not to destroy the line of Saul (1 Sam 24:21–22). As Jonathan's son and Saul's grandson, he is the living token of David's faithfulness to his former lovers.
25. For another reading of this narrative, see Fewell and Gunn, *Gender*, 160–61.

Philistines. David's first concern is for Saul and Jonathan. He first retrieves their bodies, and only then those of the executed sons and grandsons of Saul. Jonathan and Saul, his former lovers, still have absolute priority for him. All the bodies are carried to the land of Saul's father, Kish, to be entombed together. Only then does the narrator informs us that "God heeded supplications for the land" (v. 14).

The story presents us with a chain reaction of steadfast love: the love of Rizpah for her sons awakens David's steadfast love for Saul and Jonathan, which in turn provokes the return of YHWH's love for the land and people of Israel. This chain of compassion, rather than the prior events, restores a kind of rough justice that averts calamity from the land. It is David's steadfast love (incited by the example of a woman), rather than the retribution incited by YHWH, that makes YHWH yield. The narrative sequence of events thus makes it seem as though David has once again tamed the rage of YHWH through his own (perhaps belated) demonstration of steadfast love.

In all of this, one of the remarkable features of the story is the apparent distance and yet connectedness between David and YHWH. Gone is the powerful romantic current that we saw in the avowal of love or the churning passion of courtship that culminated in David's erotic dance before Adonai. These have been replaced by what may appear as a more mature relationship between busy and independent subjects. The passions of first love have receded, and in their place comes a kind of preoccupied peripheral awareness of one another, unobtrusive and yet somehow still attuned. David is now presumably an old monarch. His relationship to Adonai has been put to many a test and has been tempered by the fires of time and of mutual disappointment. He has provoked divine ire with his shameful betrayal of Uriah in order to acquire Bathsheba, and he has endured the horror of civil war and the death of his own sons (the infant son of Bathsheba, Amnon, and Absalom). Yet his relationship to YHWH has managed to survive these storms, if not to positively flourish through them. It may have grown more subdued, but it has not entirely withered.

Even more remarkable, however, than this apparent maturing of love is the complex intertwining of many loves. Here, near the end of David's life, the loves that have sustained him come strangely together. First, we have the terribly troubled relation to Saul, whose love for him brought him into the royal court and later ferociously turned against him. It would seem that David has his revenge against Saul in the extermination of his line, and yet it is his compassion that ends the tale. Concerning Jonathan, whose love surpassed "the love of women" (2 Sam 1:26), the episode has recounted the steadfastness of David's love for him through the preservation of Jonathan's son (and the last of Saul's line as well). Somehow, it is David's reawakened love for his old lovers that has the effect of softening the heart of his Great Lover, who relents at last in his punishment of Israel for ancient and obscure wrongs and brings again the life-giving rains and harvest. At the end of this discussion, we will return to the significance of this intertwining of love—human and divine.

Plague

The last episode in the narration known as 2 Samuel casts an even more somber light on the relationship between David and Adonai. Between this episode and the one we have just read, the character of David and that of YHWH have receded from the narrative. We hear of the deeds of David's companions, but David himself is removed from the action. Similarly, the name of God is not mentioned. This stark character of the narrative is interrupted by two psalms attributed to David, in which he sings his praise of YHWH: 22:1–51 and 23:1–7. Each psalm recalls the vows made between David and YHWH. The first explains the reason for praising God: "He is a tower of salvation for his king, and shows steadfast love to his anointed, to David and his descendants forever" (22:51). The second, known also as "the last words of David," who is described as "The favorite of the Strong One of Israel" (23:1), recalls that God "has made with me an everlasting covenant" (23:5). In the narrative these songs serve to bring the love of David and YHWH vividly into focus, even as David himself, and to a significant degree YHWH as well, recede from the narrative.[26]

In contrast to these songs that recall the steadfast love of YHWH for his "favorite," and in contrast to the near disappearance of David and his Lover from the narrative, the last episode in this epic romance has a tortured tone. It is the story of a plague and so of what might be called an "act of God." But unlike the story of the famine, there can be no doubt here of God's agency.

The story begins with the anger of God directed against Israel. In the story this ire seems unmotivated. Indeed, the account suggests that YHWH

---

26. If we were to try to fill out the relation between David and YHWH, we would have to take into account the relationship depicted in the psalms attributed to David. The attempt to discern which psalms may actually go back to David and which have been composed on their model is an extremely difficult task. It would take us far from our current attempt to reread the relationships inscribed in Hebrew narrative. Yet at least in terms of the pathos that they express, of passion, of intimacy, of complaint, of near despair, of love lost and rekindled, the psalms give voice to the sort of love affair that the narrative portrays from the outside. That songs of this sort were composed either by David or by an Israel that believed itself beloved for the sake of YHWH's steadfast love for David is an indication of the powerful passions unleashed between a male deity and his male beloved.

is simply in foul temper and hence seeks to stir up trouble on a pretext. Thus, in this narrative it is YHWH who puts into David's head the idea of a census of the people of Israel. And it is this census that will serve as a pretext for the unleashing of the wrath of God in the form of a pestilence spread by one of his messengers (or angels). The Chronicler will seek to mitigate the outrageous features of this story by substituting "Satan" for Adonai as the instigator of the census (1 Chron 21:1). But it is no part of the Chronicler's plan to probe the depths of David's and Adonai's passion for one another. Both characters are "cleaned up" in that later account, as we have already seen in the case of David's dance before YHWH. But in this epic in 2 Sam 24, we are presented with both a more interesting and a more troubling rendition of this relationship. In the epic YHWH seems a bit like his old self, the one who burst out upon Uzzah and had to be tamed by David before David could welcome YHWH to his new home. He is acting again with the foul-tempered arrogance of the gods of old. And so he uses David to pick a fight with Israel.

Here we need not enter into the question of why the census was such a bad idea as to seem a plausible excuse for YHWH's wrath. It is enough that for the readers of the text the use of a census to set up the levying of troops, tribute, and taxes seems to encroach upon the more direct and communal relationship both to their God and to their war-leader. In any case, a fateful change is taking place as the war-leader (*nagid*) becomes a remote king (*melek*) whose remoteness is mirrored in the receding of their god from direct relationship with the people.

David's general, Joab, protests against this plan but is obliged to carry it out, and we learn of the enormous military readiness of David's reign. Then the narrative has David realize that he has done a terrible thing. This happens somehow in David's own estimation: there is no word from God or prophet to tell him this. Nevertheless, David entreats his Lover to forgive him his rash deed (obviously, David does not know what narrator and reader both know, that YHWH is the one who has incited this act).

The response of YHWH is mediated through the prophet/seer Gad, showing one of the salient characteristics of this episode. YHWH's communication with his favorite remains indirect even though David's address is characteristically direct.

Through Gad, YHWH offers David a terrible choice between three calamities: three years of famine, three months of flight before his foes, or three days of plague (v. 13). This not only is a cruel choice; David also must be the one to make the choice. In spite of his Lover's cruelty, David will not relent in his trust in him.[27] He says: "Let us fall into the hand of the LORD, for his mercy is great; but let me not fall into human hands" (v. 14).

The plague sweeps through Israel, killing seventy thousand, but the angel in charge of the pestilence stops at the gate of Jerusalem. There David sees him and again entreats his Lover for the people of Israel: "These sheep, what have they done? Let your hand, I pray, be against me and against my father's house" (v. 17).

As the story is written, YHWH has already stopped the plague, but this is unknown to David. Accordingly, he is told (again through Gad) to build an altar where he saw the destroying angel stop, which he does. But instead of accepting the owner's offer of land and the animals for the sacrifice, David insists on paying for them so that the sacrifice will be truly his. We are told the result: "The LORD answered his supplication for the land, and the plague was averted from Israel" (v. 25). As the young David had placed himself between marauding lions and his father's livestock, so here he places himself between YHWH and the people of Israel.

The oddness of a plague that is stopped twice (without and then with the sacrifice of David) may well indicate the stitching together of a composite narrative. But the result nonetheless renders more complex the relation between David and YHWH. In this story David is the one who acts with great honor. Adonai is an altogether more disturbing character, perhaps as befits a god.

One way of reading the story would be to say that YHWH, in a fit of ill temper, sets up a pretext for attacking his own people, but then relents as the plague nears the city of David. Yet at the same time, he allows his aging beloved to play a role in the ending of the plague, just as he has given him a role in starting it. In a way YHWH seems to be toying with David. But even if this is a rather cruel game, the effect is nevertheless to cast into shadowed relief the enduring character of the relationship. YHWH determines to stop the plague at the gates of the city either because it is David's city or on account of David's supplication. In either case it seems that David is the one for whose sake the ire of YHWH is assuaged. What YHWH does in relation to Israel is mediated through the relationship to David, however distant that relationship may seem to have become.

And even if YHWH now speaks to David only through messengers, David's relationship is far more passionately immediate. YHWH may not

---

27. David has already experienced the famine in the previous episode we have discussed (2 Sam 21) and has known what it is to flee before his enemies, most recently in his flight from the rebellious forces under the command of his own son Absalom (2 Sam 15–18). And according to the narrative, YHWH sent all these troubles.

be speaking directly to him, but David is unrelenting and unwavering in the ardor of his address to his Great Lover. In the end it is David whose character shines in this story. He is the one who is utterly steadfast in his love for his Lover. And perhaps it is David's steadfastness in the face of great provocation that is a necessary part in his taming of his Great Lover—a taming that will forever redound to the benefit of the "sheep" of Israel.

In this story YHWH remains something of a dangerous, even arbitrary, and certainly unpredictable character of great power. After all, he is a god. Later narratives (such as 1–2 Kings and 1–2 Chronicles) would be inclined to give him a good motive for his irritation with Israel. The Deuteronomist would tell us how Israel had sinned, and the Chronicler gets out of the problem by making YHWH's anger the fault of David's having been seduced by the "tempter" rather than by YHWH into encroaching on YHWH's sovereignty. But the author of Samuel has no such qualms about portraying David's Great Lover as a dangerously unpredictable power. It is what one might expect of one who wields unchecked power. Kings and gods are, after all, dangerous beings, even if they are also lovers who have favorites. And those who have the risky role of being their favorites must always be astute in keeping the favor with which they have been bestowed. David appears exemplary precisely in this regard: he seems to know how to (re)awaken the love, the favor, of his Lover.

Steadfast Love

The final episodes recounted concerning the relationship between David and Adonai seem to replace the intensity of erotic passion with something more subdued, somber, and complex. Yet somehow, what will be remembered is the extraordinary intensity of the relationship. No reading of this relationship would be complete without noticing how it is recalled in the annals of Israel. So powerful is the relationship that it will be recalled as the paradigm and the motive of YHWH's relation to Israel. The steadfastness of YHWH's love for David is taken to be the model for YHWH's love for Israel. Even when the relationship grows distant and even cold, YHWH will no more abandon Israel than he could finally abandon David. Moreover, YHWH's love for Israel despite provocations will somehow continue because of YHWH's love for David. When things get bad, when YHWH seems distant and dangerous, even so the relationship will abide; it will stretch but not break. Thus, the last episodes in the relationship between David and YHWH are actually quite important. They are the episodes that provide reassurance that YHWH can be brought around by recalling his love for David.

The homoerotic relationship does not end with David's death. The covenant or "holy union" between David and YHWH has already suggested that in token of Adonai's singular love for David, Adonai will "keep the lamp burning" through the adoption of David's sons. This does not mean that Adonai enters into a similarly erotic relation with subsequent kings of David's line. We shall see that the erotic charge of YHWH's relation to David is subsequently found in relation not to the court but to certain prophets and through their words to Israel as a whole. Thus, in a certain way the relationship between David and Adonai remains "one of a kind." This in itself is a token of its singular character, its deep emotional intensity, its highly specific erotic charge.

To be sure, other singular relationships of YHWH to mortals have somewhat competing status, such as with Abraham and with Moses. But these cannot compare in personal intensity, as is evident by the way they are recalled. With Abraham, it is by reference to the covenant; with respect to Moses, by way of the law and commandments he mediates. But with David, it is on account of "steadfast love" (as in 2 Sam 22:51).[28] Accordingly, it may be useful to briefly observe how this theme of YHWH's steadfast love is connected to the recollection of David.

It is first recalled by Solomon in the account of his accession to the throne: "You have shown great and steadfast love to your servant my father David, . . . and you have kept for him this great and steadfast love" (1 Kgs 3:6; cf. 2 Chron 1:7). When it comes time to dedicate the temple, Solomon will again recall the "great and steadfast love" that YHWH had shown to David. He will remind YHWH of the promise "There shall never fail you a successor before me to sit on the throne of Israel" (1 Kgs 8:23–25; cf. 2 Chron 6:42). Following the great feast with dedicating the temple, the text says that the people "went to their tents, joyful and in good spirits because of all the goodness that the LORD had shown to his servant David and to his people Israel" (8:66). It appears that the legitimacy of Solomon and of his projects (including the temple) rests upon and derives from the abiding love of YHWH for his "favorite," who is not Solomon but his father, David. Indeed, for David's sake, the author of 1 Kings claims, YHWH does not tear the throne from Solomon in his lifetime (11:12). Not even after the kingdom is divided does YHWH forget his love for his favorite.

---

28. This theme may come to be transposed back upon the Moses saga; see Exod 34:7 and my reflections in the epilogue.

Even concerning Rehoboam and his son Abijam, the author says that despite their many sins, "nevertheless for David's sake the LORD his God gave him a lamp in Jerusalem" (15:4). The Chronicler will say much the same concerning Jehoram: "Yet the LORD would not destroy the house of David because of the covenant that he had made with David, and since he had promised to give a lamp to him and to his descendants forever" (2 Chron 21:7). Many generations later Isaiah will reassure Hezekiah, in the face of Assyrian might and power: "I will defend this city to save it, for my own sake and for the sake of my servant David" (2 Kgs 19:34; 20:6).

One of the most remarkable attestations to the bond between David and YHWH is the chorus repeated often in 2 Chronicles in praise of YHWH: "For he is good, for his steadfast love endures forever" (5:13; 7:3; 20:22). The recollection of the steadfast love of YHWH seems always to be uniquely associated with his love for David. This will indeed set the tone for the psalms that, most often when they recall the steadfast love of YHWH, claim to be bringing to expression one of David's love songs to his Great Lover.[29]

One of the most remarkable of these psalms that recall the love of YHWH for David is Psalm 89. The psalm begins with a recollection of the betrothal of David by YHWH:

> I will sing of your steadfast love, O LORD, forever;
>> with my mouth I will proclaim your faithfulness to all generations.
> I declare that your steadfast love is established forever;
>> your faithfulness is as firm as the heavens.
>
> You said, "I have made a covenant with my chosen one,
>> I have sworn to my servant David:
> 'I will establish your descendants forever,
>> and build your throne for all generations.'" (89:1–4)

After a recitation of God's mighty deeds in which his steadfast love is again recalled (v. 14), the psalmist again returns to the theme of David:

> Then you spoke in a vision to your faithful one, and said:
>> "I have set the crown on one who is mighty,
>> I have exalted one chosen from the people.
> I have found my servant David;
>> with my holy oil I have anointed him;

---

29. See, for examples, Pss 5, 6, 13, 18, 21, 25, 31, 36, and so on.

my hand shall always remain with him;
    my arm also shall strengthen him. . . .
My faithfulness and steadfast love shall be with him; . . .
He shall cry to me, 'You are my Father,
    my God, and the Rock of my salvation!' . . .
Forever I will keep my steadfast love for him,
    and my covenant with him will stand firm.
I will establish his line forever,
    and his throne as long as the heavens endure.
If his children forsake my law
    and do not walk according to my ordinances, . . .
then I will punish their transgression with the rod
    and their iniquity with scourges;
but I will not remove from him my steadfast love,
    or be false to my faithfulness."
        (89:19–21, 24a, 26, 28–30, 32–33)

The psalm then supposes that though YHWH may become enraged with his people and with their Davidic leaders, still he will be bound by his love for David forever. The psalm ends, however, with a complaint: it appears that YHWH has indeed forgotten his love of David at least insofar as one of his descendants has been utterly defeated. The psalm ends with the appeal:

LORD, where is your steadfast love of old,
    which by your faithfulness you swore to David? (v. 49)

Even in calamity the recollection of YHWH's love for David is the last best hope of the nation.

It is remarkable, therefore, that the ascription of love to YHWH basically depends upon and so recalls YHWH's great love affair with David. He is the lovely boy spotted in the fields and brought to the attention of YHWH's former favorite (Saul) so as to begin his strange career as the man who was loved by YHWH and who had a special knack for taming the testosteronic rage of his Great Lover. While traditions concerning Abraham (Gen 24:12–27) and Moses (Exod 34:6–7) may refer to YHWH's steadfast love, these references may be modeled on the relation between David and YHWH rather than the reverse. It is certainly in connection with the remembering of David that the Psalms recall this steadfast love. Is it because of the great erotic passion that seems to bind this improbable couple that it will be possible for faith to rise to the conception that "God is love"? The paradigm of love for YHWH is his passion for David. And we have seen that this passion is inscribed within the register of homo-eroticism. In this sense "homosexuality" is not the contrary of biblical faith in a loving God but is its very foundation.

This great love affair has a remarkable effect upon the character of YHWH, for we have seen that this ferocious deity was often arbitrary and bloodthirsty. But in the course of his relation with David, he begins to undergo a change. He does not cast off David as he had Saul. And David seems to have the way to charm him even when the relation grows distant. Already when YHWH burst out upon Uzzah, David seemed to tame him. And in the final episode of the plague, it seems to be David's relentless trust in YHWH that averts catastrophe at the end. YHWH is still powerful and ferocious and easily enraged. Yet he is learning from David the virtue of loy-alty to those he has chosen. So well does YHWH learn this, so deeply is YHWH transformed in the crucible of this great passion, that his faithful-ness will be relied upon even when all seems lost.

It is precisely this which will make it possible, after the last king of David's line, to project into the future the coming of another of that line who will be loved for David's sake and who will therefore be one who restores the fortunes of Israel. This is, if you will, the origin of Israel's mes-sianic hope—grounded in the homoerotics of the love affair between YHWH and David.

4. Reflections

IN WHAT FOLLOWS I will indicate some of the features of the narrative that offer themselves for thought concerning male same-sex relationships.

YHWH and Zeus

I have been suggesting that the relationship between YHWH and David may be understood in terms of a certain homoeroticism. If so, we are immediately brought up against the question of the relationship between this saga and the various accounts of homoerotic attachment between the gods and humans as found in Greek myth and legend. Most of the male deities of the Greek world come to be outfitted with accounts of relationships to beautiful young human males.[1] Nevertheless, the accounts of the relation between Zeus and Ganymede, first found in Homer (*Iliad* 20.233–35) come to be elaborated as a paradigm of pederasty, perhaps most famously in Plato's *Phaedrus* but also in a large number of texts from both classical and Hellenistic Greek literature. Indeed, so conventional does this paradigm become that it may be spoofed in (pseudo) Lucian and (in the Latin form of Ganymede's name) come to designate as "catamites" the "passive" partners of male same-sex relationships. The Renaissance recovers this

---

1. See Christine Downing, *Myths and Mysteries of Same-Sex Love* (New York: Contiuum, 1989), 146–67; and W. A. Percy III, *Pederasty and Pedagogy in Archaic Greece* (Urbana: University of Illinois Press, 1996), 53–58.

tale of desire, seduction, and abduction and elaborates it in narrative, poetic, and plastic art.[2] Although there are a number of other accounts of the love of a god for a mortal, this one has come to have a decided prominence in the Western imagination.

It is therefore useful to notice a few elements of similarity and also of contrast between the legend of Zeus's abduction of the beautiful Ganymede and the saga of the relationship between YHWH and the beautiful David. As this characterization reminds us, both relationships appear to be motivated by the extraordinary beauty of the young mortal. Both of these young mortals are described as shepherds, and in both cases their being desired and favored by the divine character means that they leave behind the paternal home. In both cases the male divinity initiates the relationship and acts upon the desire stimulated by the beauty of the mortal. Moreover, in both cases a permanent relationship between the (divine) lover and the (human) beloved is thereby initiated. In both cases a permanent status difference between lover and beloved also characterizes the relationship. To YHWH, David will become "my servant David," while Ganymede becomes the cupbearer (as opposed to armor-bearer) of Zeus. Both relationships therefore correspond to models of age or class distinctions within male same-sex relationships and are, in that sense, pederastic or asymmetrical in structure.

Within this remarkable context of shared characteristics, however, we may notice certain important contrasts. In many accounts and depictions of the relationship between Zeus and Ganymede, what comes to the fore is the scene of abduction. That Zeus takes the form of a raptor (an eagle) makes the relationship describable as rape rather than "love."[3] However, several of the retellings of this episode downplay this aspect of the relationship in order to assimilate it to the conventions of pederastic friendship (most obviously in Plato's *Phaedrus*). As we have had occasion to observe, David is by no means merely a passive partner in this relationship but also an actor, even if not the initiator.

Of even greater moment in distinguishing the saga of David and YHWH from the tale of Zeus and Ganymede is that YHWH does not extricate his beloved from the world of mortals. David remains a character in the social and political history of humanity. He remains an earthling, and in his ongoing life in society, he has other (human) lovers (Saul and

---

2. See James M. Saslow, *Ganymede in the Renaissance* (New Haven: Yale University Press, 1986).

3. This aspect of the story leads Aristides in his *Apology* to apply the term *arsenokoitai* from Paul to the tale of Zeus, thereby giving us the first and (I believe) decisive clue to the meaning of this term in the Pauline corpus. See William Petersen, "On the Study of 'Homosexuality' in Patristic Sources," in *Critica, classica, orientalia, ascetica, liturgica* (ed. E. Livingstone; Studia patristica 20; Leuven: Peeters Press, 1989), 283–88, esp. 284.

Jonathan), has wives and children, adventures and catastrophes, grows old, and dies. It is as human, all too human, that David is the beloved of YHWH, and his being the beloved does not make him divine or even quasi-divine.

To a significant degree this also bears upon the difference between Zeus and YHWH. Zeus is a member (albeit the preeminent member) of an aristocratic society of gods. His social life and his emotional and political existence are largely confined to relations with other divine beings, with only occasional sallies into the world of mortals. YHWH, on the other hand, is a rather antisocial divinity (at least as far as other gods are concerned). Virtually his entire social, emotional, and political life is lived out with human beings. He has little or nothing to do with other gods save to incite humans to revolt against their presumed dominion. In that sense he is something of a class traitor and decidedly a loner.

Thus, the YHWH of our narratives does not have even a female consort (like Hera) or divine offspring or divine companions or drinking partners. And this means that if he is to be conceived of as having an erotic life at all, it is with mere mortals. Since it is the human world with which he seems to be entirely preoccupied, there is no sense in which he is tempted to take his beloved from the earth but rather makes him a partner or companion in his historical engagements.

A second difference, closely connected to the first, has to do with the significance, for other mortals, of YHWH's relationship to a human beloved. In the case of Zeus and Ganymede, the relationship appears to have few consequences for other humans. That Ganymede is beloved of Zeus implies nothing concerning Zeus's relationship to Ganymede's place or people of origin (usually Crete). Ganymede the beloved is simply a singularly beautiful youth, not a representative of his people as a whole.

In the case of YHWH and David, however, their relationship is deeply intertwined with the relation of both to the people of Israel. David's extraordinary beauty seems to be what brings him into the center of the historical drama of YHWH and his people. Thus, David as beloved is, to a significant degree, an epitome and paradigm for YHWH's relation to Israel.

This is played out even in the moments of greatest intensity in the relationship between David and YHWH. Even when he dances before the face or eyes of YHWH, David is not alone but has around him the people (probably especially the men) of Israel. The betrothal scene of 2 Sam 7 is filled with references to David's relation to Israel and to the way in which YHWH's relation to David assimilates features of YHWH's relation to Israel. This is also true of the curious episodes of famine (2 Sam 21) and plague (ch. 24) that play out after the "honeymoon" phase of the relationship between David and YHWH has moved on to something quite different. In the story of David and YHWH, we may say that "the personal *is* the political."

Now this means that David as the male beloved of a male YHWH configures the relationship of Israel, Judah, and Jerusalem to the same deity. Thus, the homoerotic dimensions of the relationship between David and YHWH are, to a significant degree, transferred to the relationship between Israel and YHWH. Since, as I have suggested, David is, in contemporary parlance, set up as the "bottom" to YHWH's "top," this will have potentially crucial consequences for the distinctive features of Israelite and Jewish (and perhaps Christian) masculinity. Indeed, I believe that this goes a long way toward explaining the distinctive characteristics of Jewish masculinity suggested by Boyarin.[4]

The View from the Bottom

In order to make this more clear, let us briefly explore the position of David as "bottom." I have said that in the saga David is always the beloved of a more central male character. He is chosen by Saul and subsequently by Jonathan as armor-bearer, just as he has been chosen by YHWH. But David himself never has such a younger male companion.[5] He is permanently typecast as the *eromenos* (beloved one).

Yet the saga concerns itself essentially with David. To be sure, his lovers are always implicated in his adventures, but he remains the foregrounded character of the narrative. As a consequence this narrative does not depict homoerotic relationships primarily from the point of view of the *erastēs*, or lover, but primarily from the point of view of the *eromenos*, or beloved. Now this is quite different from what we find in classical and Greco-Roman literature, where we are everywhere confronted with the point of view of the lover. In that case it is with the lover of youths that we are concerned. But the youths themselves are generally the object of desire, not its subject. In fact, there is a considerable body of opinion that precludes the beloved both from desire and from pleasure.

Indeed, it is this exclusive attention to the *erastēs* as subject that makes the occasional occurrence of an *eromenos* as agent of desire so startling.

4. Daniel Boyarin, *Unheroic Conduct: The Rise of Heterosexuality and the Invention of the Jewish Man* (Berkeley: University of California Press, 1997).

5. That Abishai accompanies David on his sortie into Saul's camp (26:6–12) may seem an exception to this claim. But Abishai seems to be more of a random volunteer than a regular companion of the armor-bearer type.

Above all, in Plato's *Symposium* the protestations of the young Alcibiades of desire (and attempted seduction) in relation to Socrates is so remarkable simply because it breaks the taboo of considering the beloved as an agent at all. And one wonders if it is not precisely this irruption of subjectivity in the role of the *eromenos* that accounts for the development of Alcibiades's character as a cautionary tale (see Plutarch's *Lives*).

In contrast, David, precisely as beloved, has a fully developed subjectivity. Especially in relation to YHWH but already in relation to Jonathan and even Saul, it is David's response to his lover that is prominently displayed and narrated. David is not simply the beloved who receives; he is also a subject. He spares Saul's life; he adopts Jonathan's son. And in relation to YHWH, the answering subjectivity of David decidedly complicates the narrative of YHWH's love for him. In the episode of the ark, for example, we have noticed that David seems to seek to teach YHWH a lesson in control before he will admit him into his place of residence, and only then does he orgiastically celebrate the delayed arrival of his lover. The scene of betrothal is also one in which David appears to seek to overtake YHWH's initiative (by seeking to build him a house) and so has to be reminded concerning just who is the initiator (and so the "top") in this relationship. Yet this is by no means a mere power struggle since David is beloved, favored, and betrothed to YHWH precisely as "bottom."

It appears that this development of David as a subject results in much greater psychological complexity in the depiction of homoerotic passion. The view from the bottom that is at work here contrasts sharply with the view from the top characteristic of Greco-Roman homoerotic romance.

It is moreover the privileging of this role of being the male beloved of a male *erastēs* that will have far-reaching implications for the attitude toward male homoeroticsm in the history of Israel and indeed of Christianity.

If there is anything to Anders Nygren's attempt to distinguish Greek *eros* from Christian *agapē*[6] (which—unlike Nygren—I would attribute to Israel as well), it may be precisely this difference. It is a difference between being a subject who desires another and being a subject who is aware of being desired and favored by another.

A Question of Gender

One is tempted to speak of the feminization of the beloved by the male lover in highly gendered settings. People have often remarked upon this as

---

6. A. Nygren, *Agape and Eros* (trans. P. S. Watson; New York: Harper & Row, 1969).

the hidden dynamic and dilemma of Greek pederastic relations. But feminization in a strong sense is necessary only when the maleness of the beloved is an inconvenient detail that must be suppressed. In that case the homoerotic aspect of the relationship is actually repressed in favor of a heterosexual model. But if the homoerotic character of the relationship is more prominent, then the maleness of either partner is not itself the problem but rather is an essential aspect of the attraction. In the homoerotically suffused relationship between David and YHWH, the maleness of both characters seems essential.

As a hypothesis I would suggest that it is precisely the warrior character of the social reality portrayed in this text that prevents the masculinity of the beloved from being brought into question. In a homosocial context such as this, masculinity is not strongly dependent upon one's relationships with women but is acted out among males in terms of boldness and loyalty. As a result there is less likelihood that the relationship of lover and beloved would be transposed upon, and read in terms of, the relationship of male to female.

However, in more "domestic" settings, where the household provides the basic paradigms of relationship, there may be a stronger tendency to try to read homoerotic relationships in terms of heteroerotic ones (or even incestuous ones). In this case the beloved comes to have a somewhat unstable gender identity. And this is certainly observable in the anxieties concerning homoerotic relationships that K. J. Dover has explored in classical Greece (especially Athens in time of peace).[7]

In terms of the Hebrew Bible, we may see something of this occurring in the transgendering of Israel in Hosea, in Jer 2–3, and in Ezek 16 and 23, which we will consider in part 3. This may also lie behind the possibility of introducing the prohibition of "lying with another male as if you were a female" in the late priestly law code of Leviticus, to be discussed at the end of the present study.

In any case, I do not believe it is helpful to read the homoeroticism of this relationship as existing on a scale of "more or less" masculine or, even worse, as entailing feminization. For this essentializes binary distinctions between male and female as well as casting feminization simply as a depletion of masculinity.[8]

---

7. K. J. Dover, *Greek Homosexuality* (New York: Vintage, 1978).

8. One of the most insistent forms of this "binary" opposition of masculine and feminine may be found in the Roman world. See Craig A. Williams, *Roman Homosexuality: Ideologies of Masculinity in Classical Antiquity* (Oxford: Oxford University Press, 1999), for an analysis, esp. 125–59.

Within the limits of the androcentric, phallocentric, militaristic, and perhaps misogynistic and classist world of this narrative, we may also find a helpful clue for exceeding the ill effects of a binary opposition of male and female. Such a clue may provide a way to value the distinct masculinity of males in love, and thus the distinctive feminism of two women in love.

The Erotics of Faith

We began by noticing that Eilberg-Schwartz suggested a certain homoerotics in the relationship between God and Israel.[9] I have sought to suggest a different model of homoeroticism that also is to be read in the texts of Israel. But I want to conclude part 1 by making a simple declaration: what seems to be remarkable is not the homoeroticism that may be read in the text but that the relationship between the divine and the adherent may be read as erotic at all.

Since eroticism is an important and indeed essential aspect of human consciousness and relationship, one may suppose it only natural that this might find some place in the relationship between the believer and the divine. While I certainly agree that eroticism is a major force in human experience and that it cannot simply be put aside in representing religion, it does not seem to be true that the erotic plays an equal role in all representations of the relationship between the worshipper and the divine.

It certainly is not the case that the basic relationship, for example, between the Olympic deities and their worshippers was typically represented as erotic in character. When this did seem to occur (as in the Dionysian rites), it was a radical departure from what had gone before or what was otherwise typical. Instead, the gods of Greece and Rome seem to live out their domestic, erotic, and social lives quite apart from humanity. It is as if their relation to human beings is figured rather like that of the court to a distant peasantry, who are obliged to provide taxes (sacrifices) and occasional services (and avoid insulting their touchy cultural superiors) but are otherwise left to their own devices.

YHWH's emotional and social life is directed entirely to human beings. Insofar as YHWH is represented as a person (and even a male), the erotic finds expression not in relation to a consort but in relation to the humans he has chosen as his companions, friends, and lovers.

The erotic engagement of YHWH with Israel (and the believer) provokes an answering erotics of faith. It is this that may account for the rather

9. H. Eilberg-Schwartz, *God's Phallus and Other Problems for Men and Monotheism* (Boston: Beacon, 1994).

troubled relationship between faith and sexuality that has haunted Christianity perhaps far more than Judaism. But that would take us far afield from the erotics of the narrative we have been considering. However, at least in this narrative, the erotic character of the relationship between YHWH and David (and by extension, Israel) does not serve to inhibit the erotic life of the human characters. After all, David does have his own "love life," which is complexly but not oppositionally related to the homoerotics of his relation to YHWH. There may therefore be far more to learn from this narrative than space permits us to explore here.

Intertwining Loves

One of the most remarkable features of the narrative we have been reading concerning David and his lovers is the way in which David's relation with human males is woven into and affects the depiction of David's homoerotic relationship with YHWH. At the beginning we noticed the way in which the culture of warriors and their armor-bearers seems to include YHWH as one of these warriors—indeed, as the preeminent one. And it was from a consideration of YHWH as warrior-chief that we noticed the significant feature of male beauty as playing a decisive role in the selection of youthful companion. Thus, the stories of the selection of YHWH's armor-bearers expand and intensify our understanding of the erotics of the relationships between other warriors and their companions.

In terms of the relation between the narration of David and his (human) male lovers and the story of his relationship to YHWH, we may notice that David is introduced to the warrior-leaders of Israel after, and because of, his prior selection by YHWH. But the narration of David's love affairs with Jonathan and Saul comes to an end before the eroticism of the relationship of David and Adonai receives further narrative elaboration. It is as if David first had to learn or practice what it means to be the beloved before he could be depicted as the beloved of Adonai.

In this case David's relationships to Saul and Jonathan prepare him for the consummation of his being the beloved of YHWH.

Nevertheless, there is far more to this than a mere sequence of love affairs. Each of these relationships positively contributes to the development of David as a "beloved." In the case of his relationship to Saul, we observe how David's extraordinarily steadfast love is brought out in the narrative. In spite of extreme provocation, his lover Saul does repeatedly try to kill him. Still, David remains loyal to the man who has first taken him as an armor-bearer.

Moreover, David gains considerable practice in learning to placate his arbitrary and fickle lover. Early on, we are told of David's music as playing an essential role in wooing Saul from his evil temper. Later, David shows great ingenuity in demonstrating his loyalty to Saul even when the latter is seeking to attack him. Indeed, it is in this connection that David even pledges to defend Saul's house forever.

This apprenticeship in love prepares David for what will come. It is with music (and naked dance) that David will welcome his Great Lover to Jerusalem. And it is above all as singer that David will be recalled in later generations as one who developed an especially intimate relationship with Adonai. After all, David is remembered as much for being a psalmist, indeed, *the* psalmist, as he is for being a king.

Moreover, we see David taming YHWH's rage through the deferral of his arrival in Jerusalem. David has learned not to give in too easily to the rages of his lovers. At least as significant is David's behavior in the case of the census and the plague. Here David goes out of his way to placate YHWH, focusing the issue between YHWH and Israel into one between YHWH and himself, and then acting with boldness and vulnerability to placate YHWH's rage.

The depth of David's passion for his lovers is most strikingly narrated in connection with Jonathan. David throws himself about Jonathan's neck and weeps profusely at the prospect of separation from this lover. Thereby he anticipates some of the passion of the Psalms' articulation of an especially intimate relationship to YHWH, features that seem most likely to go back to David's own songs to his Great Lover.

In addition, David's demonstration of loyalty to Jonathan through his caring for Jonathan's son seems actually to provide a model for YHWH's subsequent demonstration of steadfast love to David. And we have seen that it is David's remembering of, and compassion for, his dead lovers that seems actually to end the famine with which YHWH has afflicted the land.

These last illustrations bear upon an even more remarkable feature of these stories: the way in which YHWH seems to be changed in the course of the narrative. When the narrative of 1 and 2 Samuel begins, YHWH has been a distant and inattentive deity. When he does pay attention, he seems astonishingly arbitrary and unpredictable as well as extremely dangerous. He abandons Israel in their need, allowing the ark to fall into the hands of the Philistines. While in his sojourn with the Philistines, he demonstrates his phallic power through something like the politics of rape. When the ark returns to Israel, he seems scarcely less ferocious, slaying those who dare to touch his "privates." This is demonstrated again in the sudden death of Uzzah when he touches the ark, even in an attempt to prevent its falling to the ground.

Nor is YHWH's comportment with Saul at all reassuring in this regard. The slightest infraction of his will results in Saul's being dismissed from his position as YHWH's favorite immediately after he has been chosen.

Yet at the end of the narrative we hear of YHWH's steadfast love. What has happened? It appears that David has tamed the ferocious desert chief. And David has done this precisely in the way he has dealt with his other lovers. For in truth the exemplar of steadfast love in this story is not YHWH but David, and the way that has been practiced and demonstrated is through David's behavior with his other lovers, Saul and Jonathan.

Although it may seem strange to say it, it would seem that YHWH has learned love from David, has learned what it is to love all the way— precisely in relation to David—and has learned steadfastness in love from David. Through being the Lover of precisely this beloved one, YHWH has become a better lover, one who can be trusted, one who can be relied upon, one in whom one can have faith.

Apart from the narrative we have been reading, it would be hard to imagine Adonai as a god who could be loved. And apart from David's relationships to Saul and Jonathan, it would be hard to imagine the love between David and YHWH. Homoeroticism therefore is the very fulcrum of biblical religion.

YHWH's Male Groupies

WE HAVE FOCUSED initial attention on the relationships between warriors as these come to expression in the sagas concerning David. But around the edges of this sort of narrative, we may also glimpse traces of a rather different sort of male same-sex eroticism. In these sagas Adonai has to do not only with warriors but also with prophets or those said to be prophets. The connecting link here is Saul, who has been portrayed as the discarded favorite of YHWH but who is also portrayed in an odd relationship to bands of prophets who roam the hills of premonarchic Israel. By attending first to this connection, we are led into a strange world of erotically charged behavior, not among warriors but among males who seem to be possessed by YHWH's erotic or phallic power. We again discover Samuel, who plays a strange role in the selection of both Saul and David and who also relates to the bands of ecstatics who seem to gravitate around him. This in turn leads us to a consideration of the bands of prophets, who are associated with the strange figures who seem to be Samuel's successors after the monarchy has been established and divided: Elijah and Elisha.

Bands of male ecstatics possessed by Adonai's erotic potency may or may not be seen to have an erotic attachment to one another. That is, their homoeroticism may simply be focused upon the divinity whose devotees they are. But in chapter 6 we examine traces of what may be a transfer of erotic potency from the prophets to younger males. This leads us to reconsider some of the elements of the story of Samuel, and especially his call to serve as the servant of YHWH's potency.

Finally for this part, in chapter 7 we turn our attention to the mysterious *qedeshim* ("the male cult prostitutes," as they are sometimes called). These mysterious men have in some way been set apart for cultic practices that come to be associated with the temple in which YHWH is honored.

The traces to which we turn our attention here are far more elusive than those we pursued in the discussion of warrior love in part 1. This may be due to several factors. First, the material itself is less tightly organized around a single compelling plot as in the case of David. Rather, it is dispersed among different narratives and indeed traditions and epochs. The male figures who emerge from these tales have in common, however, that in some way they seem to be devoted to YHWH, not as warriors but as prophets or even as cultic figures. Even so, we are accustomed to thinking of different prophets, who write, and different priests, who are the focus of priestly documents. In comparison, the figures we treat here are rather more shadowy, puzzling, and perhaps unsavory.

Also contributing to the elusive character of these traces is the fact that we know little about the kinds of shamanic and ecstatic homoerotics that may be hinted at here. We are far more familiar with the love of heroes in narratives of ancient Greece or about Alexander or even Julius Caesar.

Perhaps even more important, the sorts of homoerotic relationships and practices that may emerge from an interrogation of these texts are by no means what we normally think of as exemplary. The love that binds David and Jonathan may be mined for affecting antecedents to the sorts of relationships that some of us can imagine valorizing. But what are we to make of naked dancing prophets? Of the rapture/rape of Saul? Of the arousal (sexual or otherwise) of boys when prophets lie upon them? Of males who offer sexual services as a way of honoring their deity? These are both more alien to our experience and decidedly less usable for purposes of legitimating sexual relationships of which we may approve. So long as we approach these texts looking only for ways to validate our own experience, or relationships with which we are familiar, we hasten past the textual sites where something more strange and less savory seems to be going on.

But then, the concern of this study is rather different. It is to seek to discover the traces of homoeroticism that appear when we focus upon these ancient narratives and to see what role homoeroticism may play here.

5. Dancing Queens

THE RELATIONSHIP WE HAVE BEEN TRACING between David and Adonai
provides us with a template of homoeroticism with which we may
approach other elements of the saga material of 1 and 2 Samuel and
beyond. The material to which we now turn is certainly somewhat less
explicit in the development of homoerotic perspectives, but nevertheless it
illumines the themes we have thus far uncovered in our reading.

The basic question with which we approach this material is this:
Apart from David, has YHWH been depicted as having other homoerotic
relationships in this saga? We have already noticed the rather remarkable
account of the adventures of YHWH's ark among the Philistines. YHWH's
phallic signifier appears first to rape Dagon as the divinity of his tormentors
and then, as represented by the outbreak of hemorrhoids, to place upon all
the Philistines the mark of anal rape. But now we wish to inquire whether
there are positive suggestions of homoeroticism in Adonai's relationships
with other males. The two males who come into question in the earlier
parts of this narrative are Saul and Samuel.

Ravishing Saul

Accordingly, we begin with attention to the relationship between Saul and
Adonai. In our discussion of the generalized homosocial and perhaps

homoerotic ambience of the narrative complex as a whole, we noticed that heroes are generally accompanied by younger male companions who seem to be chosen for their beauty. In this connection we noticed that Saul appears to have been chosen for his remarkable beauty (and height) as YHWH's armor-bearer. He is introduced to the reader in this way (1 Sam 9:2), and subsequently Samuel will introduce him thus to the people of Israel (10:23–24), who immediately proclaim him their king.

Although Saul is introduced as the favorite of YHWH, he rapidly declines from favor. Indeed, in the first episode recounted of his kingship, Saul is hard-pressed by the massed Philistine forces that he has enraged by a successful ambush. As the situation worsens, he waits the appointed seven days for Samuel to come to offer a sacrifice. When the allotted time passes and the men of Israel are losing heart and slipping away, Saul determines to go ahead with the sacrifice himself. At this point Samuel arrives and tells Saul that YHWH has already chosen another "a man after his own heart" to be ruler over Israel (13:14). The narrative thus suggests that when Saul has barely begun to exercise the office of YHWH's favorite, he has already been supplanted by another in Adonai's favor. In a later episode Saul angers YHWH once again, Samuel informs him, because he has not completed the slaughter of the Amalekites as YHWH directed (ch. 15).

Later in the narrative it will appear that Saul has learned this last lesson all too well. When he discovers that the priests at Nob have fed David and his men from the "holy bread" on the altar and given him the sword of Goliath (21:3–6; 22:10), Saul orders the execution of Ahimelech and all the other priests of Nob. "He killed eighty-five who wore the linen ephod" (22:18). All the inhabitants of the town, "men and women, children and infants, oxen, donkeys, and sheep, he put to the sword" (22:19). It seems that Saul has learned the lesson about not leaving any survivors. In the worst way he has become an imitator of YHWH, his now former lover.

Incidentally, here we find another of the great ironies of this narrative. In the course of explaining why Saul is to be supplanted by another, Samuel utters an oracle that will be echoed again and again in the words of First Temple prophets: "Has the LORD as great delight in burnt offerings and sacrifices, as in obeying the voice of the LORD? Surely, to obey is better than sacrifice, and to heed than the fat of rams" (15:22). The irony is that later prophets will deploy words such as these to emphasize the importance of justice and especially justice for widows and orphans and strangers. But here the words condemn Saul for not having slaughtered every last man, woman, and child (as well as the livestock) of the Amalekites.

There is another irony in this narration of the ways in which Saul comes to be spurned by his Great Lover. It is that his "crimes" seem rather mild compared to those that will be committed by the one who will supplant him in YHWH's affections. Indeed, whether it is a crime at all may be in doubt since Saul sacrifices in 14:31–35 without any further repercussions. After all, David too will offer sacrifice at the altar; indeed, he will do so on numerous occasions (e.g., 2 Sam 6:17–20; 24:25). He will be severely rebuked for his plot to steal Bathsheba from Uriah. And the determination to make a census of Israel may also be regarded as an assault upon divine prerogatives. Yet for Saul there is little or no mercy, while for David there will be mercy even if it is sometimes severe. But we have already observed that David seems to have the knack for seducing YHWH from his ferocious ways.

All of this is background for the episode that I particularly want to examine as indicating a potentially homoerotic and even homosexual interpretation of the relationship of YHWH to Saul. It concerns the curious event at Ramah as Saul is pursuing the beautiful lad who has not only supplanted him in YHWH's eyes but also found favor in the eyes of the people. And his own son Jonathan has seduced him into becoming Jonathan's, rather than Saul's, armor-bearer. Saul has ample reason to be in a jealous rage with respect to David, his own former boy-toy.

When Michal helps David escape, he runs to Samuel in Ramah. Here we encounter the following episode:

> Saul was told, "David is at Naioth in Ramah." Then Saul sent messengers to take David. When they saw the company of prophets in a frenzy, with Samuel standing in charge of them, the spirit of God came upon the messengers of Saul, and they also fell into a prophetic frenzy. When Saul was told, he sent other messengers, and they also fell into a frenzy. Saul sent messengers again the third time, and they also fell into a frenzy. Then he himself went to Ramah. . . . He went there, toward Naioth in Ramah; and the spirit of God came upon him. As he was going, he fell into a prophetic frenzy, until he came to Naioth in Ramah. He too stripped off his clothes, and he too fell into a frenzy before Samuel. He lay naked all that day and all that night. Therefore it is said, "Is Saul also among the prophets?" (19:19–24)

The element upon which I want to particularly focus is the notice that Saul stripped off his clothes and lay naked for a day and a night. What has nakedness to do with prophetic frenzy?

Before focusing on that intriguing detail, however, we should recall that this is not the first time Saul has been spoken of as one of the prophets. It also is not the first time he has been seen in the company of a band of these mysterious men acting as people in a frenzy.

When Samuel told the youthful Saul that he was the Lord's chosen, Samuel also told him that he would receive three signs that he was indeed the one favored by Adonai. In the third sign, Samuel said:

> You will meet a band of prophets coming down from the shrine with harp, tambourine, flute, and lyre playing in front of them; they will be in a prophetic frenzy. Then the spirit of the LORD will possess you, and you will be in a prophetic frenzy along with them and be turned into a different person. (10:5–6)

The fulfillment of the first two signs is not recounted, but we do hear of the accomplishment of the third:

> When they were going from there to Gibeah, a band of prophets met him; and the spirit of God possessed him, and he fell into a prophetic frenzy along with them. When all who knew him before saw how he prophesied with the prophets, the people said to one another, "What has come over the son of Kish? Is Saul also among the prophets?" (10:10–11)

From this earlier episode we learn that the ecstatic behavior of these *nabi'im* is something with which Saul has been acquainted before. Indeed, it is the bodily sign of his having been chosen as YHWH's favorite. Fokkelman, among others, sees Saul's going to Ramah himself after three sets of messengers have been overpowered by this frenzy as a willful refusal to learn anything about the danger that awaits him.[1] However, it seems far more plausible in the narrative that being overcome in this way is unlikely to be seen by Saul as an unmitigated evil. Isn't it at least possible that Saul is looking for what he gets, a return to the ecstasy with which YHWH had first signaled his being favored? Twice Samuel has told Saul that the One who had chosen him has spurned him. His messengers have been overtaken by the ecstatic frenzy he remembers as the sign and seal of YHWH's favor. Perhaps he will succeed in destroying his rival for YHWH's favor. Perhaps he will have revenge against the seer who had made him "king" and had as

---

1. J. P. Fokkelman, *The Crossing Fates* (vol. 2 of *Narrative Art and Poetry in the Books of Samuel*; Assen, Netherlands: Van Gorcum, 1986), 278.

abruptly taken the ground out from under him. But it is also possible he will again fall under the spell that made him a new man, that demonstrated YHWH's love for him.

In this connection we may also note an intriguing parallel between the initial description of the band of prophets and the description that anticipated David's dancing before the ark. In both cases we have groups of men dancing; in both we have them accompanied by the wild music of lyre, flute, tambourine, and harp. Is the whole tale of David's dance before the ark modeled on the behavior of these ecstatic "prophets"? Is David, who is king and who will act as priest when the ark arrives at its destination, also taking the role of prophet in his own ecstatic dancing before the Lord?

There too we are told through the words of Michal that David's dancing was a naked cavorting. That is, nakedness seems to be a part of the ecstatic response to being possessed by YHWH. It was the nakedness of David there that signaled to Michal his unfitness to be king, or so she said. But more than that, it was the naked cavorting that had awakened her sexual jealousy.

This brings us back to Saul dancing, throwing off his clothes in orgiastic ecstasy, and then falling into a swoon where he lies naked for a day and a night. We first observe that Saul's stripping off his clothes is identified as something that he has in common with the others who are in ecstatic frenzy: "He *too* stripped off his clothes." Getting naked is not something that distinguishes Saul from the other cavorting *nabi'im* but rather his identification with them. Naked cavorting in ecstasy is something "prophets" do.

What this episode is suggesting is that being possessed by Adonai leads males to whirl and writhe in naked ecstasy. The possession by the spirit of the Lord is an overpoweringly erotic, indeed sexual, experience. And though for the prophets it may signal that they are simply possessed by a kind of holy madness, for Saul it has been confirmation that YHWH chose him as "armor-bearer." Perhaps this should have made him "a different man" in another way, but it has apparently left him susceptible to insane rages, in two of which he has attempted to murder his own beloved boy-toy (18:10–11).

The band of naked capering prophets, led by Samuel, appear to continue for some time whirling and cavorting like leaves tossed in the swirling winds of YHWH's phallic potency. For a time this is true of Saul, who even though possessed in this way makes his way to Naioth and Ramah and to the very vortex of this testosteronic storm: the "face" of Samuel (19:24).

Unlike the others, it is reported of Saul that the ecstasy drives him to the ground and completely out of his mind: "He lay naked all that day and

all that night." The image of male nakedness is always one of sexual vulnerability. The exposure of Noah's nakedness to Ham's gaze suggests sexual
vulnerability and perhaps even sexual violation (Gen 9:20–27). The law
codes will say that the exposure of the father's nakedness is a violation of his
masculine integrity (Lev 18:7).[2] Saul's naked swoon that leaves him exposed
to the reader's gaze for a day and a night is a rather extreme form of sexual
vulnerability and violation. Like Dagon, he lies upon the ground, immobi-
lized by the ferocious assault of YHWH's phallic potency. Has he been
raped? Is he the victim of sexual assault? We may be reminded of the fate of
the Levite's concubine, who was abused "all through the night until the
morning" by the Benjaminites and left unconscious at the door in mortal
swoon (Judg 19:25–27). Has Saul of the tribe of Benjamin suffered here the
fate inflicted upon the foreign woman at the hands of his fellow tribesmen?

Or has he, as he may have hoped, been ravished by his Great Lover? The
text at first suggests something like the latter. For in the ensuing episode
Saul seems to wonder at David's absence from his table (1 Sam 20:24–29).
Indeed, it is only when it becomes clear that Jonathan has replaced Saul as
the protector of David that Saul's old fury comes on him again, directed this
time against Jonathan (20:30–32).[3]

Thus, it would seem that being ravished by YHWH has briefly assuaged
Saul's rage. It is as if Saul is momentarily reassured of his place as the favored
of YHWH. The same erotic possession that had signaled his becoming
YHWH's favorite has come upon him with such redoubled force that his
jealous passion is temporarily spent.

But it was sexual assault after all, for Adonai has not returned to favoring
Saul. Saul's sexual submission didn't mean what Saul might have hoped.
Perhaps Saul is lucky in a way, for having been utterly possessed by Adonai's
phallic power, he is still not destroyed, as was Dagon. He remains alive for
several more chapters and is still king. Even so, Saul is torn between defend-
ing Israel from its enemies and pursuing the lad who has supplanted him in
YHWH's affections.

---

2. In both the Genesis account of Noah's nakedness and the Levitical prohibition of the uncovering of the
nakedness of the father, what seems to be (un)covered is a sexual act that violates the paternal dignity. That
Ham's (or Canaan's?) crime is more than simple voyeurism is made clear not only by the severity of Noah's
curse but also by Leviticus exclusively using the metaphor "uncover the nakedness of . . ." to refer to sexual
acts. What appears to be especially in view here is not merely sexual relations between father and son but precisely the sort of sexual act in which the son is active and the father the one acted upon—the reversal of the
role of agent. The inferior (son) acts upon the father, thereby rendering him passive. In the case of Noah this is
rather dramatically underlined by his drunken stupor that renders him vulnerable to the rape perpetrated by
Ham. That Canaan is punished rather than Ham may at first seem perplexing, but it may simply be that the
penetrator's seed is accursed.

3. In both cases Saul's rage is expressed by hurling a spear at the offending party, thus by an act of attempted
forcible "penetration."

The nakedness of the cavorting prophets that we have glimpsed through Saul's nakedness may help us to unravel more than one thread in the story of YHWH and his people. One thread leads us through the Levitical assertion that the people followed goat-demons and prostituted themselves and thence to an understanding of the supposition (as in Hosea) that the men took to the hills to prostitute themselves. What these texts have in common is that they suppose that the relation to the divine is in any case an erotic and indeed sexual one. They suppose that the YHWH who is worshiped in the high places may be seen by others as a demon, but is in any case one who takes sexual possession of his adorers. For what is common both to prostituting themselves and to being faithful is something like sexual possession and ecstasy.

Naked Prophets

But there is yet another thread that can be pulled, and it is that of prophetic nakedness. The roving bands of ecstatic prophets are not the only prophets who get naked as an integral part of their prophetic identity. Whatever may be the process of development between these roving bands (whose history stretches into the time of Elijah and Elisha and thus long after the time of Samuel, Saul, and David), the nakedness of the prophet does not disappear.

More than two centuries later, we encounter this element of prophetic vocation among prophets whom we scarcely would associate with roving bands of naked dancers: Micah and Isaiah.

In the first oracle of Micah, YHWH speaks a word of judgment on Samaria against the way in which the Israelites have prostituted themselves with the other nations. Samaria will be stripped of her wages for her harlotry (1:7).

> For this I will lament and wail;
>   I will go barefoot and naked;
> I will make lamentation like the jackals,
>   and mourning like the ostriches." (1:8)

The dramatic action of Micah, his wandering about naked and wailing, demonstrates that he is possessed by the word of YHWH and that this word, which possesses him, announces the destruction first of Israel and then of Judah. It is regularly supposed that this sign act simply enacts God's people being led into bondage. That is surely a significant part of what is happening here. But it seems also to be the case that Micah may be turning a traditional behavior of the one who is possessed by YHWH, going about naked and whirling and shouting, into a sign not of possession but of bereavement. That is, the nakedness may first signify simply that Micah is one of the prophets, that he is possessed ecstatically (and erotically) by YHWH. But its meaning is then reversed to indicate a kind of dispossession. He is naked like a prostitute who has been stripped of all the gains of her employ. His nakedness signals not only what it is to be possessed by YHWH but also what it is that will happen to those who have been possessed by other (phallic) powers. Nakedness here becomes not a badge of identification with and submission to the erotic power of YHWH but a mark of shame.

The prophet Isaiah, unlike Micah, is not from the countryside but is at home in the city and the court. Nevertheless, he shares with Micah this dramatic sign of prophetic nakedness:

> At that time the LORD had spoken to Isaiah son of Amoz, saying, "Go, and loose the sackcloth from your loins and take your sandals off your feet," and he had done so, walking naked and barefoot. Then the LORD said, "Just as my servant Isaiah has walked naked and barefoot for three years as a sign and a portent against Egypt and Ethiopia, so shall the king of Assyria lead away the Egyptians as captives and the Ethiopians as exiles, both the young and the old, naked and barefoot, with buttocks uncovered, to the shame of Egypt. (Isa 20:2–5)

The word of the Lord, like the spirit of God in the case of Saul, drives his messenger to strip naked. In his case, Isaiah goes about like this for three years. It is only after that time that the naked wandering of the prophet through the city receives an unexpected interpretation. Once again, the sign that Isaiah belonged to YHWH is reinterpreted to suggest the fate of those who resist the Assyrian juggernaut. Their nakedness is exposed to the world. Their buttocks are especially singled out as the target of violation and shame.

The nakedness of these two prophets, I am suggesting, should not be understood as an ad hoc sign, an act that comes out of the blue, but rather as the sign of their being possessed by YHWH, their being subservient to the divine potency. But in each case this action receives a new interpretation consistent with the message that each is called to convey. In the case of Isaiah, it becomes a way of emphasizing the folly of resisting the Assyrians and especially of looking for help from the other world powers (Ethiopia and Egypt). In the case of Micah, it signifies stripping Israel of the gains of the harlotries with (phallic) powers other than YHWH. In

each case the sexual vulnerability to YHWH signaled by prophetic nakedness is turned into a message concerning sexual vulnerability and violation
of another sort.

It is becoming clear how the people could suppose that Saul was one of
the prophets. His sexual vulnerability to (and perhaps violation by) Adonai,
as represented by his nakedness, actually does place him in the line of
prophets—in the line, that is, of those who are overpowered by the erotic
potency of YHWH, a potency that may also be named the "spirit of God."

It is perhaps this that helps further to explain the complaint of Jeremiah
against YHWH that the latter had raped him (Jer 20:7). It seems that the
sexual or at least erotic possession of the prophet by YHWH was a tradition
that continued long after that fateful day and night on the heights of
Ramah. There, one who had been YHWH's favorite lay stunned from rape
or ravishment and so was regarded by the people as having become like one
of the prophets.

Dionysus

The sense of being taken possession of by the god in an orgiastic scene
replete with dancing and wild music is not unique to the history of Israel.
The strange scene at Naioth of Ramah has already reminded some biblical
scholars of Dionysian ecstasy.[4] Indeed, there are a number of rather remarkable similarities and, as we shall see, a rather telling difference as well.

Although scholars have been content thus far merely to indicate the possibility of some parallel here, closer inspection reveals a rather long list of similarities. In both of Saul's encounters with the dancing ecstatics, they appear
to be in an open area on the hillside. The bands of Dionysian worshippers
are generally found capering outside the towns on the mountainsides.

Unlike the phenomenon of individual ecstatics, seers, and prophets, the
nabi'im are found in gangs or groups, as are the bacchants, maenads, and
other ecstatic adherents of Dionysus. From the eighth century BCE
onward, prophets (as opposed to the "sons of the prophets"—see below) in
Israel/Judah are either individuals or groups associated with the temple or
court. And while worshippers of Dionysus parade in the formal festivals of
city-states, they seem to be impersonators of the real phenomenon of
groups in the wilderness.

First Samuel 10 tells us of the ecstatics dancing to the music of pipe
(flute) and tambourine as well as lyre and harp. The enactment of Dionysian

---

4. J. Blenkinsopp, *A History of Prophecy in Israel* (Philadelphia: Westminster, 1983), 36.

revel seems always to require a similar musical accompaniment. Euripides
tells us of flutes and tambourines that accompany the presence of the Bacchae (*Bacchae*, lines 125–29).[5] In both cases we find the rhythmic dancing of
ecstatics as the characteristic mark of the ecstasy. Euripides speaks of "their
feet maddened by the breath of God" (1090). There is nothing here of a
contemplative mysticism.

One of the remarkable features of the Dionysian ecstasy is that it
appears to be irresistibly contagious.[6] The proximity of the bacchants, or
Bacchae, captures the sedentary and domestic denizens of town and village and sweeps them up into its ecstasy. Not only is the remarkable
contagion of the *nabi'im* represented by Saul's being drawn irresistibly
into their dance, but also, in the case of 1 Sam 19, we have three successive groups of messengers from Saul's court being swept up into the
ecstatic dance.

Remarkably as well, the phenomenon of group ecstasy is in both cases
attributed to the spirit or breath of the divinity. Twice in 1 Sam 10 and again
twice in 1 Sam 19 the phenomenon of ecstatic dance is attributed to the
spirit of God. And Euripides gives this same cause for the ecstasy of the
worshippers of Dionysus, speaking of him as "he whom the spirit of God
possesses" (*Bacchae* 74–75).

Just as the Hebrew narrative calls these ecstatics prophets (*nabi'im*), they
are also thus designated in the play by Euripides and in other Greek sources.
Euripides claims: "This is a god of prophecy. His worshippers like madmen
are endowed with mantic powers. For when the god enters the body of a
man, he fills him with the breath of prophecy" (297–301). This is reported
despite the fact that in neither case do we have any apparent disclosure of a
divine word or oracle that otherwise is associated with prophecy.

Finally, we may recognize that the frenzy produced in the worshipper
may also take the form of panic and pandemonium in the hosts of those
arrayed against the power of the god. In Euripides we hear: "Thus at times,
you see an army mustered under arms stricken with panic before it lifts a
spear. This panic comes from Dionysus" (301–5). And it is certainly the case
that the characteristic way in which the Philistines are defeated is not by
military strategy but by Adonai's unleashing a kind of panic among them
(e.g., 1 Sam 4:6–8).

---

5. Euripides' *Bacchae* is the most extensive source for understanding Dionysus; I am using William Arrowsmith's translation of it in Euripedes, *Euripides*, vol. 5 (ed. D. Grene and R. Lattimore; The Complete Greek
Tragedies; Chicago: University of Chicago, 1959).
6. Walter Burkert observes that "Dionysian ecstasy . . . is a mass phenomenon and spreads almost infectiously";
see his *Greek Religion* (trans. J. Raffan; Cambridge: Harvard University Press, 1985), 162.

In addition to these features that may provide points of contact between the worshippers of Adonai and those possessed by Dionysus, we may also identify other intriguing parallels between the two deities. Both seem to be represented as bulls. The representation of YHWH as a bull is regarded as the "sin of Jeroboam" by the writers of 1 and 2 Kings even though it appears to have been intended and regarded as a representation of YHWH.[7] In both cases the bull representation seems not to be indicative of fertility as such but of sexual potency. If I am right about the teraphim as phallic representatives of YHWH and the ephod and ark as more or less disguised phalli, then something of a parallel may also be drawn to Dionysus. He is regularly represented by a phallus; moreover, by one that is concealed in a basket.[8]

We also should not fail to notice that the god Dionysus leads his followers into a wilderness area where milk and honey seem to spring from every rock and plant (*Bacchae* 709–11); similarly, YHWH has promised to lead his people into a land flowing with milk and honey.

In spite of the remarkable similarities that I have pointed out between the Greek and Palestinian portrayals of the ecstatic relation between a male god and his adherents, there may be some resistance to seeing any relation between them. After all, Dionysus may be an overpowering divinity, but he stands in ill repute especially among the later, more sober adherents of either the OT or the NT divinity.

Yet we cannot rule out the possibility of a complex cultural diffusion. Scholars of Greek religion have observed that aspects of the cult (if that is the right word) of Dionysus seem to bear not only traces of Anatolian and Syrian influence but also marks of Semitic origin.[9]

The routes and directions of any such cultural diffusion are in the nature of the case almost impossible to identify. With their culture and destructive power, the warrior sea peoples, who appear in the guise of Philistines in biblical sources, all but extinguished the Mycenaean-Minoan precursors of Greek culture at the beginning of the twelfth century. Thereby they produced a four-century-long "dark age," which still gripped that part of the world at the time referred to in the biblical narratives we are reading.

---

7. Among many references to the appearance of Dionysus as a bull in Euripides' *Bacchae*, see lines 100, 619, 920, 1016. We may even recall that YHWH seems to be represented by a serpent (Num 21:1–9), something also true of Dionysus. That YHWH may be represented by a serpent is also clear in Exod 4:1–5 (where Moses' staff becomes a serpent "so that they may believe"). Later, in 2 Kgs 18:4, the "bronze serpent that Moses had made" was destroyed as an act of piety by Hezekiah, thereby retroactively seeking to deny the connection between YHWH and his serpent representation.

8. Burkert, *Greek Religion*, 166, notes "the significance of the phallos is not procreative. . . . It is arousal for its own sake."

9. Ibid., 163.

Indeed, Greek culture would not emerge from this period until about the time Assyria devastated Israel and brought Judah to heel as a protectorate—until the time of Hosea, Micah, and Isaiah. Accordingly, it is not until this time that the earliest sagas of the Greek people come to be written down and convey readable information concerning Dionysus. And our most extensive information comes even later, in the fifth century BCE, with the play of Euripides and the allusions of Plato.

This temporal and geographic distance (not to mention that Greece and Palestine are separated by large and more powerful cultures) would make cultural diffusion both difficult to identify and necessarily fragmentary. Already from Greek sources we may notice some remarkable transformations in the cult and representation of Dionysus. For example, in earlier times he seems to be represented as a mask of an older adult male. But by the time of the classical era, he has come to be portrayed as a languid adolescent—certainly not what immediately comes to mind from a reading of the biblical narrative.[10]

By far the most striking difference between the followers of Dionysus and those of Adonai is that the former seem typically female while the latter appear in 1 Samuel as male. The dancing ecstatics who accompany Dionysus are generally female,[11] but here on the hillside of Ramah they are male. In both cases the erotic features of the ecstatic possession by the divinity seem unmistakable, but for the Greeks this seems to have been primarily (though not exclusively) heteroerotic in character: a male divinity with female groupies.[12] However, in the case we have been examining in 1 Samuel, the ecstasy seems to be homoerotic in character. In addition, the erotic character of the ecstasy is here underlined by the nakedness of the human counterparts.[13]

It seems likely that the bands of *nabi'im* are to be understood as enacting an erotic relationship to YHWH. But to what extent does this also mean a homoerotic relationship between members of this band? To what extent

---

10. For a discussion of the role of the mask, see Walter F. Otto, *Dionysus: Myth and Cult* (trans. R. B. Palmer; Bloomington: Indiana University Press, 1965), 86–91. For the transformation, see Burkert, *Greek Religion*, 167, who dates this transformation to the middle of the fifth century BCE. By the time Dionysus has been transformed to a naked adolescent, the ecstatic or orgiastic features of YHWH adherence I am suggesting in the Samuel narratives are being suppressed by priestly writers.

11. There are important exceptions. In Euripides' *Bacchae*, while the groups in the wilderness appear to be all female, the play hinges in part on the determination of two men, Teiresias and Cadmus, to be faithful adherents of Dionysus. The former claims, "He desires his honor from all mankind" (lines 205–9).

12. The women band together in forsaking hearth and home, utterly rejecting male advances, and accepting the pervasive eroticism of the ecstasy they exhibit. These features might lead at least the contemporary interpreter to see female same-sex eroticism as the likely concomitant to the orgiastic following of the divinity most associated with liberation from patriarchy.

13. The female followers of Dionysus were characterized by flowing loose garments of an "oriental" style.

does the eroticism of the relationship to YHWH entail an erotic relation among the prophets themselves?

At the outset we must admit that the evidence is far less direct than in the case of the warrior love we have detected in the heroic saga of David and his lovers. Yet we are not completely without clues.

We begin with what we have pointed out with respect to the Dionysian ecstasy itself. Outsiders to the Dionysian revels certainly see them as erotic in character. In Euripides' *Bacchae*, for example, the doubting king bemoans the sheer eroticism of the groupies of Dionysus. However, if there is eroticism here, it does not appear at all likely that it is, apart from the relation to the god, heteroerotic. For we hear repeatedly that men are excluded from these revels. Hence, the erotic goings-on in the woods must be taking place between women. The Dionysian orgies thus are sites of female same-sex eroticism.

This comports well with what we otherwise know about the participants. They are not mere girls but are women who have left husbands and children behind in the towns to run together in abandon on the hillsides. They have left behind the trammels of patriarchy to disport themselves in the countryside. For this reason, Hera, the goddess of conventional matronly behavior, is the implacable foe of Dionysus. As the Phyllis Schafley of the pantheon, she stands for conventional marriage and family values and thus against the women's movement launched under the banner of Bacchus.

In chapter 11 we will return to the question of female homoeroticism with particular attention to ancient Israel. In that connection we will also encounter evidence of male homoeroticism in later transformations of the Bacchic cult. But this by itself will not resolve the question of whether we should imagine homoerotic practices to characterize relationships between the human males caught up in ecstatic relation to their male deity. Before taking up that issue again, it may be helpful to look at a related phenomenon in later Israel: the "sons of the prophets."

Sons of the Prophets—*Bene-hanebi'im*

In order to shed more light on the phenomenon of the group of *nabi'im* in 1 Samuel, we may turn to the apparently similar phenomenon of the *bene-hanebi'im* of Israel in the period following the division of the monarchy. These so-called prophets or sons of the prophets also appear as groups of male adherents of the divine, normally of YHWH, but occasionally of Baal as well. They appear primarily in the saga material concerning Elijah and Elisha contained in 1 and 2 Kings. The accounts refer to a period nearly two centuries later than the events recounted in 1 Samuel and are contained in a narrative with a quite different point of view (one far more reticent concerning the depiction of the foibles, sexual and otherwise, of Israel's and Judah's great heroes). Yet they may still be used, with caution, to fill out our picture of the ecstatic phenomenon that appears in 1 Samuel. One important difference is that we no longer hear of naked male dancing as a part of the phenomenon, but we would scarcely expect this from a source so markedly more nervous about "idolatry" than the Samuel saga.

If for the moment we suppose that this has simply been edited out of the accounts, what else are we able to learn about these groups of male adherents of YHWH?

In the first place we have accounts of these prophets only in the material bracketed by the appearance of Elijah and the death of Elisha (1 Kgs 17–2 Kgs 13). It is of some interest that none of the stories in which they appear has any counterpart in the more sanitized version of the history of Israel composed by the Chronicler, who barely mentions Elijah and ignores Elisha altogether.

This is not to say, however, that these prophets are consistently associated with Elijah or Elisha. For one thing, we are told of the existence of groups of prophets who are associated with Baal (and on one occasion with Asherah). For another, we encounter groups of prophets or members of such groups in stories in which neither Elijah nor Elisha appear (1 Kgs 20:35–43; 22:6–23). In other stories they appear to operate rather independently of either. Moreover, we hear of groups of prophets or "sons of prophets" only in the northern kingdom.

We first learn that they are generally found in groups. The most common feature of this group nature is that it is typically found in multiples of fifty. This is quite a regular phenomenon. In 1 Kgs 18:2–4 when the "prophets" make their first appearance, we learn that there are two groups of fifty prophets of YHWH, hidden in caves in the mountains to escape the attempt of Jezebel to exterminate them. Later in that chapter we encounter 450 prophets of Baal and 400 of Asherah (18:19). Most often the prophets are found in groups of fifty.

While such companies are often found, as in 1 Samuel, in the countryside or even in the wilderness, we do hear that they are also associated with particular towns. Thus, in 2 Kgs 2:3 we hear of a company of prophets from Bethel and later of a group from Jericho (2:5, 15), as well as a group associated with Gilgal (4:38). Though it is possible that these prophets were in some way connected with Yahwistic shrines in these places, it is even more likely that the vocation of prophet is rather part-time. The males who are called prophets engage in their ecstatic adoration of YHWH in same-sex companies but also are part of communities in which they live relatively normal lives as farmers. We do learn, for example, of one of a company of prophets who had a wife, child, and home (4:1–7). This suggests that his participation in the ecstatic bands was such as to leave him some opportunity for participating in the life of the community. Hence, it appears that the "prophets" formed a religious association of lay males who were especially devoted to YHWH and who held themselves ready to participate in orgiastic bands as occasion demanded.

Yet the level of their devotion to YHWH must have been rather extraordinary. When Jezebel seeks to impose a certain kind of religious conformity in the land, she seeks to exterminate the prophets of YHWH. This is why, at the start of the Elijah cycle, we are told that Obadiah has hidden the remaining hundred prophets of YHWH in two groups of fifty in caves (1 Kings 18:4). The attempt to eliminate the ecstatic devotees of the god is not limited to the extermination of YHWH's prophets. In a rather chilling episode we hear of Elijah first ritually defeating the 450 prophets of Baal and then summarily executing them (18:19–40). This suggests that both Baal and YHWH were regarded as inducing ecstasy among groups of males, and that these ecstatics were the most fervent devotees of their respective deities. It is even possible that we do not have to do with different deities here but with distinct versions of the "same" Israelite religion. For it does seem to be the case that Baal was regularly regarded as another name for YHWH, with YHWH taking on some of the attributes of the Canaanite indigenous religious traditions. It has been common to suppose that the ecstatic behavior of the prophets has more to do with Canaanite practices. But on the contrary, Yahwism may be responsible for the ecstatic male devotees. Perhaps Ahab's indigenizing policies carried ecstatic practice associated with YHWH over into Baalism.

If we make this connection and find the practices of the prophets of Baal also to be evidence for their counterparts among the prophets of Israel, then a new form of ecstatic behavior comes into view. The ecstatic dancing of the prophets could at times include forms of mutual bloodletting. Thus, we hear that the prophets of Baal "limped" about the altar (probably a form of ecstatic dance) and "cut themselves with swords and lances until the blood gushed out over them" (18:26, 28). This gashing of one another until they bleed is not something restricted to the prophets of Baal. We also hear later of "a certain member of a company of prophets" who gets another member of the company to strike him so that he can appear before the king with a word from YHWH (20:35–43). In this case bleeding from wounds may be an authenticating sign of prophetic ecstasy. Corroborating evidence comes from Hosea, the only writing prophet from the northern kingdom, who has YHWH complain that "they do not cry to me from the heart, but they wail upon their beds; they gash themselves for grain and wine" (Hos 7:14). At this late stage of the religious expression of Israel, it appears that the action of gashing oneself has become a form of prayer or at least a sign of devotion that seeks blessing from God. But Hosea regards it not as coming from the heart but as having become routinized.[14]

The *bene-hanebi'im* appear in the episode recounted in 1 Kgs 20 not only to be ecstatics but also to be armed, as if a military group, something that comports with the division of prophets into companies of fifties. That this is a kind of quasi-military organization we also learn from the gathering of companies of prophets who seek to find Elijah after his disappearance in a fiery chariot. Elisha is told, "See now, we have fifty strong men among your servants" (2 Kgs 2:16). Indeed, the quasi-military form of prophetic bands is reinforced by the appellation attached both to Elijah and to Elisha: "Father, father! The chariots of Israel and its horsemen!" (2:12; 13:14). Therefore, the prophets are what we might call "spirit warriors," whose ecstatically verified powers serve also as a kind of secret weapon against the enemies of Israel.

In the case of the prophetic bands of 1 Samuel, we hear of music as the accompaniment of prophetic dance. In the saga material of 1 and 2 Kings, we have little indication of this. The nearest we come to the depiction of prophetic dance is in the vain activity of the prophets of Baal "limping" about their altar. However, we do have one episode concerning Elisha that tends to confirm the continuity of the association of prophetic trance/ecstasy with music. When the son of Ahab asks Elisha to give a word from YHWH, Elisha first tells the young king to try the prophets of his mother or father (2 Kgs 3:13). But when Ahab's son refuses to be put off, Elisha asks for a musician. "While the musician was playing, the power of the LORD came on him" (3:15). In the name of YHWH, Elisha tells the king that the alliance of Israel, Judah, and Edom will be successful in taking the territory of Moab (3:9, 18). The necessity of music to induce the capacity to hear and

---

14. This form of ecstatic behavior is, of course, also known in various forms of Christianity in which devotees, usually males, display self-inflicted wounds (often from flagellation) as part of religious devotion. That gashing oneself may be viewed as a form of prayer to YHWH appears also in Jer 41:5 but is attributed to the Philistines in Jer 47:5 and prohibited in Lev 19:28 and Deut 14:1. Biblical literature thus seems to be in some perplexity about this practice.

speak the word of YHWH corresponds to the association of music and the prophetic bands of 1 Samuel.

Some features of the *bene-hanebi'im* are reminiscent not only of features of Dionysian and Bacchic rites but also of the Galli, as reported by writers in the time of the Roman Empire. These were men dedicated to the goddess Cybele. They were known to whip themselves into ecstatic behavior through music and dance, and also to inflict wounds upon themselves in the midst of such ecstasy. This sometimes culminated in self-castration. Roman writers like Martial and Apuleius regarded these male groupies of a Near Eastern mother goddess as also insatiable in their appetite for sexual access to young males.

On the one hand, we may be struck by certain similarities to the phenomena we have been examining of the *bene-hanebi'im*. The ecstatic dancing mentioned in the case of Saul and of the *nabi'im* around Samuel is also reflected among the *bene-hanebi'im* of the Israelite monarchy. We have also seen the role that ritual mutilation or wounding may play among the *bene-hanebi'im*.

There is, of course, no evidence of self-castration among these prophetic bands. However, the practice of circumcision may be regarded as a form of genital mutilation that may have rendered castration symbolically redundant even before it was specifically proscribed, at least for members of the priestly class. We should recognize, however, that the priestly class plays little or no role in the history of the northern kingdom, where we encounter the *bene-hanebi'im*.

The origin of the Galli is the same region within which the northern kingdom is situated, and as late as the Christian historian Eusebius we have the assertion of these practices as focused in the same area.

Despite these similarities, we must also notice the most important difference: the *bene-hanebi'im* are devotees of a decidedly masculine divinity, not a mother goddess. Whatever the symbolic and ritual logic of the practices of the Galli, they must be quite different in the case of the *bene-hanebi'im*. In the latter case, it is the erotic attachment to a Great Warrior that sets up the context within which ecstatic music, dance, and mutual wounding or self-wounding takes place. In the case of devotees of Cybele, the result is a kind of feminization of the devotee. In the case of the *bene-hanebi'im*, there seems to be a maculinization of the devotee, who is marked in some way as the possession of the warrior-god.

In his discussion of the Galli, Greenberg seeks to link this to the case of the "cultic male prostitutes" of the southern kingdom and seems unaware of the phenomenon of the *bene-hanebi'im*, whom in certain respects they more closely resemble.[15] For the Galli and the *bene-hanebi'im* are alike in not being associated with temples or shrines. Instead, they seem to be groups of lay males who are "groupies" of their respective divinities.

In chapter 7 we will deal with the question of males who provide some sort of sexual services in connection with the temple to YHWH in the southern kingdom, and in chapter 8 with the emergence of symbolic trans-gendering for YHWH's beloved male(s). But in the case of the *bene-hanebi'im*, we have to do neither with transgendering nor with specifically cultic practices.

Once again our examination of cross-cultural comparisons has an ambiguous result. We find several features common to other phenomena from the ancient world, but we also find remarkable differences. This is what we should expect to discover, for it is not a question of Israel being either unrelated to other cultures of the ancient world or simply an imitative adjunct to them.

The homoerotic features of northern prophetic traditions have some interesting and illuminating parallels in cross-cultural comparisons, but the distinctiveness of a religious tradition focused upon a single male deity is also quite evident.

To what extent should we see these bands of male ecstatics as an alternative site for male homoeroticism? Do they provide a model for same-sex eroticism that may serve as an alternative complement to the warrior same-sex eroticism that we have seen in the David narrative? In order to clarify this issue, we must turn to a discussion of texts that may suggest some actual or virtual same-sex sexual practices on the part of these prophets.

---

15. David F. Greenberg, *The Construction of Homosexuality* (Chicago: University of Chicago Press, 1988), 98–103. Greenberg may be right to suppose a common origin of many of these phenomena in shamanistic practices, but at least for Israel, this does not at first take the form of transgendering the male since the devotees are males assimilated to a warrior divinity. He does suppose that castration and temple "prostitution" are probably much later phenomena, "developed in the transition from a kinship order to a class-differentiated city-state" (101).

6. Boy Lovers

IN THIS CHAPTER we turn to accounts of the most notable of Israel's early "prophets," Samuel, Elijah, and Elisha, to examine episodes that appear to involve them in tales of sexual awakening.

(Res) Erection

It was in connection with Saul's naked dance that we began to focus on the question of the erotic character of prophetic possession. From the writing prophets we have seen evidence for the enduring character of this eroticism, expressing devotion to YHWH. Do we have anything of the kind in the stories of the prophets in 1 and 2 Kings?

There is one episode, or rather a pair of episodes, that may be understood as conveying the presence of homoerotic associations as characteristic of prophetic behavior. This has to do with the apparent raising of a young boy from the dead, something attributed both to Elijah and to Elisha. Elijah is abruptly introduced into the narrative of 1 Kings at 17:1, commencing a section of the narrative that continues through the death of Elisha in 2 Kgs 13:14–21. Insofar as it concerns Elijah and Elisha, this material is largely absent from Chronicles. When Elijah is introduced, it is to announce the beginning of a drought in the land. As a consequence of the drought, YHWH sends Elijah to a town belonging to Sidon (Lebanon), where he is taken in by a widow whom he rescues from the drought-induced famine through an unemptying jar of meal and jug of oil.

In spite of this mysterious supply of basic necessities, the widow's son becomes ill. It is then that the episode of the resuscitation of the boy begins:

> After this the son of the woman, the mistress of the house, became ill; his illness was so severe that there was no breath left in him. She then said to Elijah, "What have you against me, O man of God? You have come to me to bring my sin to remembrance, and to cause the death of my son!" But he said to her, "Give me your son." He took him from her bosom, carried him up into the upper chamber where he was lodging, and laid him on his own bed. He cried out to the LORD, "O LORD my God, have you brought calamity even upon the widow with whom I am staying, by killing her son?" Then he stretched himself upon the child three times, and cried out to the LORD, "O LORD my God, let this child's life come into him again." The LORD listened to the voice of Elijah; the life of the child came into him again, and he revived. Elijah took the child, brought him down from the upper chamber into the house, and gave him to his mother; then Elijah said, "See, your son is alive." So the woman said to Elijah, "Now I know that you are a man of God, and that the word of the LORD in your mouth is truth."
> (1 Kgs 17:17–24)

The story is constructed in a tight pyramid or chiasmus structure. It begins and ends with a word addressed by the mother to Elijah, the first a word of complaint and accusation, the last a word of affirmation. The second step on each side of the pyramid consists of a threefold movement. In verse 19 Elijah takes the son from the mother, carries him to the upper room, and places him on the bed. The action of verse 23 is exactly the reverse: from the bed, from the upper room, to the mother. Nearer the apex of the triangle are the two words of address from Elijah to God (vv. 20 and 21b). At the very apex of the triangle is the odd action of Elijah with respect to the boy: "He stretched himself upon the child three times." To this triple stretching out upon the boy corresponds the triple assertion of revitalization of verse 22: "The LORD listened to the voice of Elijah; the life of the child came into him again, and he revived."

The rigorous structure of this narrative draws our attention to two features of the resuscitation of the boy. The first is that, unlike the other wonders performed by Elijah, this one is accompanied by prayer.[1] In fact,

---

1. In connection with the miracles of Elijah, we are told of prayer only in connection with the calling down of the fire (1 Kgs 18:37–38) by which deed the prophets of Baal are undone.

the prayer disturbs the symmetry of the story in that if it is left out, the pyramid would be perfect, with the threefold stretching answered by the threefold assertion of revitalization of the child.

As it stands, the prayer serves to turn the reader's attention slightly away from the odd mechanics of the resuscitation: He stretches himself on the child three times. What is going on here? And why the emphasis upon the utter privacy of the action as Elijah removes the boy from his mother's embrace, takes him into his own private quarters, and places the boy upon his own bed before stretching himself (three times) upon the boy? Why does lying upon the boy bring the boy to life? What is the nature of a stretching out on someone that produces life?[2] Is the potency of YHWH being transferred to the boy through the mediation of an actual or virtual sexual embrace? Does Elijah here, by an act of sympathetic magic, draw into the boy the life-enhancing phallic potency of YHWH?[3]

In order to test this hypothesis, we must turn to the parallel story concerning Elisha in 2 Kgs 4. In general, the saga material concerning Elisha is much more complex than that concerning Elijah. Among other things, there are many more wonders attributed to Elisha, including some rather strange and apparently gratuitous episodes: changing bad water to good, having a she-bear maul forty-two small boys who teased him for his baldness, fixing bad stew, feeding a group of a hundred with twenty loaves of bread, and so on.

In the midst of this we have two separate episodes that seem to echo the story we have read concerning Elijah. In the first one, Elisha makes a jar provide enough oil to deliver the widow of one of the sons of the prophets. She is able to sell oil, pay off her debts, and prevent her children from being sold as slaves. This has certain parallels to the other jar of oil that serves to stave off hunger for the widow in Sidon, with whom Elijah stayed. The second story is a far more elaborate tale of resuscitating the son of a woman with whom Elisha lives.

When in the neighborhood, Elisha stays in a roof chamber provided by the Shunammite woman, who is childless. The story thus is well launched when we hear that Elisha intends to repay her hospitality by causing her to conceive a son despite the advanced age of her husband.

---

2. Unfortunately, several commentators focus on the rather extraneous question of whether the lad has really died; see, for example, John Gray, *I and II Kings* (Philadelphia: Westminster, 1963). While this may be an attempt at a "naturalistic" explanation or at distinguishing the act of Elijah from the later deeds of Jesus, it also diverts the reader from more intriguing elements of the narrative.

3. We may also wonder whether there is a future for the lad. In this connection we may notice the role of Elijah's "lad" (*na'ar*) in the subsequent narrative of 18:43–44. The text does not explicitly link the two episodes, but if we allow for a connection, then the relationship inaugurated through this erotic resurrection continues as the lad becomes Elijah's (erotic) companion, much as warriors have their armor-bearers.

At least on the surface level of the story, the woman conceives the child
through the word of Elisha. In this story there is no actually reported word
of Adonai, so that the conception and birth have no other agent than Elisha.
Thus, the child is in a certain sense (and perhaps in more than one sense)
the child of Elisha.

The subsequent action is set in motion by the notice that "when the
child was older, he went out one day to his father among the reapers"
(2 Kgs 4:18). When the lad complains of pain in his head, his father sends
him back to his mother. On his mother's lap, the boy expires. In an action
with curious parallels to the earlier episode, the mother "went up and laid
him on the bed of the man of God, closed the door on him, and left" (4:21).
Earlier we learned that the Shunammite woman has talked her husband
into building for this "holy man of God . . . a small roof chamber with
walls," outfitted with "a bed, a table, a chair, and a lamp" (4:9–10). Thus,
placing the boy in the prophet's private quarters and on his bed corresponds
to what has occurred in the earlier episode concerning Elijah. However,
Elisha is not now residing with the Shunammite woman but is in his accustomed wilderness retreat on Mt. Carmel.

Before we come to the actual resuscitation, Elisha sends his servant
Gehazi to the boy with his staff, which is to be laid upon the boy. Despite
the haste with which Gehazi complies with the strange orders of the
prophet, the use of the staff as a substitute for the body (?) of the prophet
does not meet with success. But Elisha is already on his way in person at the
insistence of the Shunammite woman:

> When Elisha came into the house, he saw the child lying dead on his bed.
> So he went in and closed the door on the two of them [Gehazi and the
> mother], and prayed to the LORD. Then he got up . . . and lay upon the
> child, putting his mouth upon his mouth, his eyes upon his eyes, and his
> hands upon his hands; and while he lay bent over him, the flesh of the child
> became warm. He got down, walked once to and fro in the room, then got
> up again and bent over him; the child sneezed seven times, and the child
> opened his eyes. (4:32–35)

Elijah delivers the child again to his mother.

A number of elements here echo the earlier episode concerning Elijah.
In both cases the mother delivers the son into the care of the prophet, and
at the end the child is restored to the mother. In both cases the child is shut
up in the prophet's room and laid on the prophet's bed. In both cases the
privacy of the bedchamber is the scene for the intimacy of lying on the boy,

which will have restorative effect. And in both cases the prophet cries out to YHWH as he stretches himself upon the lad. (Like Elijah, Elisha does not need to do this in order to perform any of his other wonders.)

In addition to these common elements, however, this later story fairly bristles with a barely suppressed eroticism. There is the staff as a possible phallic signifier, whose ineffectiveness seems to call out for the "real thing." The intimacy of lying on the boy (mouth to mouth, eye to eye, hand to hand) is underlined with the addition of the sexually charged verb "bent over him." We notice the warming of the boy's flesh and, oddly, that the boy "sneezed" and did so seven times. What is going on here? We may take these elements in turn.

To what extent should we read the "staff" as a phallic substitute? If this is a phallic substitute, then the report that it does not work even when laid on the face (or front) of the child suggests that this resuscitation may only be done in person with the real body of the prophet. This would be the body with a real as opposed to a virtual phallic member attached.

The English translation seeks to soften the action by inserting "on the bed" when Elisha gets up on the boy and lies on him and bends over him. The triple underlining of the action of Elisha only makes more emphatic the quasi-sexual nature of this lying upon the boy that had been expressed in the earlier account (concerning Elijah) as "stretching" upon him. The triple verb is accompanied by the triple designation of body parts in proximity: mouth to mouth, eye to eye, hand to hand.

In this narrative the erotic character of Elisha's action is answered by the response of the lad. After the first intimate action in Elisha's bed, we are told that the lad's flesh becomes warm. At first this may seem an innocent if puzzling detail—until we recall an episode from another story, this time from the last days of David. The king's diminishing potency has alarmed his advisers, and they select and send a beautiful young Shunammite girl, Abishag, to lie in the king's "bosom" in order to warm him (1 Kgs 1:1–4).[4] And we recall that in the story of Elisha, we are in the home of a Shunammite woman. But now it is a boy in bed, and it is his body that is being made warm by the man who lies upon him. In each case the warming of the body by bodily proximity seems to aim at sexual arousal as the sign of bodily vitality. Unfortunately for David, Abishag is not as successful as Elijah.

But Elisha is not yet finished with the boy. He gets up and walks to and fro. Thus refreshed, he rises up upon the boy in the bed again. And this time

---

4. The erotic overtones of this story are seldom missed in the case of David and Abishag but are universally passed over in silence with respect to the action of Elijah. On the part of biblical commentators, this is a rather clear indication of heterocentrism at least, and possibly also homophobia.

the boy not only responds with the warming of his flesh but also "sneezes" and does so not once but an astonishing seven times. Why is sneezing here the sign of new life? And why are we told that he does so seven times? The commentators regularly assert that this sneezing is a sign that the boy is breathing.[5] But there would scarcely be any need to make use of a word that does not otherwise occur in Hebrew to signify breathing.[6] There are other ways to say this; for example, the way it is said in the story in which Elijah has restored the boy. Sneezing is after all not associated with life but with a sort of convulsion more like death. But sneezing is like another act—the act of ejaculation. The liveliness of the boy is represented by a term that may well suggest ejaculation. That is why we get the otherwise inexplicable "seven times." Sneezing seven times is not a good sign of vitality. But ejaculating seven times is a sign of rather extraordinary vitality.

On this reading, what has happened here? Elisha's act of getting upon the boy, lying on him, and bending over him is an action of sexual arousal, whose success is represented not only by erection (getting warm or even "hot") but also by multiple ejaculation. The boy near death or already dead has become a sexually potent young male through being sexually awakened by Elisha.

Elisha has already been responsible for the birth of the boy. But now he has become author of the lad's sexual potency as well. The implied sexuality of the action of Elisha is answered by the phenomenal sexual response of the lad. When he is returned to his mother, he is no longer a mere child; he is a youth, "your son." He is not only restored to life; he is also astonishingly vigorous.

Reading the story in this way actually enhances its significance and gives meaning to the otherwise inexplicable activity of Elisha and the otherwise odd response of the boy. The (homo)erotic potential of the story has not always been lost on Bible readers. The twelfth-century chronicler Walter Map could rely upon his early medieval readers to get the joke when he refers sardonically to Bernard of Clairvaux's attempt to resurrect a boy by throwing himself upon him. "Dom Bernard ordered his body to be carried into a private room, turned everyone out, threw himself upon the boy, prayed, and got up again: but the boy did not get up; he lay there dead." Map then says, "I have heard before now of a monk throwing himself upon a boy, but always, when the monk got up, the boy promptly got up too."[7]

---

5. So Gray, *Kings*, 447.

6. The word occurs in biblical Hebrew only in this passage. One wonders how the translators decided on "sneezing" as its translation.

7. Walter Map, *De nugis curialium* (Courtiers' Trifles) (ed. and trans. M. R. James; rev. C. Brooke and R. Mynors; Oxford Medieval Texts; Oxford: Clarendon, 1983), Dist. 1.24 (p. 81). The tale first came to my attention through a reference in Caroline Walker Bynum's *The Resurrection of the Body* (New York: Columbia

Map continues with an elbow in the reader's ribs: "The abbot went very red, and a lot of people left the room to have a good laugh."

There are two other matters that require some consideration here. The first is the action of the prophet in calling upon YHWH. In the case of the Elijah episode, we noticed that the double invocation of YHWH seems to distort the chiasmic structure of the narrative. However, this may also serve to underline its significance. The modern reader knows only too well that sexual excitement leads one or both members of the act to call on the deity: "O God!" We have no way of knowing if this was true for the ancients, or at least for the ancient Israelites, although the eroticism of the religious texts we have been reading does not exactly discourage that association. This is plausible especially since, as we have seen, YHWH is present in some narratives as an awesome phallic power who ravishes his male companions.

This detail of calling upon YHWH is all the more significant since it does not normally accompany the miraculous deeds of these prophets. In the case of Elisha, of whom many such deeds are reported, this feature is especially noticeable. The invocation of YHWH at this point does not seem only to be a case of YHWH's special connection to life, since the work of changing bad stew into good or of producing food where there had been none is similarly connected to giving life. But what is invoked here may be precisely YHWH's phallic potency; the very potency that is otherwise directed to the prophet is now directed through the prophet to the lad. The prophet becomes the conduit of this phallic potency. The sexual connection between the prophet and the lad is made possible through the sexual connection between YHWH and the prophet. Thus, the prophet is enabled to act in YHWH's stead in an erotic encounter that (re)produces life.[8]

Finally, we may wonder whether in thus awakening the erotic potency of the lad, Elisha has not become in the important sense the "father" of the lad. We already observed how his word appears to be the agent of procreation.

University Press, 1995), in which she paraphrases the episode as "boys do usually 'rise up' when monks lie down upon them" (208n28). Her note refers to the study of Walter Map's work by Monika Otter in her work *Inventiones: Fiction and Referentiality in Twelfth-Century English Historical Writing* (Chapel Hill: University of North Carolina Press, 1996). Otter refers to this passage as "an off-color" joke (116), but she may mistake this as a reference to the actions of Jesus, which do not mirror as closely the quip of Map as do the actions of Elijah and Elisha. The footnote to the critical edition cited above makes reference to both Mark 5:40 (the raising of Jairus's daughter, suggested perhaps by "turned everyone out") and 2 Kgs 4:34 (Elisha's mediating of resurrection to the boy).

8. Scholars generally recognize that the resuscitations of apparently dead (young) people by Jesus in the Gospels echo the resuscitation narratives we have been discussing. However, the element of full-body contact is missing in the tales of the resurrection of Jairus's daughter (Mark 5) and the resurrection of the widow's son at Nain (Luke 7). This element is, however, present in the account of Paul's resuscitation of the young man (*neanias, pais*) named Eutychus in Acts 20:7–12. There we are told that Paul "fell on him" and closely "embraced" him (20:10 KJV; cf. NIV). I have discussed the homoerotic features of the account of Jesus' giving resurrection to a youth in "Secret Mark," in *The Man Jesus Loved: Homoerotic Narratives from the New Testament* (Cleveland: Pilgrim, 2003), 114–25.

But now it is his sexual potency that affects the vitality of the lad. Have the "sons" of the prophets received their own potency through this kind of intimate contact with the prophet? Is it as progenitor of their male potency that they call him "Father" and that they are called "sons"? We may recall that the head of a company of prophets may be called their "father." This was already brought to expression in the question asked concerning Saul in a frenzy as one of the prophets: "Who is their father?" (1 Sam 10:12). This may indeed suggest that the prophets "inseminate" their followers either literally or metaphorically. These followers then become the "sons of the prophets."

Samuel's Night Visitor

The twin stories of erotic resurrection that we have read in the sagas concerning Elijah and Elisha are remarkable enough in themselves, pointing as they do toward a transfer of erotic potency from or through the prophet as in some way the representative of Adonai. In our discussion of warrior love, we have noticed that YHWH's relation to Saul, and especially to David, mirrors the structure of same-sex eroticism among warriors as depicted in the relationships between David and Saul and David and Jonathan. Accordingly, we may ask whether there is something similar in the saga materials concerning the transmission of erotic power from YHWH to a "juvenile" in something like a cultic setting. To a certain degree, something like this is already inscribed in the narratives we have considered concerning Elijah and Elisha in one detail. For this miracle of erotic resurrection, it has been necessary to invoke the presence and potency of YHWH, something not true of other miracles attributed to Elijah or Elisha. Thus, in a remarkable way Adonai is already implicated in the eroticism of the man-boy relationship exhibited in these narratives. Do we have any other stories that may point in the same direction in which YHWH is more directly involved?

From this point of view, there is at least one other story in the Hebrew Bible that comes into consideration. It is the story of the relationship of the boy Samuel to YHWH, the account of Samuel's initiation as YHWH's representative.

Standing alone, the narrative may not suggest a strongly erotic or sexual reading. But we may build on what we have trained ourselves to see concerning YHWH's sexuality as it is directed to David (and Saul) and as it may be represented in the personas of Elijah and Elisha. Thereby we may glimpse more than first appears in this odd tale that takes up the first three chapters of 1 Samuel.

The first chapter concerns the distress of Hannah's barrenness and her vow to YHWH that if she has a son, "then I will set him before you as a nazirite until the day of his death. He shall drink neither wine nor intoxicants, and no razor shall touch his head" (1:11).[9]

When her prayer is answered, she declares to her husband: "As soon as my child is weaned, I will bring him, that he may appear in the presence of the LORD, and remain there forever; I will offer him as a nazirite for all time" (1:22). When the child is weaned, Hannah and her husband bring him together with a three-year-old bull (a bull that has reached the age of procreative potency) to be slaughtered as a sacrifice to accompany the presentation of the boy Samuel. Hannah's song (which serves as the pattern for Mary's Magnificat) begins the second chapter, which interweaves snapshots of the boy Samuel in the service of Eli with accounts of the corruption of Eli's sons.[10] During the unfolding account of Eli's sons (2:12–17, 22–25, 27–36), the account is punctuated by references to the boy Samuel:

The boy remained to minister to the LORD, in the presence of the priest Eli. (2:11)

Samuel was ministering before the LORD, a boy wearing a linen ephod. (2:18)

And the boy Samuel grew up in the presence of the LORD. (2:21)

Now the boy Samuel continued to grow both in stature and in favor with the Lord and with the people. (2:26)

A lengthy account of a "man of God" coming to Eli with a word of judgment upon the house of Eli takes up the rest of chapter 2. Chapter 3 gives us a narrative that focuses clearly upon Samuel. The oddity of this chapter is that it seems to make most of chapter 2 redundant. The whole business of Samuel's night visitor ends with what is in many ways a weakened version of the pronouncement of doom upon the house of Eli, already

9. Fokkelman points out that the vow of Hannah places her unborn son in the same line as Samson, who was also dedicated in this way to YHWH (Judg 13:3, 7). In both cases the dedication or "sacrifice" of the son to YHWH is regarded as beginning at birth and lasting until death. In this respect the cases of Samson and Samuel are extraordinary in that both are dedicated or sacrificed to YHWH for life, while the description of the Nazirite vow in Num 6 contemplates that this is a vow lasting for only a limited period of life. See J. P. Fokkelman, *Vow and Desire (I Sam. 1–12)* (vol. 4 of *Narrative Art and Poetry in the Books of Samuel*; Assen, Netherlands: Van Gorcum, 1993), 39. Moreover, Samson and Samuel are not the ones who take the vow for themselves; instead, they are set apart by the word of another: Samson, by the angel/messenger; Samuel, by his mother.

10. The corrupt practices of Eli's sons anticipate those of Samuel's own sons (8:3). Thus, a kind of natural paternity is unfavorably compared with the adoption of prophet, priest, and king in the saga materials. One of the general characteristics of Hebrew narrative is its regular subversion of one of the main features of patriarchy: the preeminence of the firstborn son, or primogeniture.

conveyed by the "man of God" (2:27–36). In fact, the beginning of this narrative takes us back to the beginning of the previous narrative:

> Now the boy Samuel was ministering to the LORD under Eli. (3:1; cf. 2:11)

Before launching into the main action of the narrative concerning the lad Samuel, a number of points may be made concerning the narrative thus far:

1. YHWH's own male potency is invoked for the conception of the child. This is brought to expression in two ways. First, YHWH is called upon to open the womb of Hannah. Second, Hannah calls upon YHWH to grant her "male seed." The donation of *sperma andrōn* (LXX), or male sperm (together with the act of opening her womb), appears as a rather graphic indication of the mobilization of YHWH's male potency in connection with the conception of Samuel.

2. The accompaniment of a young bull, also offered up to YHWH, puts a phallic light upon the proceedings. Fokkelman suggests that the offering "gives back this potency to the deity symbolically."[11]

3. Samuel is regularly depicted as one who is in mouth-to-mouth communication with YHWH.[12] This is the direction of Hannah's vow "that he may appear in the presence of the LORD" (1:22). And it is the place of the lad in 2:21. This alternates with the depiction of Samuel as ministering before the LORD (2:11, 18; 3:1). Thus, the lad is depicted as one who has been delivered over to YHWH.

4. One of the most intriguing aspects of the depiction of Samuel is that he is said to be wearing "a linen ephod" (2:18). We have recognized that this linen ephod designates a person as in some way belonging to YHWH. This is the distinctive garment of the "priests" at Nob who will be slaughtered by Saul (22:18–19). To the extent that this ephod represents the male potency of YHWH, that attack was an attack upon YHWH's phallic potency. However, we have also seen that the linen ephod is the garment worn by David in his ecstatic dance before YHWH. It is a loincloth that both conceals and reveals the nakedness of the wearer. Notice that the lad wearing such an (under)garment suggests to the (re)reader of this narrative a certain erotic availability to YHWH.

---

11. Fokkelman, *Vow and Desire*, 67, also suggests that the age of the bull is a way of getting at the age of Samuel when he is offered up to YHWH. While there may be some truth to this, it seems more likely that it is precisely procreative and therefore phallic potency that is at stake here.

12. As in the Hebrew of Num 12:8 for Moses.

5. We may also notice the probable age of Samuel at the point of his initiation. The text has spoken of his growing up "in the presence of YHWH" (2:21 Hebrew) and of his growing "both in stature and in favor with the LORD and with the people" (2:26). Yet at the time of initiation he is still a lad. The rabbis will subsequently maintain that Samuel is, at this time, about twelve. In Greek thought, this is the age at which a young male first becomes available to the erotic attachment of an older male.[13]

At best these are only hints at a possible erotic charge being set up in the narrative. We will have to see if these hints find more explicit attention in the account concerning Samuel and YHWH that ensues.

The story thus far has placed the reader in some suspense. The repeated juxtaposing of Samuel and YHWH must be leading to something. And the narrative suspense is heightened with a notice: "The word of the LORD was rare in those days; visions were not widespread" (3:1b).

The climactic scene is set by placing Eli at some remove from the place where Samuel, the young lad wearing a linen ephod, is curled up to sleep. Samuel's place is beside the ark of YHWH. We have already seen that this ark is the focalization of the phallic potency of YHWH. Indeed, the story that will most clearly underline this character of the ark is the one that will immediately follow concerning the ark among the Philistines. There the ark will be the concrete bearer of that phallic potency that will rape Dagon and brand the Philistines with the mark of anal rape.

But here there is no violence. The phallus is "friendly" to Samuel. It permits his boyish proximity rather than lashing out as it will another day at Uzzah.

Instead, we hear the voice of YHWH call: "Samuel! Samuel!" The boy's not recognizing the speaker of his name enhances the charm of the story. Accordingly, he supposes that it is Eli, the man to whom he has been entrusted as YHWH's representative. When this has happened twice, the reader is given the following explanation:

Now Samuel did not yet know the LORD, and the word of the LORD had not yet been revealed to him." (3:7)

When the voice resounds a third time, Eli instructs Samuel to reply to the voice as if it were the voice of YHWH: "Speak, YHWH, for your servant is listening" (cf. 3:9). Samuel returns to his place, curling up beside the

13. The Greeks did not favor erotic attachments to lads younger than twelve, and the "age of consent" in Roman sources appears to be fourteen. See Eva Cantarella, *Bisexuality in the Ancient World* (trans. C. Ó. Cuilleanáin; New Haven: Yale University Press, 1992), 40, 118. The distinction between (illicit) pedophilia and (licit) pederasty is appropriately a distinction between the attraction to persons under and over this age respectively.

ark. But now instead of a simple repetition of the voice, we are informed: "Now the LORD came and stood there, calling as before" (3:10). Samuel responds as he has been instructed (except for omitting the name YHWH), and Adonai speaks to him.[14] The content of this speaking is not remarkable since it basically recapitulates what has already been told Eli by the "man of God," that the house of Eli will be terminated. That this is already old news may account for the relative nonchalance of Eli when he persuades the lad to tell him what Samuel's odd night visitor has said.

The emphasis in the narrative as presently constructed therefore does not lie on the content of YHWH's word to Samuel but on the fact that YHWH in person accosts the lad in the shrine and reveals himself to Samuel. That this is the aim of the narrative is shown by its conclusion:

> As Samuel grew up, the LORD was with him. . . . The LORD continued to appear at Shiloh, for the LORD revealed himself to Samuel at Shiloh by the word of the LORD. (3:19, 21)

This story depicts the inauguration of an especially intimate relationship between Samuel and YHWH.

The intimacy of this initiation of Samuel is underscored in a variety of ways. We have already seen that the story places Samuel as sleeping beside the phallic signifier of YHWH. The boy's bedroom is at the same time the resting place of the divine phallus. It is here that the sleeping boy is accosted at night by the male voice. But it is not the voice alone, for we are told that the fourth time YHWH himself is standing before the boy—no longer reclining (in the ark?) but erect; no longer the concrete signifier but the signified—YHWH, in all his masculine hyperpotency.[15]

Indeed, we may even say this is YHWH in his naked potency. For the text lets us know not only that YHWH "appears" there but also that YHWH uncovers himself to Samuel (NRSV: "revealed," 3:7, 21; 9:15). The verb for "uncovering" (galah) is also used for uncovering the nakedness of Noah in Genesis (9:21–23) or for uncovering the nakedness of a person either directly or indirectly in the Levitical proscriptions (Lev 18 and 20).

---

14. Jean Luc Marion treats this scene as an exemplary case of seduction! In the course of clarifying what it might mean to receive oneself from the call (or gift) of the other, Marion takes as illuminative of the character of intersubjectivity the "most ordinary situation" of seduction. After leading the reader to notice the elementary features of any seduction (at dinner, for example), he then turns to the story of the call of Samuel, which "obeys the logic of seduction." See Jean Luc Marion, *Being Given: Toward a Phenomenology of Givenness* (trans. J. L. Kosky; Chicago: University of Chicago Press, 2003), 285–87. Indeed, it is this very seduction, the erotic ambience of which is required by Marion's analysis, that Marion also says makes possible "every prophetic message to come" (287).

15. Fokkelman, *Vow and Desire*, recognizes the contrast between YHWH's "vertical" position and Samuel's recumbent posture, although he does not attribute sexual significance to this. He does, however, allow that the lad "perhaps even sees the figure of God" (197).

Hence, here the nakedness of YHWH is, at least allusively, a sexual nakedness or nudity.[16]

This may seem to be a bit forced save that in a quite different connection no less a philosopher of language and textuality than Jacques Derrida
has pointed out the Hebrew term used here. He says it regularly signifies
the uncovering of nakedness, of what is normally concealed, and therefore
of the pudenda.[17]

In this connection what is even more striking is that YHWH seems to
be in the habit of thus uncovering himself to Samuel at Shiloh (1 Sam
3:21). The narrative lets us in on the beginning of a remarkably intimate
relationship between YHWH and Samuel, one in which the connection
seems marked by a virtual sexual intimacy. Indeed, the whole episode seems
to be oriented to explaining how it is that the boy Samuel is changed from
one who did not "know YHWH" (3:7) to one who is characterized by an
extraordinarily intimate "knowing" of YHWH. The sexual or quasi-sexual
character of such knowing, so obvious to readers in certain other texts (for
example, the story of Sodom), should be at least as obvious here.

Here Samuel seems to be inseminated by the word of YHWH, and the
result is that he himself becomes the one who utters words that YHWH
prevents from "falling to the ground" (cf. 3:19). The words of Samuel thus
become like sperm that does not fall onto the ground (as the sperm of
Onan does in Gen 38:9) but that is fruitful, efficacious, potent. The most
important fruitfulness of Samuel lies not in the production of progeny (his
sons are like Eli's in corruption; 1 Sam 8:3) but in the word by which he
makes and breaks kings.

This is indeed worth remarking upon. For the sexlike initiation of
Samuel actually makes him potent in an even more remarkable way than
we observed in the sexual awakening of the lad by Elisha. There, we recall
the potency of the lad was signified by the sevenfold orgasm. But in the case
of Samuel, this potency is already prefigured as the potency of his word.
That word is what will create Saul and David as war-leaders of Israel.

---

16. The rather revealing "uncovering" is somewhat covered over by the addition of "by the word" in 1 Sam
3:7, 21.

17. Jacques Derrida, "Of an Apocalyptic Tone Newly Adopted in Philosophy," in *Derrida and Negative Theology* (ed. H. Coward and T. Foshay; Albany, NY: SUNY Press, 1992). After mentioning the LXX use of *apokalyp-
sis* for the Hebrew *galah* (25), Derrida emphasizes the sexual or erotic charge of the term: "I reveal the thing
that can be a part of the body, the head or the eyes, a secret part, the sex or whatever might be hidden" (26).
"First of all, if we can say this, [is] man's or woman's sex" (27). He explores "the idea of laying bare, . . . for
example, the body when the clothes are removed or the glans when the foreskin is removed in circumcision.
And what seems the most remarkable in all the biblical examples I was able to find and must forego exposing
here is that the gesture of denuding or of affording sight [*donner à voir*]—the apocalyptic movement—is more
serious here, sometimes more culpable and more dangerous than what follows and what it can give rise to, for
example, copulation" (27). Derrida then points to the text concerning Noah and mentions a few of the Levitical prohibitions I have cited.

In the course of the narrative that follows, we will lose sight of Samuel. The loss and recovery of the ark seem to happen without him. Only in chapter 7 does Samuel again appear, this time as a potent "judge" who succeeds in subduing the Philistines (7:3–14). This mighty deed is followed by Israel's seeking a king—something that understandably does not please Samuel, who otherwise is the charismatic leader, judge, and prophet of Israel.

From this point onward Samuel is the instrument of YHWH in selecting a young warrior to be his armor-bearer. As we saw in part 1, this also means the selection of one to be YHWH's erotic favorite. Thus, Samuel is reduced to pimping for YHWH, procuring beautiful young men (first Saul and then David) to be YHWH's companions.

Even though YHWH turns his attentions to beautiful young male companions of a more warlike nature, still Samuel continues to represent and embody the phallic potency of YHWH, at least for a time. For at the beginning of our consideration of YHWH's male groupies, we encountered the whirling naked *nabi'im* whose ecstatic dance draws in Saul. At first he is taken to be one of them and is finally ravished by YHWH, who leaves him naked and stunned on the hillside. At the center of the naked ecstatics and indeed functioning as their leader in the testosteronic storm of YHWH's phallic power is Samuel. He is the apparent leader and founder of those who for centuries after David will be the frenzied devotees of YHWH's erotic potency. Indeed, he will be succeeded as leader of these naked dancers, the *bene-hanebi'im*, by Elisha and Elijah.

Reflections

We are thus brought, for the moment, full circle in our discussion of YHWH's male groupies. What can we learn from this consideration of the apparent "insemination" of young males by representatives of YHWH or by YHWH himself?

1. We should first point out that the erotic intimacy of YHWH makes his favorites more potent rather than less so. There is nothing in these texts to suggest that being the object of male sexual advances makes one less masculine. On the contrary, it seems to guarantee, at least for a time, that one will be the embodiment in person of that phallic potency. In the cases of Elijah and Elisha, they are themselves the embodiment of a remarkable potency that seems to be channeled through them to become the energizing, life-giving principle for lads who have been dead. The sexual embrace of the prophet or of YHWH

through the body of the prophet produces vigor where before their has been an absence of life.

Read in this way, we seem to have a story of the sexual initiation of a male child into pubescent potency. It may remind us of the sorts of rituals reported by Gilbert Herdt and others in Papua New Guinea, where the older male sexually awakens the boy and, through the donation of semen (male seed), transfers masculine potency into the child, making him ready to become a man.[18]

In the rather extraordinary resurrection stories we have read, the elements of initiation, and so of transition from childhood to adolescence, are replaced by the transition from death to life. It is impossible to know whether these stories functioned to hyperbolize more "mundane" transitions and so to give them an aura of ultimacy, or if the stories should be understood to stand alone as representing extraordinary episodes unconnected to initiatory acts generally. There is simply not enough data to be certain. It is only the detailed exhibition of the machinery of resurrection together with the tantalizing clue that prophets seem to require prophetic "fathers" (semen donors) that suggest that these stories may have had paradigmatic significance for the *bene-hanebi'im* as such.

The story of young Samuel does seem to foreground a scene of transition in this case, not from death to life, but from not knowing YHWH to knowing and representing YHWH. It is clear that the quasi-sexual initiation of Samuel on the part of YHWH empowers Samuel to be what he has been destined to be. This insemination does not weaken him but strengthens him, makes him potent as the bearer of YHWH's presence in Israel. He thus becomes the one who raises and deposes war-leaders and the one who is in charge of the naked dancing prophets who are driven into ecstasy in the presence of Samuel as the embodiment of YHWH's phallic potency.

2. We therefore see a certain isomorphism in the homoeroticism among warriors with that also displayed among "prophets." In these stories there does not seem to be a sense that being the erotic object of male desire diminishes in any way the "masculinity" of those who are thus favored. On the contrary, they become

---

18. See Gilbert Herdt, *The Sambia: Ritual and Gender in New Guinea* (New York: Holt, Rinehart & Winston, 1987), esp. 101–70, ch. 5. Also see Gilbert Herdt, ed., *Ritualized Homosexuality in Melanesia* (Berkeley: University of California Press, 1984), and the review of literature in the introduction to the paperback edition (Berkeley: University of California Press, 1993), xiv–xliv. This latter edition includes essays that deal with other groups in Melanesia demonstrating a wider diffusion of ritual semen donation as an essential part of the masculinization of young males.

the concrete representations of YHWH's phallic potency. Thus, at the stage represented both by the warrior sagas of 1 and 2 Samuel and the saga material concerning Elijah and Elisha, there does not seem to be evidence of anxiety about the "feminization" of the male that will characterize the later Athenian literature concerning pederasty.

3. The cultic or prophetic homoeroticism seems both to precede and to endure longer than the homoeroticism of warrior-companions. We have evidence of this in the story concerning Samuel that precedes the stories about David, with the material about Saul serving as a transitional case. The later Israelite stories concerning the *bene-hanebi'im* and especially concerning Elijah and Elisha follow the period indicated by the David sagas by a couple of centuries.

This situation of more or less cultic same-sex initiation preceding and then accompanying the development of warrior same-sex activity is echoed in the history of same-sex age-structured sexuality in Japan. There same-sex activity of this sort appears to originate in (Buddhist) monasteries and then becomes an ingredient for samurai warrior culture in Tokugawa Japan. The pairing of older and younger males in homoerotic bonds seems to move rather easily between cultic and warrior contexts.

Of course, the "cultic" context that we have been noticing in Israel is not associated with anything so formal as a monastery tradition, nor does it appear to be linked (as in Japanese Buddhism) with a suspicion of cross-sex (male-female) eroticism. Instead, the Israelite evidence seems more similar to shamanistic transfers of extraordinary power than either to normalized ritual practices (as in New Guinea) or to monastic establishments (as in Japan).[19] Hence, the point of noticing partial similarities cross-culturally is not to explain Israelite same-sex practices but to notice significant differences as well as similarities. We should not minimize the cultural creativity of Israel at the same time that we recognize a number of intersecting elements in comparative studies.

---

19. That the stories of Elijah and Elisha in particular seem to entail shamanistic features is the burden of the argument of Thomas Overholt in his *Cultural Anthropology and the Old Testament* (Minneapolis: Fortress, 1996). In his quite interesting study he concentrates attention on the Elijah-Elisha cycle of stories and in particular deals with the resuscitation narratives that we have discussed earlier. He remarks that these stories stand in a certain contrast to the ideology of Deuteronomy in that they introduce the ideology of shamanism (29), and this is especially illustrated in relation to the resuscitation tales (29–39). The impressive list of cross-cultural comparative materials does suggest the importance of bodily proximity, but none of them seems as sexually explicit as the Elijah-Elisha texts. The shaman typically gets into bed "beside" the patient but is not said to lie "on" them. While the similarities that Overholt suggests are impressive, they also point up the more explicit eroticism of these stories from ancient Israel.

7. Holy Hustlers

THE MATERIAL WE HAVE THUS FAR examined for YHWH's male groupies, as we have called them, is largely derived from sources depicting the northern kingdom of Israel. Here we find evidence that the phenomenon of male erotic ecstasy persisted among those dedicated to the service of YHWH. Accordingly, the continuation of the *bene-hanebi'im* (sons of the prophets) and the exploits of Elijah and Elisha demonstrate a certain continuity with the material concerning Samuel and Saul.

To this point, however, the presence of similar or related groups in the southern kingdom has not been explored. However, we have observed that in later expressions and activities of the "writing prophets" of the southern kingdom, there do appear to be echoes of the homoerotic tradition of Israel's male groupies of YHWH. Thus, the nakedness attributed to Micah and Isaiah, as well as the reference to YHWH's sexual seduction of the prophet in Jeremiah (20:7), appear to carry into late Judean literature some of the aspects of homoerotic imagery that we have explored in the northern kingdom's prophetic bands.

The question that confronts us is whether groups of male devotees of YHWH also were ongoing in Judah, with a relation to YHWH expressed in homoerotic practices. On the other hand, perhaps there was a later appropriation of this imagery, surfacing after a hiatus of more than two centuries (from David to Micah). The latter case is possible if we imagine an influx of

Israelite custom and literature following the destruction of the northern kingdom in 721 BCE. But in the kingdom that most clearly understood itself as successor to the Davidic line and as the conservator of Davidic tradition, it seems unlikely that no ongoing homoerotic tradition would reflect the relation to YHWH so prominently displayed in the traditions concerning Samuel, Saul, and David.

Suppose we ask whether there are groups of male devotees of YHWH who may be thought to express their relation to YHWH in terms of homoerotic practices reflected in the material that reports on the southern kingdom after the death of David. If so, then the principal candidate that offers itself for analysis is the group designated as the *qedeshim* (male cultic prostitutes).

Indeed, this group has often been associated, whether rightly or wrongly, with male homosexual erotic practices. In the King James Version of the Bible, every reference to the *qedeshim* is translated as "the sodomites," but more recent translations often replace this with "the male temple/cultic/ shrine prostitutes" or something of the sort. A more detailed consideration of the relevant texts will help to clarify the situation.

The Texts

The King James Version of the OT gives five references to "sodomites" (Deut 23:17–18; 1 Kgs 14:24; 15:12; 22:46; 2 Kgs 23:7), which have subsequently been identified (for example, in the RSV and NRSV) as "male temple prostitutes."[1] Typically antihomophobic exegesis is content to dismiss these passages as referring to cultic practices that do not illuminate the issue of homosexuality. Thus, the work of D. S. Bailey is content to demonstrate that these passages do not bear on the question of secular same-sex practices and thus should be discounted.[2] While this is undoubtedly a gain in clarity, especially since the mistranslation of this term served to license homophobia, it is not the case that these passages have nothing to tell us about attitudes toward same-sex practices in Israel. Indeed, they may suggest that there was little popular recognition of any incompatibility between the worship of YHWH and cultic sexuality (possibly including

---

1. *The Living Bible: Paraphrased* (Wheaton, IL: Tyndale House, 1971) simply refers in Deut 23:17 and 1 Kgs 14:24 to homosexuality, thereby perpetuating and intensifying the mistake of the KJV. Fortunately, the revision of the LB—Holy Bible, New Living Translation (Tyndale, 1996)—says "temple/shrine prostitutes" and does not say "homosexuals" in these passages.

2. D. S. Bailey, *Homosexuality and the Western Christian Tradition* (London: Longmans, Green, 1955; repr., Hamden, CT: Archon Books, 1975), 48–53.

cultic homosexuality) for virtually the entire period of the monarchy and thus for the period of the first temple.

The passages with which we are concerned are in Deuteronomy and 1 and 2 Kings. Hence, they come from material written after the time of the monarchy, although the Deuteronomic passage may go back to the time of Josiah, near the end of the monarchical period. Put another way, most or all of this material comes from the time of the exile in Babylon or from the subsequent Persian period. It is thus a retrospective look at the life of Israel/Judea from the standpoint of the collapse of national life, a collapse understood as in some way divine judgment upon Israel for failure to comply with the divine law.

The (singular) term used is *qadesh* and simply means "male holy one." In other contexts it is the same root used to designate the holiness of God, of the temple, or of the people. Thus, holiness, whether of the temple or of the people as a whole or of these individuals or groups, indicates that which is separated by YHWH. However, these "holy ones," *qedeshim* (plural of *qadesh*), may be associated with some form of cultic sexual practice.[3]

That we are to think specifically of sexual practices is suggested by the law in Deuteronomy (written after the fact, we must remember):

> None of the daughters of Israel shall be a temple prostitute [*kedeshah* = female holy one]; none of the sons of Israel shall be a temple prostitute [*kadesh* = male holy one]. You shall not bring the fee of a prostitute [*zonah*] or the wages of a male prostitute [*keleb* = dog] into the house of the LORD your God in payment for any vow, for both of these are abhorrent to the LORD your God. (Deut. 23:17–18 = MT 18–19)

The text appears to set up a parallel between the female prostitute (*zonah*) and the female holy one (*qedeshah*); and between the male holy one (*qadesh*) and the "dog" (*keleb*). Moreover, it indicates a connection between the services of these persons (female prostitutes and male holy ones) and the temple worship (house) of "the LORD your God."

We have to conclude that this law is directed against those who suppose that the worship of YHWH may include payment for the services of a "prostitute" or "holy one" as a way of carrying out a vow made in the name of the "LORD." The term "prostitute" here may indicate some specifically

---

3. The term "temple prostitute" is highly unsatisfactory. In the first place, we are concerned here with activity that, while sometimes connected to the temple, is by no means restricted to the temple. Thus, I have preferred "cultic" to "temple." It is also misleading to speak of prostitute in this connection since this suggests a purely commercial transaction rather than one that is both sexual and sacred.

sexual practice, in which case we are dealing with sexual practices
that at least some of the faithful regard as appropriate tribute to the God
of Israel.

This impression is strengthened when we turn to the accounts of the
"holy ones" in the revised history of the monarchy that scholars attribute to
the same group or groups responsible for the elaboration of Deuteronomy.
In the description of the reign of Solomon's son Rehoboam, we read:

> Judah did what was evil in the sight of the LORD; they provoked him to
> jealousy with their sins that they committed, more than all their ancestors
> had done. For they also built for themselves high places, pillars, and sacred
> poles [*Asherim*] on every high hill and under every green tree; there were
> also male temple prostitutes [*qadesh*, collective singular; KJV: "sodomites"] in
> the land. They committed all the abominations of the nations that the
> LORD drove out before the people of Israel. (1 Kgs 14:22–24)

Here it seems that the use of the "holy ones" is related to the cultic practices
attributed to the Canaanites (the nations that the Lord drove out), which
we suppose to have been associated with the fertility of the land. The proliferation of shrines with fertility symbols indicates the decentralization of
this cultic practice and thus of an accommodation to indigenous beliefs and
practices of the people of the land.

This policy of accommodation is not a departure from the policy of
Solomon himself. He appears to have constructed the temple in Jerusalem
in such a way as to give some place to elements of the worship of Baal and
Astarte. Thus, he seeks to indigenize Yahwism by incorporating some of the
beliefs and practices of the native Canaanites.

This process of indigenization was by no means uncontested. Regarding
the "holy ones," Asa, son of Abijam and grandson of Rehoboam, sought to
reverse the policy of his father and grandfather:

> [Asa] put away the male temple prostitutes [*qedeshim*] out of the land, and
> removed all the idols that his ancestors had made. He also removed his
> mother Maacah from being queen mother, because she had made an abom-
> inable image for Asherah; Asa cut down her image and burned it at the Wadi
> Kidron. But the high places were not taken away. (1 Kgs 15:12–14)

Here it seems that Asa's policy was determined by a power struggle within
the royal family. Thus, the destruction of the female image of the divine, the
deposition of the queen mother, and the partial expulsion of the "holy

ones" are related to one another. Since we are told that Asa ruled for forty-one years, he must have acceded to the throne quite young. Hence, we may suppose that his mother was quite powerful in the early part of his reign, and he may have taken the steps described to limit her influence.[4] The editors of Judea's history, however, ascribe this policy to Asa's piety.

It would appear, however, that Asa's policy was determined not by religious zeal but by more pragmatic considerations, for we subsequently learn that his expulsion of the "holy ones," despite forty-one years of rule, was at best partial. We are told that although his son Jehoshaphat did not take away "the high places . . . , and the people still sacrificed and offered incense on the high places" (1 Kgs 22:43). Nevertheless, "the remnant of the male temple prostitutes [qadesh] who were still in the land in the days of his father Asa, he exterminated" (22:46 = MT 47).

It is rather chilling to reflect that the translation of qadesh/qedeshim as "sodomites" together with the approving reference to their extermination (as about the only good thing reported of his reign) are triumphs of homophobic extremism.

The story does not end with the extermination of qedeshim under Jehoshaphat. After all, the infrastructure that made their services necessary remains in place (the high places). Thus, it comes as little surprise that at the very end of the monarchy in Judea, the reforms of Josiah include yet another attempt to purge the "fertility cult" from the temple in Jerusalem. From 2 Kgs 23 we learn that this is a massive enterprise, illustrated by these excerpts:

> The king commanded the high priest Hilkiah, the priests of the second order, and the guardians of the threshold, to bring out of the temple of the LORD all the vessels made for Baal, for Asherah, and for all the host of heaven. . . . He deposed the idolatrous priests whom the kings of Judah had ordained to make offerings in the high places at the cities of Judah and around Jerusalem; those also who made offerings to Baal . . . and all the host of the heavens. He brought out the image of Asherah from the house of the LORD. . . . He broke down the houses of the male temple prostitutes [qedeshim] that were in the house of the LORD, where the women did weaving for Asherah. . . . The king defiled the high places that were east of Jerusalem, . . . which King Solomon of Israel had built for Astarte. . . . (2 Kgs 23:4–7, 13)

4. For an extended treatment of the role of the "Queen Mother" in Israel, see Susan Ackerman, *Warrior, Dancer, Seductress, Queen: Women in Judges and Biblical Israel* (New York: Doubleday, 1998), 128–80.

Here it becomes clear that the worship of Baal, Asherah, and Astarte has been completely integrated into temple worship in Jerusalem from the time of Solomon until the time of Josiah—for the entire period of the monarchy and the temple in Jerusalem! Moreover, it appears that the "holy ones" were also an integral part of the cultic practices that had been assimilated into the worship of YHWH during this period.

Who are these *qedeshim*, and what are we to make of their apparently complete integration into the religious practices of the people of Judah? The texts suggest that they may in some way be related to functionaries of fertility rituals, for this is the apparent significance of the *Asherim* ("sacred poles," 2 Kgs 23:14) with which they are often associated.

Are these functionaries of fertility rites to be associated with sexual practices of any kind, and are they to be associated with *same-sex* ritual sexual practice? The principal association between these functionaries and sexual practices of any kind comes from the law in Deuteronomy (cited above) that makes them parallel to female prostitutes.[5] By itself, we could not conclude with any certainty that the term "prostitute" is used here in a specifically sexual sense because idolatry is regularly called prostitution whether or not sexual practices are involved. Hence the phrase "whoring after [other] gods" (Exod 34:15 KJV; Deut 31:16 KJV; and so on). The context of the passage in Deuteronomy, moreover, does not concern itself significantly with sexual practices. Immediately preceding is a prohibition of returning escaped slaves to their owners; immediately following is a prohibition of charging interest on loans to another Israelite. Hence, the texts, taken in isolation, would not force the conclusion that we have to do with sexual practices of any kind. All that is clear is that we have to do with practices that some deemed appropriate to secure the favor of the divinity and that others opposed, at least in retrospect.

A more definite association between *zonah* (prostitute) and *qadesh* (holy one/cultic prostitute) comes from the story of Judah and Tamar, which takes up the whole chapter 38 of Genesis. This story is later evoked by Matthew in the genealogy of Jesus; Tamar is one of the four women (two of them prostitutes) mentioned in Jesus' lineage.

Judah's firstborn son is conceived through a liaison with a Canaanite woman. In due course, after siring two other sons, Judah selects a wife (Tamar) for his firstborn, but the latter dies without siring progeny. The second son, Onan, refuses to perform his duty of begetting a son for his older

---

5. This law *may* date from the time of Josiah, as a rationale for his policies of cultic consolidation. However, there is no likelihood that it is earlier, and it may well be later—produced by exiles in Babylon who express nostalgia for the days of Josiah as the zenith of Israelite independence and power.

brother with Tamar, instead spilling his semen on the ground (and thereby giving masturbation the name of Onanism). Onan also dies, and Judah, fearing that his third son (Shelah) too will die if linked to the apparently unlucky Tamar, puts off requiring Shelah to perform his duty of siring a son with Tamar to be heir of Er, the firstborn.

Tamar fears she will never bear sons in this household. Hence, she disguises herself as a prostitute (*zonah*) and places herself where Judah will find her. The result is that she bears two sons to Judah himself, who become the twin progenitors of the tribe of Judah.

What is significant about the story for purposes of this discussion is that Judah identifies Tamar not only as a prostitute (*zonah*, Gen 38:15) but also as a female "holy one" (*qedeshah*, 38:21), a cultic (NIV: "shrine"; NRSV: "temple") prostitute. This latter designation agrees with the extravagant payment offered by Judah for her services (a kid from the flock of goats) and the still more extravagant pledge offered in lieu of immediate payment: signet, cord, and staff—all the emblems of his chieftainship. Surely more is going on here than a wayside adventure with a country prostitute who by now is no longer in her prime.

The story makes clear that real rather than virtual sex has been involved: Tamar has the twins to prove it. And even if the proper mode of sex with a cultic prostitute was anal rather than vaginal intercourse, this only shows that the ever resourceful Tamar has tricked Judah in more ways than one. The Tamar story thus strongly supports the surmise that the holy ones (*qedeshim*) provided services that were sexual in nature.

In order to come any nearer to unraveling the mystery of the *qedeshim*, scholars have often considered the character of fertility cult practices generally, especially in the cultural region adjacent to Israel in the time of the first temple.

In his discussion of the situation, Bailey cites Westermarck as supposing that they were "male homosexual prostitutes." But he asserts that "there is no reason to assume that they were required or accustomed to perform or submit to sodomy or any other homosexual act for sacred purposes."[6] Bailey does suppose that some sexual practices were involved in the duties of the *qedeshim* but argues that these must have been heterosexual in character:

> Homosexual coitus would be meaningless in the ritual of a fertility cult, with its exclusively heterosexual rationale, and there is no evidence that it was ever practiced in this connection.[7]

6. Bailey, *Homosexuality*, 50.
7. Ibid.

However, in a more recent survey of the studies of fertility cults, Greenberg has reached a quite different conclusion.[8] He supposes that sexual intercourse with temple prostitutes (male or female) was anal intercourse. The female priestesses were to avoid pregnancy. Indeed, the fertility goddess herself does not become pregnant but bestows fertility upon the land and people who worship her. Nevertheless, the debate has by no means ended. Richard Henshaw has recently surveyed the evidence and found no basis for imputing sexual practices of any kind to the *qedeshim* in Israel or in Mesopotamia generally.[9] While the evidence he cites is impressively thorough, he does not account for the association between prostitute (*zonah*) and female holy one (*qedeshah*) either in the Deuteronomy passage with which we began or in the story of Judah and Tamar in Gen 38.[10]

Interpretation

Most of the scholarly discussion of these passages has been preoccupied with the question of the relation of sexuality to fertility cults. Scholars have sought to indicate the relation or possible relation of Israelite or Judean cultic functionaries to the role and activity of cultic functionaries in Mesopotamian or Canaanite practices associated with fertility. The references to Asherim, to Astarte, and to pillars and poles give some grounds for such an interpretative pursuit. But we have also seen that the attempt to link the *qedeshim* with what we can discover about the practices of fertility cults in the region has yielded little confirmation or clarity.

---

8. David F. Greenberg, *The Construction of Homosexuality* (Chicago: University of Chicago Press, 1988), 94–106.

9. Richard A. Henshaw, *Female and Male: The Cultic Personnel: The Bible and the Rest of the Middle East* (Allison Park, PA: Pickwick Publications, 1994), 218–36.

10. Joan Goodnick Westenholz gives a different study of the evidence in "Tamar, Qedesa, Qadistu, and Sacred Prostitution in Mesopotamia," *Harvard Theological Review* 82, no. 3 (1989): 245–65. She is also critical of the supposition that the female "holy ones" performed sexual services in the cultic sphere. However, she does report that in Akkadian literature there is reference to female holy ones whose "social position . . . is hardly different from that of the prostitute" (251). Where there is evidence of the profession of prostitute (*harimtu*), at least in the city of Sippur, "this status is held by men as well as women" who exercise "prerogatives designated as those of a goddess" (259). Thus, some of the evidence she cites tends to confirm rather than deny the association between sexual services and cultic status. Westenholz suggests that Tamar is designated as a holy one not because of her sexual services to Judah but as a way of deflecting attention away from the sexual nature of these services (247–48). This is a way of accounting for the evidence, but it seems something of a stretch. Similarly, Tikva Frymer-Kensky, *In the Wake of the Goddess* (New York: Free Press, 1992), 199–202, has also argued against the sexual function of the female "holy one." She rightly points out that much of the attractiveness of the contrary notion may lie in the inability to conceive of a sacred function for women apart from sex (202). Neither of these authors attempts to apply their case to that of the male holy ones. Phyllis Bird has investigated the general notion of harlotry in the Prime Testament, in "'To Play the Harlot': An Inquiry into an Old Testament Metaphor," in *Gender and Difference in Ancient Israel* (ed. P. Day; Minneapolis: Fortress, 1989), 75–94. She focuses upon Hosea's comments about female holy ones (*qedeshot*, Hos 4:11–14), who in her view may indeed be understood by the prophet as performing some sort of sexual activity with the men of Israel (87–88). In a subsequent article Bird does consider the specific question of the male "holy ones," and some of her suggestions will be explored below.

What has not been considered is whether we may have to do here with a significantly different practice, one that is indeed indigenous to Yahwism. Such a practice may fit better into the picture of male homoeroticism in the service of YHWH that we have been exploring in this interpretation of Davidic and post-Davidic traditions.

One indication that we may have to do here with a practice that is not identical with alleged fertility practices comes from considering a rereading of this same period of time. This is the one undertaken not by the authors or editors of 1 and 2 Kings, but by the later authors/editors of 1 and 2 Chronicles. One of the remarkable features of this latter retelling of the sad story of Israel and Judah is that the *qedeshim* entirely disappear from view. This is not because the Chronicler wishes in general to absolve Israel from sin or idolatry. On the contrary, in this text we also meet with condemnations of idolatry and, in particular, of the apparatus of fertility cults (Asherim, Astartes, pillars, and poles), in both the temple and the "high places" of the countryside. But there is no mention whatever of the *qedeshim*, still less of the campaigns launched periodically to eliminate them from the temple or other sites where YHWH may have been worshipped.[11] What are we to make of this strange silence?

The Chronicler, while not setting out to expurgate the record of Israel and Judah's cultic unfaithfulness, is concerned to clean up the record of sexual deviation. On reading the text of Chronicles, one would have no idea of David's relationship to Bathsheba. Chronicles never identifies her with Uriah (named in 1 Chron 11:41) and thus does not report David's adultery (and complicity in Uriah's murder). As a consequence, the difficulties of David's reign that follow from this adultery (civil war with Absalom and so on) are unmotivated.

But this "cleaning up" process goes even further. For virtually nothing that lends itself to homoerotic interpretation in the books of Samuel and Kings is left. Thus, there is nothing to be found of David's particular relationship to Saul and Jonathan, nothing of the *bene-hanebi'im*, nothing of the odd adventures of Elijah and Elisha. Even where the Chronicler does report

---

11. The LXX seems also to be somewhat perplexed. Thus, the translation of 1 Kgs 14:24 replaces *qadesh* (collective singular: "cultic prostitutes") with "conspiracy" (*syndesmos*), giving us "There was a conspiracy in the land." In the case of 1 Kgs 15:12 (concerning Asa), *qedeshim* is translated as "initiates" (*tas teletas*), which, in addition, is feminine rather than masculine. This term, according to Liddel and Scott, may have been common for initiates of Dionysus, suggesting a link to the phenomena discussed in chapter 5. The reference to *qadesh* in the story of Jehoshaphat is eliminated by the stratagem of eliminating the entire verse (1 Kgs 22:46). Finally, in the reference to *qedeshim* in the reforms of Josiah, the LXX simply transliterates the term (2 Kgs 23:7). The references in Deut 23:17–18 (18–19 LXX) are complicated with "prostitute" being replaced with something like "initiates," as in 23:15, albeit in conjunction with other terms that refer to prostitution. Thus, the process of erasure begun by the Chronicler ends in apparent confusion in the Greek translation of the passages from Deuteronomy and denial in 1 and 2 Kings.

something like what we have read in Samuel, as for example in the case of David's naked dance before YHWH, we are confronted with a fully clothed David leading a purely liturgical procession. The Chronicler's editing is incomplete, however, for we are told that when Michal saw David dancing, "she despised him in her heart" (1 Chron 15:29). But the text gives no reason for her contempt and no reply of David to her and no repercussions for her. Thus, the Chronicler's editing actually introduces incoherence into the narrative. This purgation of homoerotic elements from earlier accounts is so systematic that Chronicles may be read as a kind of reverse index to the earlier material. What the Chronicler leaves out is what for our purposes is the most interesting part of the history of Israel.

What would it mean to follow up this clue? We gather that the Chronicler does not seek to eliminate cultic infidelity from the history of Israel. But he does eliminate references to sexual deviation on the part of its heroes and especially eliminates passages that lend themselves to homoerotic interpretation of the relation among YHWH's favorites or between them and YHWH. If so, does this not at least make plausible an interpretation of the *qedeshim* that would view them as functionaries of Yahwism, whose very relation to YHWH may have entailed homoerotic practices?

Before indicating what might count for or against such a hypothesis, we should first indicate more concretely what this would involve. On this hypothesis the *qedeshim* would be understood as somewhat parallel to the *bene-hanebi'im* of Israel. They are associated with the devotion to YHWH and, like them, are associated with the cultic shrines, perhaps including the temple in Jerusalem. They are holy ones precisely as separated to YHWH in some way. And our previous reading of YHWH's male groupies would suggest that we take their relation to YHWH as entailing a homoerotic relation to the deity. They may be understood as being the sexually initiated devotees of the phallic potency of YHWH. In short, they view themselves and are viewed by others as males who have been "penetrated" or sexually possessed by YHWH. As we have seen in the case of Samuel and the *bene-hanebi'im* generally, this does not mean that they have necessarily been feminized. Rather, it may mean that they become the living embodiment of YHWH's male potency. As such, they become the transmitters of this male potency. But if this is so, then they would in turn become penetrators or inseminators of other males, of males who seek similarly to be devoted to YHWH. Thus, we would imagine that it made a certain sense for male devotees of YHWH to seek to be erotically or indeed sexually possessed by the "holy ones" who represent and embody the male potency of YHWH.

Such an interpretation would at least serve to make sense of the designation of these functionaries as "holy ones." It would also indicate why their appropriate location would be the temple of YHWH as well as at "high places" that had not as yet succumbed to the centralization of the state cult at Jerusalem. In addition, it would suggest how Judean practices had a certain parallel to Samaritan or Israelite practices that appear in the *bene-hanebi'im*. Thus, it would show how the identification of the representative of YHWH as one who was sexually possessed by YHWH (as in Jeremiah's striking image) would have a certain resonance in Judah as well as in Israel.[12]

Is there any other evidence that would support this hypothesis? There is at least one further piece of suggestive evidence that would count in its favor. The Chronicler, in one of the passages in which the parallel from Kings would suggest mention of the *qedeshim*, does not simply erase that reference but provides a substitute: the goat-demons. The process of substitution is actually rather complex. The sins of Rehoboam in Judah (1 Kgs 14:23–24) seem to be displaced onto Jeroboam. The latter is said to have prevented the Levites "from serving as priests of the LORD, and had appointed his own priests for the high places, and for the goat-demons, and for the calves that he had made" (2 Chron 11:14–15). We recall encountering goat-demons or satyrs in our exploration of the erotic features of David's dance before YHWH. His "capering" before YHWH, we observed, is expressed in a term otherwise used of goat-demons or satyrs in the priestly writings. Indeed, it is only in these priestly writings that we discover goat-demons, and Chronicles is a significant part of that literature. Satyrs are associated with phallic prowess and are equal-opportunity phallic penetrators of male and female alike. Thus, they would fit the hypothesis of the function of the *qedeshim* that we are developing. The displacement, if that is

---

12. In a more recent article, Phyllis A. Bird, "The End of the Male Cult Prostitute," in *Congress Volume: Cambridge 1995* (ed. J. A. Emert; Supplements to Vetus Testamentum 66; Leiden: Brill, 1997), 37–80, maintains that the attribution of male cultic prostitutes to the religious practices of Judah may rest upon a series of mistakes. These may include a mistaken attribution of practices on the part of the Deuteronomist as well as on the part of his translators. Without engaging her argument in detail, I do find certain of her suggestions fruitful for the quite different interpretation that I am proposing. She does, for example, declare that the Ugaritic evidence for a class of holy ones restricts this to what seem to be "lay temple servants" (44). She further reports that the use of a term to refer to both male and female religious functionaries seems to be restricted to "charismatic" specialists, most notably prophets (45). This tends to support at least that part of my interpretation that makes the *qedeshim* of the southern kingdom parallel to the *bene-hanebi'im* of the northern kingdom. I also tend to agree with the notion that the Deuteronomist no longer has (and therefore cannot provide us with) a clear idea of what the *qedeshim* were or did. Moreover, I can also agree that the *qedeshim* may not have been defined by sexual practices any more than the *bene-hanebi'im* were—even though I maintain that they may be understood as engaging in same-sex practices as an (occasional?) extension of their representation of YHWH's male potency. That kings, who in some way also represented the male potency of the divine (on Hos 3:3–4, see ch. 8, should have instigated purges against them may reflect that the *qedeshim* were, at least in this limited respect, competitors with the role of the king.

what it is, of the *qedeshim* into goat-demons now relocated in Israel rather than Judah shows their association with Jeroboam's "calves"—with the bulls that represent the phallic potency of YHWH.[13]

Our hypothesis also serves to suggest why the search for parallels in Canaanite religion may have been fruitless. For the *qedeshim* are indigenous to the cult of YHWH. They make whatever religious sense they make not in the framework of a fertility cult but in the context of a phallus cult, in the context of the adoration of a male deity on the part of male (and possibly also female) devotees.

To be sure, there was available in Jerusalem also an attempt to indigenize Yahwism into the fertility apparatus. Astarte and probably also Asherah represent this process. If in such places female devotees provided sexual services to males for the fertility of the land, then a certain isomorphism of sexual practices might evolve. Male devotees of YHWH and female devotees of Asherah could be viewed as providing functionally similar services. Hence, we see the possibility of associating them together as occurs in some of the passages in Kings (1 Kgs 14–15; 2 Kgs 23; but not in 1 Kgs 22 or in Deuteronomy). However, the only definitive association is in 2 Kgs 23:7, where the *qedeshim* are located "in the house of the LORD, where the women did the weaving for Asherah."

Such an assimilation or even parallelism would have fateful consequences, even more so if the *qedeshim* serviced both male and female worshippers. For it would be but a short further step to associate the males who were penetrated or sexually possessed by the *qedeshim* with feminization. In such a case the specific rationale for Yahwistic *qedeshim* would be endangered.

The evidence in support of our hypothesis is admittedly quite circumstantial. However, the case might be strengthened if we found that there was a significant tendency to regard YHWH's relation to his (male) adherents as sexual. And the intervening parallelism with fertility practices would then result in regarding the male adherents not as masculinized by divine possession but as made somehow the equivalent of YHWH's wife, and thus feminized. But as we shall see, this is precisely what we do find in the prophetic literature that reflects on the relation of Israel/Judah to YHWH. It is therefore to a consideration of the transgendering of Israel that we next turn.

---

13. In chapter 8, on the transgendering of Israel, we will turn to a discussion of the phallic signifiers in Israel in connection with a discussion of Hosea.

PART THREE

Transgendering Israel

To THIS POINT IN OUR STUDY of homoeroticism in the literature of ancient Israel, we have encountered two types of eroticism among males that strongly emphasize what might be termed the masculinity of those who are characterized by these relationships. In the case of the warriors of Israel, we have seen a strong emotional bonding between males engaged together in tales of adventure and derring-do. These relationships seem to develop within a structure in which one of the males (the lover) is more powerful or prestigious than the other. Nevertheless, the junior partner in the relationship (most evidently David) is the central character who, as war-chief, king, and founder of a dynasty, may be regarded as a paragon of male virtue. It is of some interest, therefore, that David's very success as a male seems significantly to depend on how he negotiates his role as the youthful, beautiful, and faithful companion of more powerful males, culminating, as we have seen, in his relationship to YHWH. It is precisely as "boy-toy" or as "bottom" in contemporary parlance that David is also exemplary male.

In part 2 we explored another quite different form of homoeroticism, one that is located not in the warrior camp but in groups of males devoted to YHWH, whose characteristic expression seems to be something like ecstatic possession by YHWH's phallic potency. This form of homoeroticism appears in narratives that precede the institution of kingship in the David saga. After that institution begins, it seems to have its home among figures whose relationship to the religiopolitical institutions of Israel is more marginal. Thus, traces are found both in the characters who prefigure the institution of kingship (Samuel, Saul) and in the sagas concerning those who are troublemakers for that institution once it has taken shape (Elijah, Elisha). What seems characteristic in both sets of appearances, however, is instantiation in bands of males who are devoted to YHWH. Even when we find traces of such groups of males (*qedeshim*) associated with the temple, we seem to be dealing with figures and groups whose relation to that institution is somewhat marginal.

A consideration of the admittedly fragmentary and illusive traces that we find of this sort of shamanic/ecstatic homoeroticism leaves us with the impression of a homoeroticism that enhances rather than diminishes the "masculinity" of those who are possessed by this erotic and phallic power.

The material to which we now turn does suggest a transgendering of the (male) object of homoerotic attention. In connection with David we saw that Israel is loved with steadfast love on account of YHWH's love for David. But in the quasi-narrative depictions of Israel's relation to YHWH provided by the later prophets, this same Israel is depicted as if female. So successful has this transgendering operation been that commentators often simply attend to this material as if it depicted a heterosexual couple: YHWH as male, Israel as female. What is often lost sight of is that the prophets are dealing with a male Israel dressed in metaphorical drag. While one might speak of "feminization" in this case, one cannot suppose that Israel has therefore become female. Israel remains a male, but one that is (somewhat) transgendered. In these quasi-narrative depictions of Israel's relation to YHWH, it is YHWH who does the transgendering of Israel, in order first to accuse Israel of being an unfaithful bride and later to call Israel back to becoming a faithful bride. What these texts never actually forget is that the bride, whether faithful or not, is a male that is being addressed by a male deity.

In the following chapter we turn to ask whether, apart from these prophetic narratives, there are others that depict the transgendering of a male subject. This leads to an exploration of the narratives concerning Joseph, who, it turns out, is transgendered by Israel (Jacob), his father. (Hence comes the ambiguity of the title "Transgendering Israel," which I have chosen for this discussion: Israel is not only the object but also the subject or agent of transgendering.) As we shall see, the figure of Joseph suggests a quite different cultural context than the sagas concerning David or the early prophets. It seems to reflect a situation in which Israel has become the ward of other great empires, precisely the situation anticipated or articulated also by the later prophets in their transgendering of Israel.

8. Transgendered Israel

To this point we have concerned ourselves primarily with narrative texts from the Hebrew Bible that lend themselves to homoerotic interpretation. In what follows we consider prophetic texts dealing not with individual characters (as in the saga of David and his lovers) or with specialized groups (as in the *bene-hanebi'im* or *qedeshim*, YHWH's male groupies), but with Israel as a whole. What relates the texts that we here consider with those that have gone before is that they continue to imagine the relationship between YHWH and his adherents as erotic in character, even as specifically sexual in expression. What distinguishes these passages from those that have gone before is that they deal with Israel (or Judah) as a whole or as a people. YHWH obviously remains a male character in these texts, but his counterpart is now represented alternatively as male or as female. In some of these texts, the male counterpart to YHWH (Israel) is transgendered as female. Because of the distinctiveness of our approach to these texts, some preliminary remarks may help to orient the discussion.

Perhaps the most difficult yet also most evident character of the material with which we will be dealing is that it concerns the deliberate transgendering of a typically male subject. Still today, the theme of transgendering is one that gives pause to those who try to think through the nature of marginalized sexual identities and practices. Even counterhomophobic discourse is frequently at a loss as to what to do with the linking together of gay, lesbian, bisexual, and transgendered people in the now-familiar conglomerate designation "queer sexuality." And it is often assumed that transgendering is even more problematic for the Hebrew and Greek sources of Western reflection.

There is a certain plausibility to the supposition that transgendering is difficult for Greek (and perhaps especially Roman) representations of gender. Highly gendered societies seem to find the blurring of gender distinctions or gender binaries especially difficult. It is often supposed, with some reason, that this would also hold true of the attitudes of ancient Israel. In the saga materials that we have considered, there is some evidence that the slippage of male into female identity was by no means unknown. One of the misfortunes that may befall a man's lineage or house is that there may be sons who adopt a feminine role, at least with regard to gendered domestic activity. This is what seems to be the meaning of someone taking up a spindle, as found in the curse that David pronounces upon the house of Joab because of the latter's assassination of Abner:

> May the guilt fall on the head of Joab, and on all his father's house; and may the house of Joab never be without one who has a discharge, or who is leprous, *or who holds a spindle,* or who falls by the sword, or who lacks food. (2 Sam 3:29)[1]

However, the appearance of this condition in a list of common misfortunes (hunger, falling by the sword, etc.) suggests that we are not dealing with something rare or unheard of. And the legal codes of Israel do find it necessary to prohibit transvestism as perhaps an especially troubling instance of category confusion (Deut 22:5).[2]

Whether aspects of transsexuality are regarded as an unfortunate condition or as proscribed activity, what seems self-evident about these attitudes, in some ways mirroring those of our own society (not excepting gay and lesbian community perspectives), is a discomfort with phenomena that destabilize gender identity.

What is therefore surprising about the biblical materials to which we now turn is that they do engage in a deliberate transgendering of a standardly male subject. What the oracles that we will examine have in common is that they describe a stereotypically male collective (Jacob, Israel,

---

1. See also Prov 31:19, using the "spindle" image as part of describing a "capable wife," who is "far more precious than jewels" (31:10).

2. This legal text seems to be a later insertion into the Deuteronomic legal code that interrupts the continuity of items concerned with the welfare of others. See chapter 9, on Joseph.

Ephraim, Judah, and so on) as female. It is the normally male collective that is the counterpart of YHWH. We will be considering prophets who most often represent the people of God as male, the counterpart of YHWH. But in some of their most striking images, this same counterpart is represented as female.

This transgendering of a typically male subject as female occurs in a number of ways in prophetic literature. Sometimes, as in Amos or Isaiah, it seems to be an image that evokes pity for the unfortunate and vulnerable people as they are made the victims of aggressive powers operating on the world stage. Sometimes the transgendering occurs as an extension of the parent-child figuration of the relation between YHWH and his people. But in these texts the transgendering occurs in such a way as to bring to the fore an extraordinary emotional intensity and indeed erotic passion as determinative of the relation between YHWH and his "people." It is precisely this eroticism that links these texts to the narrative materials that we have considered in previous chapters. And it is in attempting to hold together this eroticism with a consideration of the transgendering of Israel that the distinctiveness of our approach consists.

What makes this especially difficult is that the gendering of the people of God as female has in the meantime, especially for Christian readers, come to seem commonplace. After all, the gendering of the church as female has become rather a cliché of theological literature dependent, perhaps, on the idea of the church as the bride of Christ. Accordingly, the oddity of this gendering has disappeared under the weight of a certain theological conventionality. Yet for all that, it remains distinctly odd even in Christian discourse. For until at least the time of Vatican II, the Catholic Church, by far the majority of all Christians, had defined the church not simply as the people of God but as the institution that was identical with the clergy and hierarchy. And this collectivity was and is exclusively male. That the church as an exclusively male corporate entity should be cast as female is itself quite remarkable. But it had become so conventional that it was relatively easy to transpose this identity back upon the people of God of ancient Israel. Precisely as "precursor" of the church, it would make an odd sort of theological sense to retroactively gender Israel (or Ephraim or Judah or what have you) as female. In this way the startling and provocative transgendering undertaken by the prophets is made to disappear "right before our eyes," in a remarkable feat of hermeneutical legerdemain.

As a result, when one consults commentaries on these remarkable passages, the gender question is simply taken for granted. Thus, we may hear of a kind of romantic wooing of Israel (for example, in reflection on Hosea).

Or we may find reflection on YHWH's husbandly role.[3] Psychiatrically inclined readers may focus on an allegedly irrational fear of female sexuality in Ezekiel.[4] More recently, feminist interpretation sees the metaphor as leading to a general characterization of female sexuality as promiscuous or even to a licensing of abusive relations between male and female generally.[5] But what is generally missing from these reflections is the observation that the so-called female here is a male in metaphorical drag.

Two discussions of this material come closest to the perspective that will be developed here. The first is that of Renita Weems, whose focus is primarily on the way in which the metaphor of YHWH's relation to his "spouse" may, for a certain class of readers, legitimize male abuse of women, especially of their wives. But within that framework she makes two observations particularly pertinent to our study. The first is that the gendering of Israel as female is by no means self-evident but rather must have had quite a shocking impact on its male audience.[6] Although she does not draw out the implications of this provocative act of transgendering, she has, unlike many readers, noticed it and drawn attention to it. The other insight important for our purposes is that the metaphor does permit a kind of narrativizing of the history of Israel that sets the fate of Israel and Judah in some sort of synoptic perspective.[7] It is precisely as a device of narration that the elaboration of this metaphor links these oracles to the narrative material with which we have been primarily concerned.

The other approach that requires special mention is that of Eilberg-Schwartz, who has drawn attention to the implications of the male gender (and genitalia) of the biblical God for a "people" that is typically understood as male.[8] In connection with such groundbreaking reflections, Eilberg-Schwartz draws attention to these passages as serving to disguise the homoerotic character of the relation between Israel and God.[9] I am not persuaded that the transgendering of Israel does function as a disguise of homoeroticism. In fact, I am rather inclined to the idea that it actually fosters or incites a homoerotic relation to the divine on the part of male devotees. This goes together with my supposition that these texts do not

---

3. Nelly Stienstra, *YHWH Is the Husband of His People* (Kampen, Netherlands: Kok Pharos, 1993).

4. David J. Halperin, *Seeking Ezekiel: Text and Psychology* (University Park: Pennsylvania State University Press, 1993), esp. 141–66.

5. Renita J. Weems, *Battered Love: Marriage, Sex, and Violence in the Hebrew Prophets* (Minneapolis: Fortress, 1995).

6. Ibid., 80.

7. Ibid., 59.

8. H. Eilberg-Schwartz, *God's Phallus and Other Problems for Men and Monotheism* (Boston: Beacon, 1994).

9. Eilberg-Schwartz suggests that the shifting of metaphors "obscured the implied homoeroticism between the loving father and the loving son" (ibid., 132). My interpretation also differs from that of Eilberg-Schwartz in that I do not privilege the father-son relationship as the fundamental domain of homoeroticism.

stand alone in representing the relation between YHWH and his male
devotees as a homoerotic one. But if the transgendering of Israel does not
occur in order to disguise homoeroticism, and if that homoeroticism is
already deeply embedded in important traditions of Israel, then how does it
happen that this transgendering is introduced?

In the discussion of David as well as that of YHWH's male groupies, we
observed no suggestion that an erotic relationship with another male
brought the masculinity of the beloved (or the lover) into question. Even
the quintessential beloved, David, remains Israel's war-leader, the founder of
the line of kings upon which Judah's future depends, and so on. As far as we
can tell, the same is true of the *bene-hanebi'im* and other males who fall
under the erotic spell of YHWH's phallic potency. We speculated that this
has to do with the character of warrior or shamanistic subcultures. In such
cultures or subcultures the erotic or even sexual relation between males is
not comparable to the sexual relation between male and female. However,
when the dominant metaphors of a culture are agrarian, with a strong
emphasis on fertility, and the primary social unit is not the warrior band or
the male group but the household, then male sexuality tends to have a different set of meanings attached to it. The cross-sex relations come to have
greater cultural saliency. In such a case it is almost inevitable that sexual relations are incorporated into the male-female structure so prominent in
agrarian or household contexts. Hence, the analogy of male-female relations is more ready to hand us a template for understanding (or misunder-
standing) erotic relations between persons of the same gender.

In the case of relations that involve YHWH, this is all the more so as
YHWH takes on the functions of Baal in ensuring the fertility of the land.
Thus, the male potency of the divine is expressed not in warrior-like
pursuits but in husbanding the land. From the time of Solomon onward,
the more settled life of Israel even seems to find it necessary to supply
YHWH with a female consort, which may lie behind the assimilation of
Astarte and Asherah into the temple cult. In this connection the homosocial
bonds of the *bene-hanebi'im* (and perhaps also of the *qedeshim*) may represent
a protest on the part of the tradition over against the heterosexualization of
the cult and of life generally.

The upshot of the heterosexualization of life and cult is that the same-sex
relationship between YHWH and Israel comes to be fraught with heterosex-
ualizing metaphorical representation. In prophetic faith YHWH has no other
consort than Israel. The divine female is still held at bay. Thus, the male Israel
becomes the feminized consort of YHWH. The relationship is still erotic,
perhaps even more so. But it is imagined as if it were like a relationship

between male and female. However, it is never simply such a relationship. For Israel remains male even if sometimes dressed in rhetorical drag.

In order to become clearer about how this works, we will survey many of the relevant texts that explore the image of YHWH's erotic relation to Israel. While the transgendering of Israel already appears in Amos, the metaphor is first truly elaborated in Hosea. In both Amos and Hosea we are dealing with oracles addressed to the northern kingdom. The metaphor is applied to Judah only after the collapse of the northern kingdom and indeed as Judah (now also the remnant of Israel) confronts a similar fate. The metaphor resurfaces in Jeremiah and receives remarkably graphic elaboration in Ezekiel (and is even present in Second Isaiah). In what follows we first take up the oracles addressed to the northern kingdom and then those addressed to the situation of national calamity in relation to Babylon.

From Amos to Hosea: Ephraim Is a Slut

The transgendering of Israel appears for the first time in prophetic literature in an oracle from Amos:

> Fallen, no more to rise
> is maiden Israel;
> forsaken on her land,
> with no one to raise her up. (Amos 5:2)

This brief oracle anticipates the devastation of Israel as viewed by the Judean prophet Amos. It has the character of a lament spoken by the prophet or by YHWH through the prophet. In this lament there is, as yet, no suggestion of an erotic relationship between the speaker and the figure of Israel; instead, the relationship seems to be one of pity or compassion for a young girl left unprotected and thus at the mercy of male marauders. However, the transgendering of Israel does appear connected to the association of Israel and the land. Thus, it may be that the association of Israel with "her land" is what makes it seem apt to describe Israel as female in relation to the male gaze of prophet/YHWH; it is the view of the sower of seed (Hos 2:24 = 25 MT).

Yet here Israel is not only female but also "virgin" or maiden. Israel is imagined as a female not (yet) betrothed or sexually bound to a male. While this image may express pity and horror at the fate of Israel, it also may provoke the question of how it comes to pass that this female or feminized figure comes to suffer such an unseemly and unsettling fate. It is almost as if the complex imagery of the prophet Hosea sets out to answer precisely this question.

Hosea, Overview

While the book of Hosea is notoriously difficult in terms of exegesis, it remains a favorite of readers because of the powerful passions it expresses. Indeed, so given is the book to expression of YHWH's anger, heartbreak, and love that it is often difficult to know what it is precisely that occasions these passionate outbursts. It is more concerned to give expression to the emotions of the wronged lover than it is to indicate what it is that the beloved (typically Ephraim/Israel, although occasionally Judah as well) has done to provoke this howl of protest on the part of the lover. We have relatively little of the bill of particulars concerning the practice of injustice that characterizes other prophetic literature from Amos onward.[10] Only rarely do we find the kind of indictment that we associate with prophetic literature: "Swearing, lying, and murder, and stealing and adultery break out; bloodshed follows bloodshed" (Hos 4:2; cf. 7:1; 10:13). More common is the allegation of a kind of faithlessness that expresses itself in something like idolatry, in the sense of fashioning images for worship (8:6; 13:2).

Yet what is most striking is the linking together of an almost bewildering array of objects and forces to which Ephraim gives himself instead of being faithful to YHWH. These include the calves or bulls that mark the sanctuary of YHWH (8:5–6; 10:5–6), which the books of Kings regularly characterize as the sin of Jeroboam (1 Kgs 12:28–30; 2 Kgs 10:29; 17:16). These bulls, representing YHWH's phallic potency, seem similar to the "golden calf" that Aaron fashioned in the wilderness to represent the presence of YHWH (Exod 32). In uncertain connection to the bull/calf of the Yahwistic sanctuary is the confusion of YHWH with Baal as the giver of fertility and prosperity. We are probably not to suppose that Israel has simply exchanged the worship of YHWH for another deity named Baal, but rather that YHWH is worshipped as Baal, as the giver of land, fertility, and so of prosperity.[11] In addition, we are given pictures of a more diffused erotically charged worship in the countryside, which involves (at least as

---

10. What Sherwood says about the first chapter of Hosea seems apt for the book as a whole: "Hosea 1 determinedly avoids reference to the social milieu in which it is situated." See Yvonne Sherwood, *The Prostitute and the Prophet: Hosea's Marriage in Literary Theoretical Perspective* (Sheffield, UK: Sheffield Academic Press, 1996), 121. However, Gale Yee has made a convincing case from the perspective of historical, economic, and political considerations that may be brought to bear on the text. She claims that some of the allusions, for example, to cash crops such as oil, wine, and grain, may be understood in relation to conditions of a tributary economy in crisis. See Gale A. Yee, "'She Is Not My Wife and I Am Not Her Husband': A Materialist Analysis of Hosea 1–2," *Biblical Interpretation* 9, no. 4 (2001): 345–83, esp. 347.

11. With respect to many of these items such as calves, high places, baals, and so on, Yee (ibid., 351) states: "What stands condemned as Baal worship in Hosea . . . [includes features that] were for centuries accepted components of the worship of YHWH. In other words, Hosea condemns not Canaanite encroachment into Yahwism, but rather early Yahwism itself."

far as the prophet is concerned) the orgiastic adoration of pillars and other phallic symbols and cultic practices that may involve sexual acts. Finally, we are presented with the image of an Israel that seeks aid, security, and prosperity through alliance with neighboring powers such as Assyria and Egypt (Hos 7:11; 8:9).

What unites this strange mixture of apparently diverse elements is everything being suffused with an overpowering erotic passion. Thus, any or all of these elements (and I have mentioned only the most prominent among them) come to be characterized as adultery, promiscuity, prostitution—illicit sexuality. Indeed, the prophet presents us with a Felliniesque pastiche of sexuality run rampant. In this context of exuberant sexuality, we encounter the metaphor of Israel as female counterpart to YHWH. Accordingly, we should examine this context more closely.

Promiscuity

The atmosphere of rampant sexuality is expressed throughout but seems most clearly expressed in oracles grouped in chapter 4:

> For a spirit of whoredom has led them astray,
>   and they have played the whore, forsaking their God.
> They sacrifice on the tops of the mountains,
>   and make offerings upon the hills,
> under oak, poplar, and terebinth,
>   because their shade is good.
>
> Therefore your daughters play the whore,
>   and your daughters-in-law commit adultery.
> I will not punish your daughters when they play the whore,
>   nor your daughters-in-law when they commit adultery;
> For the men themselves go aside with whores,
>   and sacrifice with [female] temple prostitutes (*qedeshot*).
>   (4:12b–14b)

The description of rampant sexuality concludes:

> When their drinking is ended, they indulge in sexual orgies;
>   they love lewdness more than their glory. (4:18)

What are we to make of this scene? At the beginning we seem to have a description of simple excess of sexual transgression (on the part of women),

expressed as adultery and promiscuity. But then this is related to what seem
to be particular cultic practices, especially as this concerns the men who not
only engage as their daughters do in sexual excess but also "sacrifice with
qedeshot," the female counterparts of the *qedeshim*. There seems to be an easy
passage between depictions of promiscuity and depictions of cultic behavior. Any attempt to identify one pole of this activity as the signified and the
other as the signifier seems to be arbitrary. Indeed, it may be that each is
understood to entail the other, thereby producing a dizzying effect.

The consequence seems to be that Israel as a whole or Ephraim (understood as a male subject) is accused of promiscuity and prostitution. Thus,

> I know Ephraim,
>   and Israel is not hidden from me;
> for now, O Ephraim, you have played the whore;
>   Israel is defiled. (5:3)

Moreover,

> In the house of Israel I have seen a horrible thing;
>   Ephraim's whoredom is there, Israel is defiled. (6:10)

Furthermore,

> You have played the whore, departing from your God.
>   You have loved a prostitute's pay
>   on all threshing floors. (9:1)

The description of Ephraim as a slut who is chasing multiple lovers does
not by itself seem to require the device of transgendering. The accusation of
whoring around or being a slut, while having a primary association with
the derogation of female philandering, may also be used in relation to
males. (Indeed, the fancier term, "philandering," is quite regularly used of
males, even heterosexual males, even though it comes from a Greek word
etymologically meaning "lover of males.") Just as in modern gay parlance a
male may be accused by other males of being a slut, so also here.

The term used here in Hosea, like the corresponding term in Greek, is
applicable both to cases of "promiscuity," where what is involved is multiple
"lovers," as well as to cases of "prostitution," where what is involved is the
receipt of material reward for sexual services performed. Indeed, Hosea
seems to make no distinction between promiscuity and prostitution. As in

many languages, the terms seem to be the same.[12] The meaning depends upon whether what is most in view is the casual multiplication of lovers or the derivation of material support from this diversification of lovers.

Double Trouble

Although transgendering is a decided possibility in the accusation of promiscuity/prostitution, it only becomes fully evident as the first three chapters of Hosea deploy the metaphor of marriage. There Hosea's relation to Gomer serves as a template for exploring the relationship between Israel and YHWH. These two relationships so mutually condition one another that it becomes notoriously difficult for the reader to know where one (Hosea/Gomer) leaves off and the other (YHWH/Ephraim) begins.[13]

What the marriage metaphor does for the accusation of Israel's slutty behavior is to set it within the framework of adultery, and so make Israel's behavior a transgression of the law. Interestingly, there is no thought here of applying the law as it comes to (probably later) expression in Deuteronomy and Leviticus, which would require the death of the adulteress.[14] Thus, Deuteronomy (probably compiled at least a century later) specifies that in the case of adultery when the parties are caught in the act, "both of them shall die, the man who lay with the woman as well as the woman" (Deut 22:22). The Holiness Code (probably compiled several centuries later) contains a similar provision: "If a man commits adultery with the wife of his neighbor, both the adulterer and the adulteress shall be put to death" (Lev 20:10). We have already recognized that no such law seems to have been known to the author of 2 Samuel in the account of David and Bathsheba.[15] It appears that at the time of the composition of Hosea, there is also, as yet, no knowledge of these legal requirements.

---

12. This appears true also in the case of the legal code of Deuteronomy, which finds that a young woman who is not a virgin when married shall be charged as "prostituting herself in her father's house" (Deut 22:21). Thus, the charge of something like fornication and prostitution are one and the same even though there is no suggestion that the sexual act was committed for any reward. Yee (ibid., 371) makes a similar point even more emphatically by choosing to translate Hos 1:2 as "promiscuous wife" rather than "prostitute," arguing that the former would be less tolerated than the latter. Hosea seems to make use of both possibilities.

13. Sherwood (*Prostitute*, 135) remarks concerning chapter 2: "It is impossible to perceive where the signifier ends and the signified begins." This also makes it hard to know which is the signified and which the signifier. Thus, she can also say: "In Hosea 2 there is no stark contrast between signifier and signified, but rather an amalgam" (136).

14. That the text knows no such legal requirement of death for adultery is manifest. But this also means that it also knows no legal prohibition of same-sex relationships (a prohibition known only to Leviticus). In the world of the text, same-sex relationships are available to symbolize the relationship between Ephraim and YHWH, as is an adulterous cross-sex relationship within which the male suffers ignominy but the woman does not suffer automatic execution. Both are equally necessary to the text, and in both ways the world of Leviticus is completely foreign to the text.

15. The supposition on the part of Weems that the wronged husband has the right to have the adulteress wife put to death is based on the application of legal codes that in all probability have not yet come into existence at the time of Hosea, and perhaps even of Jeremiah. See Weems, *Battered Love*, 27 et passim.

Hosea's relationship is constructed on the basis of his knowing what he is getting into. The beloved is always already promiscuous and a prostitute, a notorious chaser after men. This seems to be true whether one starts from the prophet's relationship to Gomer in 1:2 ("Take for yourself a wife of whoredom") or from the related description in 3:1 ("Go, love a woman who has a lover and is an adulteress"). Of course, the "client" of a prostitute or hustler has no reason to complain if the hustler has other "clients." And it is hard to know on what basis, apart from sheer willfulness, someone who sets their sights on a relationship with a notorious slut should have reason to complain of unfaithfulness if the promiscuous one does not change his/her ways. Human nature being what it is, however, the absurdity of the lover's complaint does not seem to preclude its being both felt and uttered. What gives the complaint some semblance of a reasonable basis is the fiction of marriage. That presumably gives the lover a claim to the body of the beloved as exclusive sexual property and so places the unfaithfulness of the beloved in the realm of adultery, as wronging the honor and rights of the "husband." It is the fiction of such a marriage that seems to require the further fiction (in the case of Israel) that the beloved slut be a female.

Second, the Gomer analogy also serves to set up the possibility of ascribing the production of progeny to the relationship.[16] Thus, Hosea's three children by Gomer all have symbolic names that seem to designate the people as a whole ("God sows," "Not pitied," "Not my people"). It is not clear whether they really are Hosea's children. But this also permits Hosea to affirm that the people of Israel as the progeny of Ephraim are "illegitimate" and thus have no claim on their putative "father" (1:2; 2:4; 4:6; 5:7). Hence, the transgendering of Israel serves to permit the ascription of progeny to Israel as the (unfaithful) beloved of YHWH.[17]

Third, the transgendering of Israel permits the appropriation of Baal fertility images into the relationship between Israel and YHWH. Thus, Israel may suppose, "I will go after my lovers; they give me my bread and my water, my wool and my flax, my oil and my drink" (2:5 = 7 MT). But according to Hosea, these gifts associated with the fertility of the land come not from Baal but from YHWH. "She did not know that it was I who gave her the grain, the wine, and the oil, and who lavished upon her silver and gold that they used for Baal" (2:8 = 10 MT). This is a dangerous game; it would appear that the whole problem is that the people suppose they are

---

16. Thus, Sherwood, *Prostitute*, 83: "Hosea must be a husband so that he can be a father."

17. Once transgendering begins, it multiplies. Thus, Sherwood (ibid., 206) observes that Jezreel, initially portrayed as a male (Hos 1:4), also becomes "female" when YHWH promises to "sow" him/her (2:23 NRSV with "him" = 25 MT with "her"). Here there is little question of the copulatory nature of the relationship. Yet it may not be sex but rather fertility that makes the object of YHWH's amorous action "female."

worshipping YHWH when they are said to be worshipping Baal. Indeed, in the image of restoration, the confusion seems to be, if anything, compounded: "On that day, says the LORD, you will call me, 'My husband,' and no longer will you call me, 'My Baal'" (2:16 = 18 MT). What this suggests is that YHWH takes on the features of Baal as the giver of prosperity from the land.[18]

In this connection it is important to see that YHWH becomes the "husband" of Israel precisely as the one who gives true prosperity. YHWH is certainly no longer the warrior-god who takes on male favorites. Instead, he becomes (somewhat like Baal) the male provider of prosperity for "his" woman. The difficulty is that the only "woman" YHWH has is Israel/Ephraim. This is another male who must, at least for metaphorical purposes, be thinly disguised as a female.

Sex Toys

One of the most intriguing images in this text comes in the description of the way in which Hosea (YHWH) disciplines the wayward spouse (Israel). Hosea 3 seems oddly related to the extended image of chapters 1–2 that dealt with Hosea's relation to Gomer. Though it is possible that the same relationship is being redescribed here, this is by no means certain.[19] In any case, Hosea "purchases" the woman indicated by YHWH but tells her: "'You must remain as mine for many days; you shall not play the whore, you shall not have intercourse with a man, nor I with you.' For the Israelites shall remain many days without king or prince, without sacrifice or pillar, without ephod or teraphim" (3:3–4). A woman who appears to enjoy sex with multiple partners is somehow made to undergo a period of sexual abstinence as preparation for eventual consummation of the relationship. The emphasis here is on abstinence from erotic play. And it is this that somehow suggests that Israel will have to do without "king or prince, sacrifice or pillar, ephod or teraphim." In other words, Israel will have to make do without sex toys in order to prepare for "real sex" later, when "they shall come in awe to the LORD and to his goodness in the latter days" (3:5).

The middle term of this trio of parallel items is the one that we most often encounter in the text. We are told that the people of Israel are quite

---

18. Sherwood's analysis of this situation is especially acute: "Baal is perceived by the woman as lover and provider, and to reclaim her affections, YHWH describes himself in precisely the same terms" (ibid., 224). Sherwood goes on to demonstrate that the text renders problematic any hard and fast distinction between YHWH and Baal, still less any absolute priority.

19. "The analogies that exist between the two texts [chs. 1 and 3] are complex and ambiguous, and cannot be reduced to the verdict that they are two versions of the same event . . . or even that they are two ways of expressing a similar meaning" (ibid., 127).

taken with their "pillars." "The more his fruit increased, the more altars he built; as his country improved, he improved his pillars" (10:1). But YHWH "will break down their altars, and destroy their pillars" (10:2). It appears that the pillars are phallic representations celebrating the fertility of the land, "male" counterparts of the poles associated with Asherah. But Hosea associates them with sacrifice as such. The cultic expression of faith is, as such, discarded by Hosea (as by other prophets), for after all, what YHWH requires is clearly stated in opposition to any cult whatever: "For I desire steadfast love and not sacrifice, the knowledge of God rather than burnt offerings" (6:6). The point is that sacrifice, like pillars, is regarded as a sex toy, providing cheap thrills but not the consummation of the relationship that matters.[20]

Earlier we encountered the third pair of sex toys. In the discussion of David's dance "before the LORD" (2 Sam 6), we had occasion to notice that the ephod appears there at least to have the character of a kind of loincloth or jockstrap that both conceals and draws attention to the male genitals.[21] Consider the case of the teraphim Michal used to make it appear that David was still in his bed when Saul was out to kill him (1 Sam 19:16). It must have had the shape of a (very large) phallus, what goes into an ephod.

If the second and third pair in this series are to be understood as phallic signifiers, what of the first, king and prince? The text is certainly critical of those who have posed as kings of Israel: "They made kings, but not through me" (8:4). Yet the text as it stands incorporates into the image of restoration a return to "David their king" (3:5). It is possible but by no means certain that, as several scholars suppose, this is an insertion made by Judean editors. For the image of steadfast love is critical to Hosea, and we recall that this is generally associated with David. What may be in view, then, is a king like David who is the beloved of YHWH, and for whose sake Israel also becomes the beloved of YHWH after his smutty behavior has been expunged.

One of the sex toys that figures most prominently in Hosea's imagining is the bull or calf that Israel erected to represent the phallic potency of YHWH.[22] We hear, for example: "Your calf is rejected, O Samaria. . . . For

---

20. Yee makes the point that the institution of sacrifice was also an instrument of political and economic domination ("She," 360). This is something scarcely unknown in the history of Christianity, whether we are thinking of the "sacrifice of the mass" or of the willing collaboration of Protestant worship in systems of political economy.

21. We should also recall Judg 8:27, perhaps from an editor influenced by Hosea, saying that in the time of Gideon, Israel prostituted itself to the ephod of YHWH.

22. James Luther Mays, *Hosea: A Commentary* (Philadelphia: Westminster, 1969), 118, states: "The bull was not meant to be an idol, but rather a pedestal or throne of the invisible deity, similar to the ark." In this respect, Jeremiah exploits the bull's similarity to the ark (see below).

it is from Israel, an artisan made it; it is not God. The calf of Samaria shall be
broken to pieces" (8:5–6; cf. 10:5–6). Indeed, the "calf" seems to have been
the object of religious-erotic adoration: "People are kissing calves!" (13:2).
We are told as well, "In Gilgal they sacrifice bulls" (12:11), and recall that we
encountered this practice at Shiloh, as part of the cult of YHWH when the
young Samuel was dedicated to the shrine managed by Eli (1 Sam
1:24–25). The importance of the bull as a representation of YHWH thus is
no great surprise. In Hosea, this in turn suggests to him the image of Israel
as a heifer, as the object of the bull's phallic attention: "Ephraim was a
trained heifer that loved to thresh, and I spared her fair neck" (10:11). Yet
"like a stubborn heifer, Israel is stubborn" (4:16). Just as Hosea seems somewhat ambivalent about the confusion of YHWH and Baal, both opposing
and contributing to that confusion; so also does he seem ambivalent about
the bull-heifer image. Indeed, perhaps he agrees that YHWH "is" a bull but
supposes that the mistake of Israel is to fabricate a bull of heavy metal that
gets in the way of the real bull's access to "his" heifer. Hence, the problem is
one of using a sex toy to substitute for the sexual consummation of the relationship between Ephraim and YHWH.

What is most remarkable here is the virtually complete focus on Israel's
sex toys as simulacra of the phallus. Only once do we hear of the *qedeshot*
(4:14, female cultic prostitutes), never of the poles, the Asherah, or Astarte
as representing the "temptation of the feminine" or the goddess.[23] Israel
seems to be addicted to the phallus whether as bull or pillar, as teraphim or
ephod, as sacrifice or king. The religious and political life of Israel seems to
consist, in the prophet's view, in a bewildering array of dildos.

Return of the Male

Now this feminization of Israel/Ephraim by no means eliminates the essential maleness of YHWH's beloved. In the same text this maleness is
recalled in a number of ways, in addition to the use of names such as Israel
and Ephraim that insistently recall to the reader the male ancestors of this
name. The original love of YHWH for Ephraim is recalled, for example, in
these terms:

> When Israel was a child, I loved him,
>   and out of Egypt I called my son. . . .
> Yet it was I who taught Ephraim to walk. (11:1, 3)

---

23. Yee remarks: "Hosea does not explicitly refer to or condemn devotion to the goddess Asherah, her cult
object, or the female figurines" ("She," 353). This is so in spite of the supposition by many (male) scholars that
this cult is the object of Hosea's censure. Male scholars may be more (consciously) aware of dangers in worshipping a goddess than aware of the allure of the phallus.

And the goal of return is expressed in terms of the renewed beauty of this same Israel:

I will be like the dew to Israel;
    he shall blossom like the lily. . . .
    His beauty shall be like the olive tree,
    and his fragrance like that of Lebanon. (14:5–6)

What is striking about this image of a restored Israel is that it images Israel as a male while retaining the warmth of erotic passion for "his" beauty. Throughout, Israel/Ephraim is also regarded as male when his sins are enumerated, whether in terms of building idols (10:6) or engaging in the construction of altars or pillars (10:1) or engaging in orgiastic rites on the hillside (4:14) or in the worship of Baal (11:1–2; 13:1). Even the quest for lovers may be attributed to the male subject (8:9).[24] Hosea never lets the reader forget that the object of YHWH's love and anger is male.

It is the all the more striking that precisely this male object of YHWH's affection and passion is also prominently transfigured as female.

The problem with which Hosea deals is clearly not that the relation between divinity and devotee should be an erotic one. This seems to be taken for granted in the text as a whole. There is no suspicion toward eroticism as such or toward the erotic and indeed sexual relation between Israel and his lover. On both sides, that of lover and beloved, the relationship is and indeed ought to be suffused with erotic passion.[25]

The transgendering of Israel seems not to be occasioned by the erotic character of YHWH's love for Israel or Israel's erotic attachment to YHWH. It does not appear that the device of transgendering serves to conceal the essentially homoerotic character of this relationship (as opposed to Eilberg-Schwartz). It is not the erotic character of this relationship that feminizes Israel. Instead, the transgendering seems to come about in order

---

24. Stienstra (*YHWH the Husband*, 145) translates Hos 8:9–10: "Ephraim has rented lovers, and because he has rented them from the nations I am now going to round them up." She comments: "It is interesting to note that here it is male promiscuity that is used to depict the Israelites' disloyal attitude to YHWH, but this is not embedded in an extended metaphor such as the marriage metaphor." It is questionable, however, that the marriage metaphor can be treated apart from its context in a metaphorical transgendering. By focusing on "marriage" apart from "transgendering" as its antecedent condition of possibility, the usefulness of her study, at least for our purposes, is limited.

25. Sherwood (*Prostitute*, 234–35) rightly criticizes the tradition of commentary that seeks to desexualize the relation between YHWH and Israel. She observes that in descriptions of the Baal cult "commentators tend to overplay the sexuality of the Baal cult and underplay the sexuality of YHWH." Then she states that YHWH functions "as a graphically sexual deity." At no point in her excellent book, however, does she suspect that the most remarkable fact about the allegory is that it transgenders Ephraim and so presupposes a (heterosexualized) same-sex relationship.

to characterize the promiscuity of Israel as adultery, and to give an account of the apparent "fruitfulness" both of this adultery and of the relationship to YHWH. Transgendering thus serves to enable the writer to speak of promiscuity/adultery and of the progeny of the union of Israel with his lover(s).

Passionate Embrace

We should not leave off our discussion of Hosea's remarkable image of YHWH's passion for Ephraim without underscoring its most central characteristic: that of the power of erotic passion itself. For the love of YHWH for Ephraim is the passion of a lover for a beloved. Whether in fond remembrance of the days of falling in love, or in wounded and bewildered rage of a jilted lover, or in the deep yearning for the return of Ephraim's "steadfast love" for his first lover—the poems of Hosea give expression to an overpowering passion. And we can only wonder, What would it be like to be the object of such unbridled desire and yearning? What would it be like to be the male object of this male passion? For the whole articulation of this passion aims for the return of this love, aims to have Ephraim with equal desire return the desire of his Great Lover. Who would Israel be if Israel, precisely as male (for the women of Israel are not addressed by these oracles[26]), were to be awakened to a corresponding passion for this "husband"? Does the text not incite homoerotic passion? A passion that can only be assuaged by the consummation of this love affair?

And if the text incites homosexual desire, can we suppose that this desire can be expected to confine itself to the plane of Israel's relation to a single great male? Or will this incited desire not also play itself out in relationships among the males who together constitute Ephraim? Will not their relationship to the divine also serve as a template for their relationship to one another? Is that not what a relationship to the divine should do, always and everywhere?

---

26. Weems rightly makes much of the fact that the audience of these oracles is decidedly male (*Battered Love*, 41). She also observes: "To characterize elite, socially prominent Hebrew men as whores and to imply that there was very little difference between them and sexually impure women must have caused quite a stir, to say the least" (80). What Weems does not reflect on is that the alternative offered to these men of Israel to being whores is to be faithful and adoring wives to YHWH. It is also for this reason that I am not persuaded by the view that the transgendering of Israel is a device aimed at shaming the male elite by symbolically castrating, emasculating, or feminizing them. The problem identified by the prophets is not that of gender slippage or transformation. If that were the problem, the prescription would be "Act like a man." Rather, the problem is something like promiscuity, for which the prescription is "Love me as much as I love you."

Jeremiah: Judah Is (an Ass) in Heat

Hosea had largely exempted Judah from his indictment of Ephraim's slutty behavior. Judean prophets such as Isaiah and Micah had largely avoided the provocative metaphorical transgendering of YHWH's beloved, choosing instead to emphasize the call of Amos for justice and for reliance on YHWH alone for the defense of Judah.[27] To be sure, both Micah and Isaiah exhibit the sign of erotic possession by YHWH in their symbolic nudity, but they do not, for all that, seem to be transgendered; they remain clearly male, as does Judah.

A century later than Hosea, as Judah was facing the same kind of threat that had overwhelmed Israel, another prophet takes up the metaphor of a transgendering of YHWH's beloved. The metaphor is, occasionally, more reminiscent of the brief oracle of Amos that lamented the exposure of "virgin Israel." Jeremiah can make "virgin Israel" the object of hope and longing: "Return, O virgin Israel" (Jer 31:21), paradoxically suggesting that she is a "faithless daughter" who resists the entreaty (31:22). More to the point, Jeremiah can seemingly combine in one breath the ascription of virginity and of blame to Israel: "The virgin Israel has done a most horrible thing" (18:13). The ascription of virginity to Israel invites, as we saw, an explanation for her plight, and this is provided by the adaptation of Hosea's imagery of God's people not as a virgin but as a slut.

One thing Jeremiah will not do is adopt the prophetic strategy of marrying a prostitute or adulteress, as Hosea seems to have done. Instead, he adopts the almost equally remarkable behavior of remaining a bachelor at the behest of the Great Lover: "You shall not take a wife, nor shall you have sons or daughters in this place" (16:2). This has two consequences. First, Jeremiah's own passionate expression is directed entirely to his relationship with YHWH and his people. As a result, second, Jeremiah's expressions of passion are somewhat clearer than those of Hosea; we are not left in the position of trying to figure out whether we have Hosea speaking about Gomer or YHWH speaking about Ephraim; signifier and signified line up in a more intelligible fashion.

In order to appropriate the metaphor of transgendering developed by Hosea, Jeremiah is able to conflate Israel and Judah so that what was said of Israel is now applied to Judah. Where there is a distinction, it will be said that Judah's promiscuity is even worse at least because Judah did not take

27. In 3:22 Isaiah does use a transgendering metaphor (similar to that which we found in Amos 5:2), which evokes the readers' pity for fallen Jerusalem. And Isa 1:21 even alludes to Jerusalem as a harlot, but this image is not developed in such a way as to evoke the erotic dimension of the relationship between YHWH and his people.

warning from the plight of Israel (3:6–10). And where they must be spoken of together, Jeremiah will introduce the image of them as sisters (3:7–8, 10), an image that Ezekiel will greatly expand.[28]

The consequence is that Jeremiah repeats many of the images of Hosea.

> On every high hill
> > and under every green tree,
> > you sprawled and played the whore. (2:20)

> Look up to the bare heights, and see!
> > Where have you not been lain with?
> By the waysides you have sat waiting for lovers,
> > like a nomad in the wilderness.
> You have polluted the land
> > with your whoring and wickedness. (3:2)

> She polluted the land, committing adultery with stone and tree. (3:9)

> You have . . . scattered your favors among strangers under every green tree. (3:13)

> I have seen your abominations,
> > your adulteries and neighings, your shameless prostitutions
> > on the hills of the countryside. (13:27)

It appears that Judah has learned only the joys of promiscuity and not its dangers from the example of Israel.

In this connection Jeremiah develops a striking image of Israel/Judah's promiscuity. He compares YHWH's beloved to an animal in heat:

> Look at your way in the valley;
> > know what you have done—
> a restive young camel interlacing her tracks,
> > a wild ass at home in the wilderness,
> in her heat sniffing the wind!
> > Who can restrain her lust?
> None who seek her need weary themselves;
> > in her month they will find her. (2:23–24)

---

28. Because Ezekiel expands this image, we will postpone discussion of its rather scandalous implications until then. Many scholars also suppose that Jer 3:6–11 is a later insertion, itself dependent upon Ezek 16 and 23, thus making it doubly appropriate to postpone dealing with this extension of the metaphor until we discuss Ezekiel. See William A. Holladay, *Jeremiah: A Commentary on the Book of the Prophet Jeremiah* (2 vols.; ed. P. D. Hanson; Hermeneia; Minneapolis: Fortress, 1986–89), 1:116.

So eager is YHWH's beloved for lovers that they don't even have to try to find or seduce her. She advertises herself to them, as insatiable for their attentions as a wild ass (onager) in heat.

While the image of promiscuity may not of itself require transgendering, Jeremiah does exploit it in order to speak about divorce. Jeremiah still seems not to know that the penalty for adultery will be stoning to death any more than he believes that YHWH gave any instructions concerning sacrifice in the Sinai covenant (7:22). But he does suppose that divorce is obligatory for cases of adultery, and so he cannot adopt the idea that Israel/Judah was an adulteress or prostitute before being betrothed by YHWH. Indeed, the assumption that Israel/Judah was first a virginal bride before becoming an adulteress is one of the ways that Jeremiah can make sense of the history of Israel. In this way he clarifies the transition from the early days to the current sad state of affairs. Accordingly, he changes Hosea's image of Ephraim as a youth "adopted" by YHWH (11:1, 3) into one of virginal betrothal: "I remember the devotion of your youth, your love as a bride" (2:2). In addition, Jeremiah can explain the fate of Israel as the result of a legitimate bill of divorce that YHWH enacts on account of "her" adultery (3:1, 8, 20). Thus, Jeremiah/YHWH can ask:

> If a man divorces his wife
>   and she goes from him
> and becomes another man's wife,
>   will he return to her?
> Would not such a land be greatly polluted?
> You have played the whore with many lovers;
>   and would you return to me? (3:1)

That Israel has done far worse than simply marry another man but has indeed taken many lovers is here supposed to be the grounds for not taking her back. This appears to be in keeping with a provision of Deuteronomy. A man may not take back a wife whom he has divorced and who has become the woman of another man. "That would be abhorrent to the LORD, and you shall not bring guilt on the land that the LORD your God is giving you as a possession" (Deut 24:4). The later description of the divorce of YHWH and Samaria seems to echo provisions of the same law code. For here we hear of sending Samaria away with a "writ of divorce" (3:8 NASB), which echoes the provision of Deut 24:1. At this point, however, there still seems to be no awareness of the possibility of stoning the wife for adultery as in Deut 22:22.

Judah does not seem so well provisioned as Ephraim with sex toys, how-ever. We hear nothing now of the "calves" or bulls, nothing of teraphim and ephods. We do hear of trees and stones, and these seem to have a certain phallic character: "[They] say to a tree, 'You are my Father,' and to a stone, 'You gave me birth'" (2:27),[29] in addition to "committing adultery with stone and tree" (3:9). But what is most remarkable is that Jeremiah regards the ark of the covenant itself as a kind of substitute phallus: "They shall no longer say, 'The ark of the covenant of the LORD.' It shall not come to mind, or be remembered, or missed; nor shall another one be made" (3:16). In our discussion of David's relation to the ark, we saw that it seemed to be inter-changeable with the totemic ephod as a kind of phallic sheath. And it would appear that, for Jeremiah at least, it has come to be a substitute fetish that distracts from "the real thing."[30]

This does not mean that, for Jeremiah, YHWH has somehow been "desexed." On the contrary, it is Jeremiah who develops the astonishing image of YHWH's loincloth as representing Israel/Judah's appropriate clinging to YHWH (13:1–11). He is instructed to acquire a linen loincloth and wear it about his loins (genitals). Then the Lord instructs him to hide it in a cleft of a rock in the Euphrates. When he goes to retrieve it, as instructed, "now the loincloth was ruined; it was good for nothing" (13:7). YHWH gives the following explanation:

> Thus says the LORD: Just so I will ruin the pride of Judah and the great pride of Jerusalem. This evil people, who refuse to hear my words, who stubbornly follow their own will and have gone after other gods to serve them and worship them, shall be like this loincloth, which is good for nothing. For as the loincloth clings to one's loins, so I made the whole house of Israel and the whole house of Judah cling to me. (13:9–11)

That Israel and Judah are made to cling to the divine phallus like a loin-cloth emphasizes the intimacy of the relationship even more graphically than does the suggestion of transgendering. The clinging or cleaving is what Gen 2:24 ascribes to male and female as they become "one flesh."

---

29. Holladay (ibid., 104) admits the possibility of a sarcastic transgendering of the tree and stone since the tree is a female symbol or Asherah while the stone may be a phallic signifier. Once transgendering is let loose, its myriad metaphorical possibilities seem to multiply, as we already observed in the case of the gender of Jezreel in Hosea's oracles.

30. For Jeremiah, as for Hosea, there seems to be no concern about the various possibilities of representing a female divinity; the sex toys are precisely those of the cult of YHWH.

But here we have not male and female but two male subjects: YHWH and Israel/Judah.[31]

This makes clear further that the transgendering is not essential either to the depiction of Judah's unfaithfulness or to his desired intimacy with YHWH. It is his idolatry that is represented by the ruined loincloth just as it is his proper function to cling to the genitalia of his Great Lover. What this means for our purposes is that when Israel/Judah is transgendered, the guise remains rather transparent. The male figure of Israel/Judah is always peeking out of the extravagantly donned vestments of assumed femininity.[32]

Hence, it is not surprising that when we are told of Israel/Judah's female attire, we are given an "over the top" depiction:

And you, O desolate one,
what do you mean that you dress in crimson,
    that you deck yourself with ornaments of gold,
    that you enlarge your eyes with paint? (4:30)

It is as if Israel, like a transvestite in a drag show, overdoes her/his imitation of "femininity" in such a way as to betray the falsity of the impersonation. Nor should we overlook the fact that the impersonation is one that YHWH actively seems to be staging:

Can a girl forget her ornaments,
    or a bride her attire?
Yet my people have forgotten me,
    days without number. (2:32)

It is YHWH as lover who decks out Israel in the costume of a "wife."

This means that the transgendering of Israel/Judah is a transparent fiction, for the relationship is still one of male to male. Even in the midst of developing the metaphorical transgendering, Jeremiah still speaks of Israel as a young man:

31. The verb "to cleave" also is used in connection with the relationship between Ruth and Naomi, thereby suggesting another dimension of homoeroticism. See chapter 11.

32. There are several points in the depiction where the shift between masculine and feminine designations of Israel/Judah is rather startling. Among the points Holladay identifies are Jer 2:2–3 (ibid., 1:84). At 3:19–21 we seem to have the "wife" treated as if she were a "son" or at least a movement among these ways of describing Israel (ibid., 1:122). A similar juxtaposition occurs in the transition from 3:6–11 to 3:12 (1:117). The point is simply that the transgendering always betrays itself as an activity in which the "true" gender never completely disappears behind the metaphorical "drag."

Is Israel a slave? Is *he* a homeborn servant?
    Why then has *he* become plunder?
The lions have roared against *him*,
    they have roared loudly.
They have made *his* land a waste;
    his cities are in ruins, without inhabitant. (2:14–15, emphasis added)

The repeated and insistent use of the masculine pronoun reminds us that the transgendering going on here is rather a matter of transparent metaphorical drag.

This may be true even at the level of the punishment that is inflicted on or threatened for Judah/Israel. In addition to the threat of divorce, we have the threat of exposure:

It is for the greatness of your iniquity
    that your skirts are lifted up,
    and you are violated. (13:22)

I myself will lift up your skirts over your face,
    and your shame will be seen. (13:26)

On one level we are to think of the exposure of Judah to his enemies, on another of the exposure of the woman to those who would violate her. But there is, I contend, yet another level of supposing that this exposure results in the display of the falsity of the feminine guise in which Judah/Israel has been covered. This "drag" serves not only the purpose of making a marriage between Israel and YHWH intelligible but also the purpose of causing Israel to attract other (male) lovers.[33] "Her" exposure provokes the outrage of those who have been lured by "her" false pretenses.[34] Thus, the prophet warns: "Your lovers despise you; they seek your life" (4:30). But why would her lovers attack her unless the exposure of Israel's pudenda reveals that they have somehow been duped? The identification of her/his lovers as the great powers (Assyria/Egypt) makes this outrage of the

---

33. Don Kulick has done an ethnographic study published as *Travesti: Sex, Gender, and Culture among Brazilian Transgendered Prostitutes* (Chicago: University of Chicago Press, 1998). He makes it wonderfully evident that the main motivation for at least certain forms of transgendering is the desire of a (transgendering) male to lure the attention and desire of another (conventional) male (a recurring theme: 48, 221, 233). Kulick also observes that this is quite different from the first-person accounts of transgendering males in Europe and North America (48).

34. One of the principal dangers for transvestite prostitutes comes from slippage in the guise of femininity, which regularly results in their being battered by their clients. For an in-depth study of the lives of transvestite prostitutes, see Annick Prieur, *Mema's House, Mexico City: On Transvestites, Queens, and Machos* (Chicago: University of Chicago Press, 1998).

lovers all the more clear. The prophet warns: "You shall be put to shame by Egypt as you were put to shame by Assyria" (2:36). Indeed, it is this that really makes the analogy work as a depiction of historical events. That Israel has turned for protection to the great powers is as much her self-prostitution as is her invoking other gods. And it is concretely these great powers that will in turn spurn and violate her/him.

That the exposure of the genitalia of Israel is precisely the exposure of *male* genitalia may also be suggested by the recollection of the shaming of males that figures in the saga material of 2 Samuel. The Ammonites attack David's envoys in the following way:

> So Hanum seized David's envoys, shaved off half the beard of each, cut off their garments in the middle at their hips, and sent them away. When David was told, he sent to meet them, for the men were greatly ashamed. (2 Sam 10:4–5)

What is suggestive here is that the symbolic assault on the masculinity of the men of David not only takes the form of cutting off half the beard (this both makes them look odd and also demasculinizes). It also takes the form of cutting their garments so that their genitals (and buttocks) are exposed.[35] We have no comparable indication that the public exposure of nakedness similarly is a shaming device relative to women. Nor is it at all clear how the public exposure of Israel/Judah's nakedness (in the guise of an insatiably promiscuous prostitute) could otherwise be a source of great shame since in every other way she/he has been advertising "her" availability.

The elimination of the prophet/prostitute relationship means that Jeremiah's use of metaphorical drag to identify the character of Israel/Judah's unfaithfulness in relation to YHWH gains in clarity over the sometimes bewildering complications of Hosea's passionate outburst. Even so, the metaphor remains, perhaps of necessity, somewhat unstable. It is necessarily unstable, not only because Israel/Judah is a transparently masculine name and male corporate identity, but also because, as transparent, it facilitates the sense of shame that the prophet seeks to evoke. Yet this in turn provokes the question of Israel's proper response to the outrage of YHWH. For it is clear that the Lord hopes that the male Israel will be seduced by the one who claims: "I have loved you [the now male Israel] with an everlasting love" (31:3). And if Israel/Judah is thus seduced, will he not turn to cling to the loins of the great male lover of Israel? Nor are we permitted to suppose

---

35. This form of humiliation made headlines recently in the scandalous treatment of Iraqui prisoners by the U.S. military.

that this will not entail a virtual sexual embrace. The prophet himself knows
that YHWH's love is a seductive and indeed a sexual love. He accuses the
Great Lover of seducing and even of ravishing him:

> O LORD, you have enticed me,
>   and I was enticed;
> you have overpowered me,
>   and you have prevailed. (20:7)

The homoerotic character of YHWH's love for Israel or for his prophet
cannot be concealed.[36] Nor can the desire for an answering passion on the
part of the beloved be silenced. But will this not also provoke the desire,
precisely of the devotee of YHWH, to be possessed by another male? That
is, does not the metaphor, precisely on account of its power, serve to
awaken, if not to express, homoerotic passion?

Ezekiel: Jerusalem Is a Size Queen

Perhaps the most systematic use of the metaphor of Israel as transgendered
is that developed by Ezekiel. The result is an almost nightmarishly maniacal
rationalization of the metaphor into a schematic of the history of YHWH
and his people. The oracles of Ezekiel that make use of this metaphor are
found in chapters 16 and 23. To a significant degree the metaphor seems
confined to these chapters rather than being dispersed throughout the text,
as in Hosea or even Jeremiah. This concentration, however, seems to provide the opportunity for even sharper focus on the metaphor and its development. Even so, the metaphor is developed in significantly diverse ways
within this set of oracles, making it notoriously difficult to harmonize them
into a unified vision. For purposes of presentation, I will focus first on
16:1–43, next turn to the allegory of two sisters in chapter 23, and then
return to 16:44–63.

Ravishment, Pornography, and Prostitution

The first set of images seems to elaborate on the previous work of
Hosea and Jeremiah while developing the metaphor in various ways.
Unlike Hosea and Jeremiah, who used references to Israel and Judah

---

36. Kathleen M. O'Connor, in *The Confessions of Jeremiah* (Atlanta: Scholars Press, 1988), 70–71, maintains
that a sexual meaning is not required by the text. But Holladay is more persuasive when he flags the "semantic
field of sexual violence" that pervades the verse and links it to legal depictions of sexual violence as in Exod
22:15 and Deut 22:27 (*Jeremiah*, 1:553).

throughout, Ezekiel focuses attention on the capital city of Jerusalem (and subsequently Samaria). Some scholars have mentioned that it may have been customary to refer to capital cities as female consorts of the local deity.[37] While this observation may be pertinent up to a point for the oracles of Ezekiel, they do not explain the transgendering of Israel and/or Judah in Hosea and Jeremiah. And it is this transgendering of male subjects that lies in the background of Ezekiel's development of the image far more clearly than any alleged supposition that cities are "naturally" female. Thus, although the metaphorical drag is less transparent in Ezekiel (because it is more consistently carried through in these oracles), it still betrays its artificiality.

The oracle with which we begin thus seems to have Jerusalem as its subject. It addresses Jerusalem: "Make known to Jerusalem her abominations" (Ezek 16:2). Jerusalem is said to be from a different father and mother, and hence to be a basically Gentile city (16:3). At its birth it is an abandoned child, "thrown out in the open field" (v. 5), in a metaphor that may suggest to the later reader the custom of exposing unwanted infants in the Roman Empire. As thus exposed to the elements, "she" is seen by YHWH, who somehow gives her strength to live (16:6–7).

Jeremiah pushed the metaphor back to the betrothal of a virgin by YHWH, but Ezekiel pushes this further, making YHWH into a surrogate parent or at least benefactor of this baby at birth. Yet Ezekiel pushes the image of betrothal further in another way as well, into a graphic depiction of sexual possession:

> You grew up and became tall and arrived at full womanhood; your breasts were formed, and your hair had grown; yet you were naked and bare.
>   I passed by you again and looked on you; you were at the age for love. I spread the edge of my cloak over you, and covered your nakedness. (16:7–8)

The reader is presented with a kind of pinup picture of a lovely nubile and naked pubescent female, the sort of picture that one would be jailed for possessing in our own culture ("kiddie porn," it is called if the subject is under eighteen). But things go further than a simple picture of naked nubility. For the spreading of the cloak seems to serve as a euphemism for sexual consummation (see ch. 11). In our society YHWH would be arrested for pedophilia and for statutory rape. Yet in the cases of the boy Samuel and

---

37. Among others, Weems makes much of this (*Battered Love*, 44–45) even though it would seem to apply, if at all, only to references to Jerusalem rather than to Israel/Ephraim/Judah. Even when Jerusalem is in view, as often in Ezekiel, it is not the city alone but the whole people of God, a collective that is otherwise masculine, even for Ezekiel.

(by means of prophetic surrogates) the boys sexually awakened by Elijah and Elisha, we have seen that Adonai's behavior corresponds more to ancient than to modern notions of an "age of consent." Actually, there is here no question of consent in any recognizable sense. But it is here that the notion of covenant is interposed: "I pledged myself to you and entered into a covenant with you, says the LORD God, and you became mine" (16:8; cf. Ruth 3).[38]

Here we read an extended depiction of YHWH's generous bestowal of "favor" on Jerusalem (Ezek 16:9–13), with the result that

> you grew exceedingly beautiful, fit to be a queen. Your fame spread among nations on account of your beauty, for it was perfect because of my splendor that I had bestowed on you, says the Lord GOD. (vv. 13–14)

Here there is no question, as in Hosea, of the source for the fine things with which Ephraim is decked out. Moreover, the prophet elaborates the brief suggestion that YHWH is the origin of her jewelry (and thus of her feminine allure). If transvestism is to be discerned here, it is clear that YHWH is the one who dresses up his beloved. Since YHWH takes credit for Jerusalem's beauty, it clearly is clothes (and jewelry) that make the woman; something many transvestites at least seem to hope is true.

Now we get the familiar image of the beloved of YHWH as a slut. This image is developed in three ways, each more consistent than, but building upon, what has gone before. First, the claim is made that Jerusalem takes the jewelry and other fine things with which YHWH has made her pretty, and fashions them into shrines and images with which "she" plays the whore. Since there seems to be no question at this point of other lovers, what is involved is an elaborate development of the image of sex toys.

> You also took your beautiful jewels of my gold and my silver that I had given you, and made for yourself male images, and with them played the whore. (16:17)

---

38. In other texts of the Hebrew Bible, this type of commitment, coming after the fact of sexual desire and possession, could still be understood as rape. Thus, in the story of the rape of Dinah that occupies the whole of chapter 34 of Genesis, this daughter of Jacob is first desired and raped by Shechem (v. 2). Immediately, however, he seems to fall in love with the girl: "His soul was drawn to Dinah . . . ; he loved the girl, and spoke tenderly to her" (34:3). He pledges to marry her and offers to "put the marriage present and gift as high as you like" (34:12). Neither this nor the acquiescence in the demand to be circumcised mollifies the outraged brothers of Dinah, who launch a genocidal campaign against the males of the city. When Jacob protests that they thereby will incur the hostility of the peoples of the region, the brothers reply: "Should our sister be treated like a whore?" (34:31). The parallel between what Shechem does with respect to Dinah and what YHWH does with respect to Israel is unmistakable.

As in the case of Hosea and Jeremiah, the sex toys strikingly are basically regarded as dildos (male images). It is not clear whether this refers to ephods and teraphim (as in Hosea) or to the ark itself (as in Jeremiah) or in general to everything that passed for the worship of the divine under the name of YHWH. Given what Ezekiel supposes about temple worship in this period (see, e.g., chs. 8–9), it is safe to suppose that what the prophet here recognizes as substitute phalluses is the whole paraphernalia of temple worship.

At this point Ezekiel introduces the image of child sacrifice as a part of the cult of Israel/Judah/Jerusalem (16:20). It would take us too far afield to examine the various texts indicating the significance of this practice in Israelite religious tradition. Nevertheless, it is crucial to Ezekiel's argument that child sacrifice was widely practiced within Israel. Jeremiah is the first to formulate the denial that YHWH has ever really instituted this practice (Jer 7:31), even though he also claims that YHWH instituted no sacrificial practices whatever (7:22). Denying that YHWH ever instituted child sacrifice or maintaining that people must have been mistaken in claiming that YHWH instituted it—either track looks like a case of "protesting too much." Whatever may be the case about this troubling subject, Ezekiel supposes that the practice was as widespread as the making of (phallic) representations of YHWH that become the object of veneration in the cult.

As a result, Ezekiel can claim that YHWH's consort has not only created sex toys to substitute for YHWH but also sacrificed YHWH's children to these images:

> You took your sons and your daughters, whom you had borne to me, and these you sacrificed to them to be devoured. As if your whoring were not enough! You slaughtered my children and delivered them up as an offering to them. (16:20–21)

That both sons and daughters are offered up to be "devoured" by fire reminds us of Jephthah's daughter, who was sacrificed as a result of a pious vow made to YHWH (Judg 11:29–40). That she was to be a "burnt offering" (12:31) makes all too clear what is meant by being "devoured." But Ezekiel, like Jeremiah, denies that YHWH sanctioned child sacrifice, whatever may have been claimed in the past. Thus, Ezekiel uses the charge that Adonai's consort is the murderess of his children to justify Jerusalem's punishment. For here the rights of the "husband" to his progeny have been violently denied by "Jerusalem." Moreover, Ezekiel is able to accuse Jerusalem of a pitiless forgetfulness of the plight of abandoned children:

You did not remember the days of your youth, when you were naked and
bare, flailing about in your blood. (16:22)

The logic seems to be that in the pitiless sacrifice of children, Jerusalem
does not imitate the pity of YHWH, who rescued her when she was a
helpless infant (16:4–7).

Ezekiel has thus filled out the idea of Jerusalem fabricating sex toys
upon which she has lavished her erotic attentions, even to the point of sacrificing children. Next the prophet turns to a second way of developing
the metaphor of promiscuity. Here we no longer have sex toys but other
males. These other males are not gods as we might have expected but the
world powers, the great empires of Egypt (16:26), Assyria (v. 28), and
Chaldea (v. 29). The supposition that Israel's whoring has included liaisons
with other imperial powers is certainly hinted at in Hosea (7:11) and
openly asserted in Jeremiah (2:18, 36), but Ezekiel is the prophet who
deploys this metaphor to greatest effect. In this oracle (ch. 16) it is already
developed more fully than in earlier prophets. In chapter 23 it will receive
its greatest elaboration, and so we will discuss it more fully at that point.
However, it is important to notice that for Ezekiel it is only with the mention of Egypt and Assyria (and Chaldea) that we have references to other
male paramours for God's consort. Ezekiel has been quite clear that previously he was speaking not of other males but of simulacra of the male, that
is, of dildos. Monotheism has developed at least to the point that it is no
longer plausible to suppose that there are other divine males to compete
with YHWH. But this oracle has the somewhat unsettling effect of identifying the superpowers as YHWH's rivals in male prowess. Perhaps it is
because YHWH is still recalled as the warrior familiar to us from the saga
material that the warlike superpowers are now plausibly cast as his competitors for the affections of Israel.

The third extension of the metaphor is to push it beyond the informal
prostitution that seeks material benefits from one's lovers (after all, even husbands like YHWH are measured by their provision of these benefits). Prostitution becomes flagrant promiscuity in which "Jerusalem" not only gives
her favors to her lovers (the superpowers) but also actually seems to pay
them to be her lovers:

You were not like a whore, because you scorned payment. . . . Gifts are
given to all whores; but you gave your gifts to all your lovers, bribing them
to come to you from all around for your whorings. So you were different
from other women in your whorings: no one solicited you to play the

whore; and you gave payment, while no payment was given to you; you were different. (16:31b, 33–34)

Without shifting, as Jeremiah had done, to the image of a camel or wild ass in heat, Ezekiel is thus able to remain within the metaphor and yet invoke the image of flagrant promiscuity, not even dignified by mercenary advantage.

Not only is the sex unmotivated by mercenary need; it is also "public sex." For she builds "a lofty place in every square" and "at the head of every street" (16:24, 25). By emphasizing the publicness of Jerusalem's sexual escapades, Ezekiel can also lay the groundwork for the publicness of Jerusalem's punishment.

The actual punishment has three causes: the idols, the murder of children, and the wanton pursuit of lovers (16:36). These may even be reduced to two: "I will judge you as women who commit adultery and shed blood are judged, and bring blood upon you in wrath and jealousy" (v. 38). Yet it is not YHWH himself who will actually do the punishing but rather Jerusalem's erstwhile lovers, into whose hands she is delivered. And here we again see the odd connection between being exposed naked to one's lovers and their being enraged against their paramour. What is it about the nakedness of Jerusalem that will so enrage "her" lovers? What, moreover, makes it occur to Ezekiel that this should occur "in the sight of many women" (v. 41)? Do we again have the outrage provoked by the recognition that they (the lovers) have been duped? That they wrongly supposed they were dealing with a "real woman"? Is the presence of the "real women" here precisely to shame the male who has been exposed, as Michal supposed that David would be shamed by the women who saw his nakedness as he danced before YHWH (2 Sam 6:20)?

Men in Uniform and Big Studs

In many ways the oracles of Ezek 23 seem to depend on those that we have considered in chapter 16. Here we also have the reference to the offering of child sacrifice (23:37–39) and the use of idols or sex toys (vv. 29, 37), as well as the supposition that YHWH's beloved will be punished for the guilt "of adultery and of bloodshed" (v. 45). In addition, the image of punishment is elaborated far more, even though here too it is the former lovers (great powers) who will do the actual punishment. They "uncovered her nakedness; they seized her sons and daughters; and they killed her with the sword" (v. 10). This chapter clearly gives historical reference to how the Assyrians treated Samaria (722 BCE) and the Babylonians treated Jerusalem

(586).[39] The actual form of punishment, it is carefully specified, will be in accordance with "*their* ordinances" (23:24). This makes it dubious to derive from the punishment of Samaria or Jerusalem anything definite about Israelite law at this time. Even the reference to stoning (23:47; 16:40), which seems compatible with the Levitical instructions, may actually predate by a considerable time the formulation of the laws of Leviticus.

The metaphorical transgendering, however, is developed further in two ways. In the first place, there is a much more elaborate description of the relationship to the great powers or empires as the actual referent of Israel's adultery or promiscuity. And in the second place, the metaphor is doubled in that YHWH now has two female consorts who, moreover, are sisters!

The emphasis on the great powers as YHWH's rivals for the affections of Jerusalem/Samaria is already present in chapter 16:

> You played the whore with the Egyptians. . . . You played the whore with the Assyrians, because your lust was insatiable. . . . You multiplied your whoring with Chaldea, the land of merchants. (vv. 26, 28–29)

But now this image is developed in wonderfully graphic terms. In the first place, we are treated with an odd fixation on men in uniform who represent Assyria. Indeed, what is most remarkable is the almost delirious portrayal of handsome young cavalrymen:

> [Samaria] lusted after her lovers the Assyrians, warriors clothed in blue, governors and commanders, all of them handsome young men, mounted horsemen. (23:5–6)

> [Jerusalem] lusted after the Assyrians, governors and commanders, warriors clothed in full armor, mounted horsemen, all of them handsome young men. (23:12)

> All the Assyrians with them, handsome young men, governors and commanders all of them, officers and warriors, all of them riding on horses. (23:23)

What are we to make of this fixation on the youthful beauty of these proud young men on horseback? Whose fantasy is this anyway? Is it Ezekiel or YHWH who can't get this erotic picture out of his head? Its triple repetition looks like an obsession with the beauty of these stern officers. Indeed,

---

39. Gale Yee, in *Poor Banished Children of Eve* (Minneapolis: Fortress, 2003), ch. 6, esp. 131, provides a useful parallel between Ashurnasirpal's bragging about his devastation of conquered cities and the punishment meted out to Oholibah in Ezek 23:25–27.

given the way it ends, it almost seems like stage directions for a sado-masochistic scene, with the muscular types decked out in the uniforms of authority to administer appropriately alarming discipline.

But these stern and handsome cavalrymen only whet the appetite for more. And now it is Jerusalem whose lust is further spurred on by "dirty pictures":

> She saw male figures carved on the wall, images of the Chaldeans portrayed in vermilion, with belts around their waists, with flowing turbans on their heads, all of them looking like officers—a picture of Babylonians whose native land was Chaldea. (23:14)

Whatever may be the case with other forms of pornography, in this case the pictures are enough to give rise to a real desire, which authors the deed:

> When she saw them she lusted after them, and sent messengers to them in Chaldea. And the Babylonians came to her into the bed of love, and they defiled her with their lust. (23:16–17)

For some reason the Babylonians, earlier said to be mere merchants (16:29), wind up disgusting promiscuous Jerusalem. Perhaps they weren't "butch" enough compared to the dashing young cavalrymen of Assyria. Yet those who disgust Jerusalem will be the primary instruments of her punishment (23:24–26).

We gather a further idea about why the Babylonians may be unsatisfactory lovers when we hear of what draws YHWH's "women" to their first great love affair: the Egyptians. This love affair goes back to their youthful infatuation with Egyptians:

> Their breasts were caressed there, and their virgin bosoms were fondled. . . . She did not give up her whorings that she had practiced since Egypt; for in her youth men had lain with her and fondled her virgin bosom and poured out their lust upon her. (23:3, 8)

It is unclear how we are to "locate" this original affair with Egypt. In chapter 16, constructed far more tightly as a story about Jerusalem, the most likely candidate, I believe, is the marriage of Solomon and Pharaoh's daughter that resulted (as did Solomon's other marriages) in the importation of "foreign" cult objects and practices (1 Kgs 11:1–9). This also has the irony of entailing a double transgendering. For Egypt was then represented by a woman (Pharaoh's daughter) and Israel by a male (Solomon, son of David). Thus, it is really Solomon's breasts that are being fondled by the Egyptian princess!

However, the recollection of Egypt produces even more startling images:

> She increased her whorings, remembering the days of her youth, when she played the whore in the land of Egypt and lusted after her paramours there, whose members were like those of donkeys, and whose emission was like that of stallions. (23:19–20)

One of the great innovations of modern porn movies and videos was the invention of the so-called "money shot," in which the viewer was allowed to witness the external ejaculation of the male upon the body of his (usually female) counterpart. In this way the viewer received visual proof of "real sex."[40] But it seems that Ezekiel (the most visually oriented of the prophets) may have been the real inventor of the money shot, for he invites the reader to visualize stallionlike spurts of semen. (This may also be behind the allusion to Egyptian lovers who "poured out their lust upon her," in verse 8.)

What is especially in view here is the astonishing size of the male member (big as a donkey dick)[41] and profligacy of the seminal emission (comes like a horse). Perhaps it is this that makes the Babylonians seem inadequate (Ezekiel thus gets in a dig at his current tormentors); but it may also be what keeps her looking for love anywhere but in the arms of the one who first had sex with her in the wilderness (Ezek 16:7–8). For it may well be, in terms of the visible expressions of power, that YHWH can't measure up to the astonishing Egyptians or the dashing Assyrians.

Once again, we ask ourselves, Just whose fantasies are being invoked here? Who is astonished at the sheer size of Egyptian penises, or the awesome fountains of sperm they ejaculate upon Jerusalem? Who is taking at least vicarious delight in the breast-fondling and caresses of this aggressive lover? Is it YHWH, whose words are simply repeated by Ezekiel? Is it the prophet, who in trancelike state allows images of subconscious homoerotic desire to burst forth? But the words are directed to Israelite males, elite males, one supposes. Is it their wondering and admiring gaze that is being solicited here? For even

---

40. See, e.g., Linda Evans, *Hard Core: Power, Pleasure, and the "Frenzy of the Visible"* (Berkeley: University of California Press, 1989).

41. Gale Yee (*Banished Children*, 128) observes that "the preoccupation with the size of Egyptian genitalia may allude to the ithyphallic Egyptian god Min-Amun, who is often portrayed with an erect penis." For the fascination with large penises as an important part of travesti subculture, see Kulick, *Travesti*, 149: "The attraction of a large penis is something travestis talk about continually."

if the drag in which Jerusalem/Samaria is draped remains largely in place, there can be no question about whose identification with "her" lustful desire is being solicited, who is expected to be obsessed with handsome cavalry officers and hugely endowed Egyptians. It is the male readers of Ezekiel. For this is a fantasy by men, for men, about men.

Weird Sisters

In Hosea's version Ephraim/Israel and Judah seem to be male siblings (4:15; 6:4; 11:12). It is Jeremiah who first supposes that they may be represented as sisters (3:6–11), although this is done in a rather cursory fashion.[42] The difficulty with casting the two kingdoms (and their capitals) as sisters, in spite of the advantages gained for representing parallel elements of their history, is that the Levitical law code prohibits the taking of sisters as wives as a kind of incest (Lev 18:18). It is, of course, not certain when that law code, as we know it, came into existence. Certainly, the story of Jacob's marriage to Leah and Rachel in Gen 29–30 could not have been recorded in a time when the prohibition was in effect. And the same may well be true of the analogy of the sisters developed in Jeremiah and Ezekiel (although the latter is generally supposed to have more in common with the priestly ideology that stands behind the codes of Leviticus). In any case, this is yet another indication that the attitudes toward sexuality (as well as other matters) represented in narrative or even prophetic texts cannot be reconciled with several positions inscribed in the legal codes of Israel.

It is all the more striking, then, that Ezekiel is even less inhibited than Jeremiah in adopting this image in order to integrate a more complete allegory of the history of the two kingdoms as the sad history of two sisters. Thus, in chapter 23 Ezekiel sets up a parallel between the history of Oholah (Samaria) and Oholibah (Jerusalem), who become YHWH's wives and who bear him sons and daughters (23:4). The basic aim of this extension of the metaphor is to suggest that Jerusalem not only does not learn from the fate of Samaria but actually goes even further in her whoredom.

Chapter 23 seems to end with the pronouncement of doom. But the oracles at the end of chapter 16 open up something more, the prospect of eventual reconciliation. Already in 16:42–43 there is the sense that at last the fury of the Great Lover will be spent:

> So I will satisfy my fury on you, and my jealousy shall turn away from you;
> I will be calm, and will be angry no longer. (16:42)

---

42. We have also pointed out that this may be an insertion into Jeremiah, dependent on Ezekiel.

While this image contents itself with depicting the calming of YHWH's savage fury and testosteronic rage, the subsequent oracle goes further in suggesting actual restoration, but not before taking the image of the sisters in new and surprising directions. For now we have not only Samaria and Jerusalem but also Sodom—three sisters who are the consorts of YHWH. The function of this extension is to suggest that Samaria and especially Jerusalem are even worse than Sodom in their faithlessness. In this accounting, the sin of Sodom has nothing to do with "homosexual practices." It will be several centuries before that bromide is invented. Ezekiel has a rather sober assessment of that sin:

> This was the guilt of your sister Sodom: she and her daughters had pride, excess of food, and prosperous ease, but did not aid the poor and needy. They were haughty, and did abominable things before me; therefore I removed them when I saw it. (16:49–50)

Only with the phrase "did abominable things before me" do we find a parallel to the forms of unfaithfulness with which Samaria and Jerusalem have been charged. As we have seen, these include sex toys (representations of YHWH), adultery (alliances with the great powers), and the sacrifice of children.

The destruction of Sodom had become a byword. But Ezekiel maintains that because of the greatness of Jerusalem's sins, Sodom and Samaria look rather good by comparison: "For you have made your sisters appear righteous" (16:52). As a result Ezekiel proclaims the restoration not merely of Jerusalem but, out of fairness, also of Samaria and Sodom (16:53). This will also have the result of shaming Jerusalem's haughtiness. She will not be the only one to be restored and will have to "share" with Sodom and Samaria the favor of YHWH. Samaria and Sodom will be her "daughters" (16:61). Still, the import seems to be that they will always be there, like concubines, to serve as potential rivals to Jerusalem in order to keep her humble.

The recollection of Sodom may also serve another purpose in this allegory; it puts the reader in mind of another element in that saga, the story of Lot and his daughters. For it was after the destruction of the cities of the plain (Sodom and her daughters, in Ezekiel's image) that Lot was "seduced" by his own daughters, who through him thereby gained progeny who became the people of the Moabites and the Ammonites (Gen 19:30–38). This rather egregious case of incest results in the supposition of the uncleanness of the Moabites, with whom Israel will be forbidden to have dealings.[43] The connection is not just allusive here since Ezekiel has supposed that the three sisters are daughters of one mother "who loathed her husband and her children" (16:45). This sets up the suggestion that YHWH is also the "husband" of the "mother" of the three sisters. Here it makes little difference whether this original relationship is with the Hebrew people who eventually founded Samaria and Jerusalem as capitals, or whether we are to harmonize this with the suggestion that "your father was an Amorite, and your mother a Hittite" (16:3).[44] In any case, it seems that here we are to suppose that YHWH is the father of his wives who are therefore sisters. This has been lurking in the metaphor all along since the transgendering often includes the subtext of reference to YHWH's not only as "son" but also as "daughter" (e.g., Jer 4:31).

Ezekiel's oracles do not shrink from the attribution of a kind of incest to YHWH, whether in the taking of sisters or of sister/daughters as "wives." This should at least make clear that no reference to presumed legal codes of Israel can be used to preclude the homoerotic and transgendering elements of these oracles that I have been suggesting. The point is that the prophets do not shrink from the attribution of almost any kind of eroticism to the relation between YHWH and his people. Since the relationship is one between subjects that are typically cast as male, the eroticism involved is essentially homoerotic in character. Even where YHWH's beloved is dressed as female, the result is not so much the depiction of a conventional heterosexual relationship but one between a male and his transvestite beloved.[45]

Deutero-Isaiah: Lover, Come Back

The last extensive use of the metaphorical transgendering of YHWH's male beloved is found in the oracles of Deutero-Isaiah. The identity of YHWH's beloved seems to vary considerably in the oracles so that scholars often debate about the specific referent of YHWH's counterpart (for example, when is his servant the people of Israel as a whole, or Cyrus, or a prophet, or a remnant?). Yet the ability of Isaiah to play with gender remains one of the most intriguing features of his poetry. That YHWH's beloved is

---

43. This sets up problems that the book of Ruth (the Moabitess) will exploit and which will result in the reductio ad absurdum of David and his house being declared unclean or cursed. See the discussion in chapter 11.

44. My own view is that harmonization is not to be undertaken here because the material of Ezek 16:44–63 seems to be an independent revision and extension of the metaphor in the earlier part of the chapter.

45. In Kulick's ethnographic study, *Travesti*, the relationships between travestis and their "boyfriends" mimic some conventions of heterosexual relationships while subverting others. Neither member of the couple supposes that the travesti really is a woman. Accordingly, the relationship is always different from a more conventional heterosexual "marriage."

male is clearly recalled in some of the oracles. Thus, for example, we hear the invocation of "Israel, my servant, Jacob, whom I have chosen, the off-spring of Abraham, my friend" (Isa 41:8). In an oracle that may refer to Israel (or possibly Cyrus), we hear:

> Here is my servant, whom I uphold,
>> my chosen, in whom my soul delights. (42:1)

Another oracle that again may refer either to Israel or to Cyrus announces:

> The LORD loves him. (48:14)

This rather conventional gendering of YHWH's counterpart, however, does not seem to be eroticized.

One of the most remarkable features of Isaiah's transgendering comes in the application of the notion of sister/daughters not to Israel or Jerusalem but to Babylon/Chaldea. Here if anywhere we find something that seems a bit like Ezekiel's reference to sisters:

> Come down and sit in the dust,
>> virgin daughter Babylon! . . .
> Your nakedness shall be uncovered,
>> and your shame shall be seen.
> I will take vengeance. . . .
> Sit in silence, and go into darkness,
>> daughter Chaldea!
> For you shall no more be called
>> the mistress of kingdoms. (47:1, 3, 5)

The transgendering of the empire(s) again is remarkable since it uses terms of judgment familiar to us from Jeremiah and Ezekiel. Yet there seems to be no suggestion of an erotic connection even if the punishment of nakedness and shame would recall to the reader the more erotically charged use of this metaphor in Jeremiah or Ezekiel.

Babylon/Chaldea is not the only daughter referred to here; Jerusalem also is not only gendered as female but also called "daughter":

> Loose the bonds from your neck,
>> O captive daughter Zion! (52:2)

Indeed, references to Zion seem to be rather consistently female (51:3, 18).

The development of the metaphorical transgendering of the people of God seems to take as a starting point the suggestion of Jeremiah relative to Samaria, that YHWH had divorced her on account of her promiscuity. However, Isaiah seems to deny that any actual or legal divorce has really taken place:

> Thus says the LORD:
> Where is your mother's bill of divorce
>   with which I put her away? (50:1)

In a subsequent oracle YHWH even seems to regret the separation from his people as a kind of youthful rashness on his part:

> For the LORD has called you
>   like a wife forsaken and grieved in spirit,
> like the wife of a man's youth when she is cast off,
>   says your God.
> For a brief moment I abandoned you,
>   but with great compassion I will gather you. (54:6–7)

The tone of divine repentance contrasts markedly with the tone that has typically characterized the transgendering of Israel. But what remains consistent is the sense that the bond between YHWH and his beloved is one of conjugal intimacy.

The transgendering that we have been noticing has blurred the typically masculine identity of YHWH's beloved. But when gender binarisms are blurred, additional possibilities open up. One of the most remarkable features of the transgendering that occurs in these oracles is that YHWH also may be transgendered.[46] In one especially striking juxtaposition of images, we hear that YHWH "goes forth like a soldier, like a warrior he stirs up his fury" (42:13). In the next verse we hear: "Now I will cry out like a woman in labor, I will gasp and pant" (42:14). In another oracle God claims:

> Can a woman forget her nursing child,
>   or show no compassion for the child of her womb?
> Even these may forget,
>   yet I will not forget you. (49:15)

---

46. Kulick remarks on the way the relationship to a travesti results in quite surprising ways in the "feminizing" of the macho boyfriend of the travesti (ibid., 131).

Thus, YHWH himself, so regularly portrayed as fierce warrior or more recently in the oracles we have been discussing as aggrieved husband, comes toward the end of this process to be susceptible to a similar kind of transgendering.

The transgendering of the divine that we discover here and that has been discerned elsewhere in the Hebrew Bible does not seem to take on the erotic tone that so often characterizes the transgendering of Israel. It is typically maternal rather than amorous. Of course, it is probably mistaken to wholly separate the relation of mother-child from that of lover-beloved as though it were possible to invent another binary opposition (now between relationships erotic and nonerotic, or even sexual and nonsexual). This could not make up for blurring a gender binarism and so keep everything "straight" and prevent confusion. For this would simply be to reinscribe (or replace) the binarisms that these texts have unsettled and perhaps even deconstructed.

Reflections

In what follows I want to indicate some of the possible consequences and questions that arise from attempting to take seriously the act of transgendering that appears to be at work in the prophetic imagination as we have traced it in this chapter. As we shall see, this will open up further avenues for exploration.

The Transgendered Imagination

What does it mean for males to imagine themselves as part of a female collectivity in relation to a male divinity and to imagine that relationship as profoundly erotic? In order to pose this question, I turn to a rather peculiar image in the oracles of Jeremiah.

The image in question occurs within the context of a remarkable series of images of restoration that anticipate the return and renewal of God's people represented as Jacob, Israel, Ephraim, and Judah. Jeremiah 31 turns from depictions of destruction and judgment to evocations of "homecoming." All but two of these oracles depict YHWH's beloved as a male. In the first oracle the gendering of Israel changes in midimage. Jeremiah proclaims: "When Israel sought for rest, the LORD appeared to him from far away" (31:2–3). Then the prophet speaks in the name of YHWH: "I have loved you with an everlasting love" (v. 3). Abruptly, however, we hear:

> Again I will build you, and you will be built,
>> O virgin Israel!
> Again you shall take your tambourines,
>> and go forth in the dance of the merrymakers. (31:4)

The love of God for his male beloved seems to slide into the image of Israel as a maiden leading a festive dance. Here the transgendering is occasioned not by the perspective of desolation nor of unfaithfulness but of glad merrymaking.

After images that identify YHWH's beloved as Jacob/Israel/Ephraim (31:7–14), we seem to have an image of the collectivity of God's people as "Rachel," who weeps for her children but is not to be comforted (vv. 15–17). In this case we have what appears to be not a transgendering of Israel but a gendering of the people of God as female, under the name of Rachel. For the first and only time in the materials we have been considering do we have the image of the people of God not as an ersatz female but as an actual one.

Next we switch to oracles that return to the image of Ephraim, this time as YHWH's "dear son" (31:18–20). At this point we get one of Jeremiah's most provocative and obscure images in the context of the regendering of YHWH's beloved as virgin (v. 21) and daughter (v. 22):

> For the LORD has created a new thing on the earth;
>> a woman encompasses a man. (31:22)

The images then change to speak of Judah as well and to the vision of a new covenant.

Many of these images have come to have a significant place in the theology and piety of the peoples of this book. But the image of a woman "encompassing" a man has remained obscure as an image of the new thing that YHWH is undertaking. I do not intend to solve the knotty exegetical issues that arise here.[47] But I do want to suggest that this image is a fitting depiction of the metaphorical transgendering that we have been considering.

---

47. Holladay persuasively argues that the text must refer to the sexual role of the female that is, in some way, transcending what is normally understood to be the role of the female. He maintains that "the female undertakes the male role" (*Jeremiah*, 2:193) and suggests that the significance is that "the female shall be the initiator in sexual relations" (2:195). Holladay concludes: "The reassignment of sexual roles is innovative past all conventional belief" (2:195). My reading differs from his: I am suggesting moving beyond the binarism male/female, as this is constructed from the side of the male, and thus taking more seriously the sense of surround or encompass, which he also observes in the image. I believe my reading is substantiated by the puzzles that he identifies in the passage.

For whatever else is going on here, a typically male subject has been enclosed within the depiction of a female subject.

On one level this is a description of the transgendering process. On quite another it is the breaking through of a suppressed recognition. For the male begins as enclosed within a woman's womb. And the sex act between a male and a female may be understood as penetration (by the male), but may as well be represented as being encompassed by the woman. Of course, this would not be a new thing, but it would be something that is denied or repressed by masculine imagination and would in that sense be something "unheard of."

Now what would it mean that a male (whether deity or prophet) speaks in this way? Would it mean that the male identifies here in a remarkable way with the sexual activity that is stereotypically female, the act of encompassing, not as a passive "being penetrated," but as an active taking in and enclosing and incorporating? In this way the male who has been "transgendered" now takes on the active sexual role of the female, while the male subject (YHWH here) renounces the male view of sexuality to become the encompassed, the enclosed rather than the penetrating invader of the "female" body.[48] Now I do not suppose that the miracle of a male actually being a female has occurred here. The speakers remain male. But a certain act of sympathetic imagination does seem to be at work, which seeks to take seriously the perspective of a feminine sexuality. Now in what way does it become possible for a male to imagine such a feminine sexuality as actively encompassing rather than as passively being penetrated?

There is one way in which this point of view is potentially engendered in the text itself. It has to do with Jeremiah's imagining himself as one who has been seduced by YHWH. In that image it seems that Jeremiah speaks of this quasi-sexual encounter as one of being penetrated, the "female" role in a masculinely conceived sexual encounter, or put another way, as the bottom in a male-male sexual encounter. But is this what the subjectivity of a "bottom" perceives if that bottom becomes the subject of desire rather than its object? Or is the subjective desire of the bottom not instead a desire to encompass the male? The point is that the desire of the "bottom" is not simply the desire to be "possessed" or "penetrated" (to be the object of a male sexual subjectivity). It is also the desire to encompass, to actively take in or incorporate the phallus (to be the subject of a different sexuality, a sexuality figured as feminine). It is precisely as one who has been sexually seduced by

---

48. All of this is quite tentative, but in a certain way it is suggested by Luce Irigaray's reflections on what it might mean to think from the perspective of a woman; see esp. her book *An Ethics of Sexual Difference* (trans. C. Burke and G. C. Gill; Ithaca, NY: Cornell University Press, 1993).

the male that Jeremiah suggests something quite new: the subjectivity of the "bottom" as the subject of a female-like sexual activity.

Once again, I do not suppose that this is the "same thing" as female sexuality.[49] However sympathetically imagined, it is still imagined from a male perspective, but a male perspective that has adopted a new subject position, the position that desires the male not on the "top's" terms but on the terms of the "bottom."

This may seem to have taken us rather far from the texts into a form of gender speculation. But it is germane in two ways—first, because what I have been suggesting throughout is that the relation to YHWH as male lover incites erotic desire for the (sexual) consummation of that relationship. We have already seen how this entails making the figure of David into that of a kind of "ideal bottom" for YHWH who is imaged as top or *erastēs* (lover). What I am now suggesting is that the exploration of models of transgendering in the Prophets permits a sympathetic identification with a "feminine" sexuality. Such sexuality is, at heart, the interiority of sexual desire from the subject position (rather than object position) of the bottom—or of the one who desires to draw in and encompass the maleness of the other.[50]

The thoughtful reader will have noticed the unsatisfactoriness of the various ways of trying to account for this "new thing." The language for thinking about sexual or erotic relations is always already constructed in a masculinist way. Hence, we find the oppositions of male and female, masculine and feminine, top and bottom, all of which are rendered deeply problematic by the very theme we are exploring here.

Social Context

In the discussion of David and his lovers, we were able to point to what appeared as a supportive cultural context for the development of homoerotic relations. We observed that the pairing of a hero and his younger male companion serves as a background within which the foregrounded relationships seemed to make a certain amount of sense. The homoeroticism of the relationships between David and his lovers (including YHWH) was embedded within a cultural context in which homoeroticism seemed to be at least an available option for the males of Israel. This in turn seemed to depend upon a warrior culture, which did not compare male-male relations

49. There is good reason to be suspicious of the attempt of the male to render the perspective and voice of the female superfluous by simply appropriating the place of the female. I am suggesting not substitution by which the place/voice of the female becomes superfluous, but sympathetic imagination by which the possibility of a certain solidarity may be broached.

50. This will help to clarify why it is that in the proscriptions of Leviticus what is particularly in view is precisely the subject position we are exploring, the desire of the male to have sex with a male in a womanly way.

with male-female relations. These, we supposed, could operate in separate spheres, so that there seemed to be no question of feminizing the male beloved of a male lover.

However, in the texts we have now been considering, it seems that the homoeroticism of the relation to YHWH does require a certain transgendering in order to become fully intelligible. At the beginning of these reflections, I suggested that this may have to do with the disappearance of the all-male groups (whether of warriors or shamans) that served as a supportive social context for the imagination and perhaps enacting of homoerotic relationships. The greater saliency of domestic and agrarian social structures entails that erotic relations will inevitably come to be understood in terms available from those contexts and thus "heterosexualized." Does this mean that the practice of a transgendering homoeroticism is confined to the religious imagination? Or is there to be discerned here a supportive social context of "secular" homoeroticism, perhaps also inclusive of gender malleability or even transgendering?

Insofar as I can see, the answer, if it is to be sought in the prophetic oracles themselves, must first be one of historical agnosticism. The prophets are not concerned to proscribe same-sex eroticism or transgendering. How could they, since they so deliberately deploy images that depend on some, at least minimal, acceptance of these possibilities? On the other hand, they give us no direct evidence of the homoerotic practices of their contemporaries. They are fixated on the relation between YHWH and his people and take umbrage at what they take to be deviations from loyalty to YHWH that violate justice or a total devotion to YHWH. If same-sex relations are not the primary sites of injustice or of cultic deviation, there would be no particular reason for the prophets to take notice of them.

Instead, what they do is focus on what are imagined as fascinations with men in uniform, large penises, and dildos as if they were the preoccupation of a certain female subject, but a subject who is, in reality, a male subject in drag. Here there may be three possibilities: (1) The supportive social context is one in which men know or believe women to be plausibly fascinated with sex toys, big dicks, and men in uniform. (2) Or men know that they, or at least a significant number of other men, are similarly fascinated. (3) Or these images are conjured out of "thin air." The third option seems to me to be simply implausible. The first would mean that the transgendering remains opaque, an impenetrable disguise (such as saying, "That's just the way women are. Men don't do that, but the prophet is only talking about women anyway, so that's okay, plausible"). There are two difficulties with this view: (1) It must "forget" that the transgendering is occurring without seeing its instability, an instability we have seen to be inscribed in the very texts that perform the operation. (2) It supposes that the social contexts that had fostered a kind of homoeroticism in earlier epochs have now disappeared without a trace, that homoeroticism has suddenly and inexplicably vanished from the social fabric of Israel.

I incline to the middle position, that homoeroticism has not vanished at all but has rather undergone certain transformations similar to the transformations that have taken place in the representation of the relation of Israel to YHWH. Therefore, these images reflect a continuing lively same-sex eroticism within the culture itself. I do not (yet) allege direct evidence for this, save that of a certain cultural plausibility. But in the absence of more direct evidence, it does seem to me to be the most likely view. In the next chapter we will see at least one narrative that does seem to suggest transgendering as a live option apart from the effects of the relationship with YHWH.

In any case, the elaboration of these images does seem to me to be likely not merely to reflect homoerotic practices within the culture, but also and more importantly to incite both the feelings and the practices that express homoerotic relationships. For those who are invited to imagine themselves in the position of Israel, whether as promiscuous slut or as desiring wife, are precisely males. To the extent that these vividly articulated images actually do their work of inciting identification and engagement, they also will give form and impetus to the homoerotic feelings they express and the practices they suggest.

But this means as well that there is no way in which these feelings or practices can be hermetically sealed away into some separated "religious" or cultic sphere any more than we would expect heteroerotic representations to be thus isolated from intrahuman feelings and practices. To put the matter differently, relations between the deity and the devotee mirror and solicit interhuman loyalty among friends and lovers. Also, betrayal of relations among persons reflects betrayal of covenant between God and human beings, according to these prophets. Likewise, the evocation of strong erotic attachment between deity and devotee may be conjectured to awaken at the same time erotic feelings (and concomitant practices) among those who are affected by these images. Whether or not God really is a sexual being (as these narratives suggest), human beings are; and the evocation of homoerotic passion may be expected to create as well as reflect homoerotic potentialities among those who are addressed and incited by these images.

The Becoming of the Divine

The images articulated in these passages may both reflect and provoke corresponding feelings and behaviors. This is at the heart of feminist protests lodged against some potential effects of these images. We might forget that the "female" subject of these portrayals is "really" a male and focus on the rage of the wounded male attributed to the divine spouse. If so, then readers who identify with the female object of this rage may be particularly struck by the psychological and even physical violence that this metaphor seems to express. They observe the relentless characterization of a certain female sexuality as nymphomaniacal promiscuity, the accusation of flagrant violations of every form of decency, coupled with the evident desire to restrain, cage, expose, and see violated the object of this scorn. These cannot but evoke comparison with the abusive behavior of many men toward many women as well as the ways in which this inexcusable violence is not only excused but also legitimated.

We may notice that what is involved here is a relationship between subjects of the "same" gender, one of whom has been "transgendered." But that does not go far toward mitigating the force of feminist protest against the effect of these images, either on those who have been battered or on those who do the battering. For, unfortunately, spousal abuse is not confined to the "straight" world, nor is its extent limited to the gay male world.

On the other hand, we do not have to wait for the development of this metaphor to discover that the divine is imagined in violent and indeed abusive ways in the material at which we have been looking. To recall only tales from Samuel, we have encountered a deity who seems not above the anal rape of his human enemies and divine rivals in the story of the ark's sojourn among the Philistines. We have seen the testosteronic storm that leaves Saul naked and stunned on the hillside of Ramah, and the bursting forth of YHWH when Uzzah reaches out to steady the ark. Nor does this aspect of the divine wholly disappear in later representation, as we have seen in Jeremiah's protest against having been seduced by YHWH.

However, we also noticed that, in the course of the saga of David, the character of YHWH as Lover seems to undergo incremental transformation. David's steadfast love for his lovers, including his steadfastness in devotion (if not obedience) to YHWH, has a noticeable effect upon the character of YHWH. Thus, YHWH is tamed by David's love, enters into covenant betrothal, and steadfastly stands by Israel for the sake of his love for David, even long after David himself has died.

That transformation of YHWH has not been reversed in the adoption of this metaphor of the transgendering of Israel. To be sure, the history this metaphor is burdened to represent is itself astonishingly violent. Ephraim was violently assaulted by Assyria, Judah by Babylon. And the practices of those great powers toward those they conquered were horrifying in their brutality (something not unknown in the contemporary world, as CNN daily reminds us). But even when the fate of Israel and Judah is well known, the prophets seek to immunize the deity from direct implication in the violence. At most, YHWH has permitted Israel's lovers to do with her/him as they will, according to *their* customs and statutes. The old warrior-god had his policy of scorched earth and renounced Saul because the latter seemed too "merciful" to his enemies. This same god is later imagined to have repented even of passive complicity in Israel's woes (e.g. Isa 54:7; Jer 31:19) and to swear that never again will he turn a blind eye to his beloved's misfortunes, even those one supposes that Israel may bring upon himself.

What I am suggesting is that through the exploration of this metaphorical transgendering, in a way similar to the exploration of the homoerotic relation between YHWH and David, Israel comes to know a much different deity than the one it first imagined in such ferociously macho terms. To be sure, this reimagining of the divine does not occur ex nihilo. It occurs through time, through history, through long and painful experience and reflection. But it does reach out toward the imagining of God as one of steadfast love and limitless compassion. And the transgendering of Israel plays an important role in this history. Indeed, one of the things this process makes possible, in spite of the misogyny it may also reflect, is precisely the males' sympathetic imagination for the position of the female beloved, as which they are invited to imagine themselves. It is precisely this kind of sympathetic imagination that makes it possible for male or female readers, on behalf of the female, to protest the abusiveness of the male. One of the "effects" of the transgendering imagination is precisely that it may create space for a feminist reading.

The Future of Gender Transformations

At the developmental end of the metaphor of a transgendered Israel, as this reaches a kind of conclusion in Second Isaiah, we recognized that the gender instability produced by this process finally reaches out to include the destabilizing of God's gender as well. Already with Hosea we encounter a barely disguised transgendering of the deity in the image of a mother bear protecting her cubs (13:8). But the tenderness of maternal love evoked by Deutero-Isaiah certainly makes this more explicit. Hence, it is no accident that the prophets are among those to whom contemporary feminists turn for images of the divine that break open the monopoly of androcentric imaginings of the divine.[51]

---

51. See Virginia Ramey Mollenkott, *The Divine Feminine: The Biblical Imagery of God as Feminine* (New York: Crossroad, 1983); Phyllis Trible, *God and the Rhetoric of Sexuality* (Philadelphia: Fortress, 1978).

To be sure, developments in this direction seem to be limited. In large part this limitation comes through the distanciation of the divine from the human so that the gender and "sexuality" of the deity become of less apparent significance. As the divine threatens to recede from view in transcendence, the protest against this disappearance seems to be carried, at least in Judaism, by the vividly imagined figures of Lady Wisdom or of the Shekinah of YHWH. Similarly, the comfort of Mary may compensate for an overly distant divinity in Christianity. Thus, the feminization of the divine continues, but under other names.

But if the divine is in a certain way "feminized," so too is the devotee. I do not mean here the odd image of the church as female. But I do have in mind the development of alternative styles of masculinity that may appear (in a gender-dichotomized world) as feminine. Daniel Boyarin has suggested that adherence to the God of the Hebrew Scriptures may in any case entail a quite different way of being male that partakes in important ways in what is otherwise described as feminine.[52] He even suggests a corresponding transformation in the imagining of what is appropriately "female."

This is not the place to explore these themes. The point rather is that the act of transgendering Israel in the materials we have read has set in motion processes of reimagining the divine and the human that we are still striving to articulate.

We may even glimpse here a possibility not explored by the men who wrote/edited these documents. If Israel may be imagined as female, the destabilization of gender may reach out to imagine the divine as female. And the relation between deity and devotee may be imagined as erotic. If truly so, then it seems by no means impossible to understand the relation between the divine and the human homoerotically, in terms of a relation between female and female, on the model of a lesbian relationship.

This is a step not taken, as far as I can see, in the texts that together make up the Hebrew Bible. One of the things that would be necessary to make this step plausible would be the sympathetic description of the love of two women for one another. This would match the development of the "love story" involving David and Saul, or David and Jonathan, which gives concreteness to the love story of David and YHWH. In chapter 11 I will argue that this element, at least, is not missing from the Prime Testament.

---

52. Daniel Boyarin, *Unheroic Conduct: The Rise of Heterosexuality and the Invention of the Jewish Man* (Berkeley: University of California Press, 1997).

9. Joseph as Sissy Boy

IN READING THE PROPHETS we have encountered the transgendering of Israel. In this chapter we ask whether there is in the narrative material of Israel anything that corresponds to the metaphorical transgendering that we encounter in Hosea, Jeremiah, Ezekiel, and even (Deutero-)Isaiah. The narrative material at which we had previously looked seemed to eschew any transgendering. The males who are either lovers of males or beloved of males seem nonetheless to be rendered as otherwise more or less "conventionally" masculine. This is true both for the warrior sub-culture that seems to be presupposed in the David saga and for the quasi-shamanistic subculture that appears under the surface of the tales of the *bene-hanebi'im*, of Elijah/Elisha, and of Saul/Samuel.

There is, however, at least one narrative that lends itself to a reading from the standpoint of transgendering, that of Joseph, which occupies almost all of Gen 37–50 (with anticipatory material: 30:22–25; 33:2, 7; 35:24). It is therefore comparable in length to the saga material concerning Abraham. It has not, however, attracted anything like comparable interest from theologians and religious commentators generally. This owes in part to the way in which YHWH recedes from the narrative, seeming to leave the reader with a long narrative of little more than "secular" interest. But it may be more than the relative absence of the divine character from the plot that has served to marginalize the narrative. The way in which the story troubles gender roles may also help to account for this marginalization.[1]

The Robe

Insofar as the tale of Joseph plays any role in the religious imagination, it seems to have to do with Joseph's "coat of many colors" (Gen 37:3 KJV), and in some obscure relation to this, Joseph's troubled relationship with his brothers.

But what is this garment with which Joseph is "vested"? In the early part of the tale, it has a strangely prominent role. It is introduced as the token of the special favor with which Jacob, his father, regards Joseph, and it becomes the sign of Joseph's alleged death (37:31–33).

Before looking at the relevant texts, however, it is important to ask about the garment as such. For centuries the description of the garment was translated as the "coat of many colors." More recent scholarship has corrected this to a more accurate "long robe with sleeves." Thus, the "technicolor dreamcoat"—the object of lavish description in Thomas Mann's extraordinary novelistic expansion of the story[2] and of the Broadway play that owes something to that retelling—has disappeared in favor of a "long robe with sleeves." With that in mind, we may now indicate the texts with which we must initially concern ourselves.

> Now Israel loved Joseph more than any other of his children, because he was the son of his old age; and he had made him a long robe with sleeves. But when his brothers saw that their father loved him more than all his brothers, they hated him, and could not speak peaceably to him. (37:3–4)

The story goes on to tell the story of Joseph's dreams, which have as their apparent content a foretelling of Joseph's ascendancy over his brothers and therefore provide additional motivation for his brothers' hatred. Yet we seem to have here already adequate motive for what will follow. Accordingly, some scholars suggest that the whole dream narrative is basically irrelevant to the unfolding of the plot.[3] I follow that suggestion in my own rereading of the text and move to the next appearance of the robe. Joseph has been sent to spy on his brothers, who are out doing the work of sons

---

1. The term "sissy boy" that appears in the title of this chapter refers to the study by Richard Green called *The "Sissy-Boy Syndrome" and the Development of Homosexuality* (New Haven:Yale University Press, 1984).

2. Thomas Mann, *Joseph and His Brethren* (trans. H.T. Lowe-Porter; 4 vols.; London: M. Secker, 1934–45).

3. Claus Westermann observes:"What is narrated here [vv. 12–17] could follow directly on vv. 3–4; nothing would be lost from the progress of the narrative." See *Genesis 37–50: A Commentary* (trans. J.J. Scullion; Minneapolis: Augsburg, 1986), 39.

by shepherding Jacob/Israel's flocks. From some distance the brothers see Joseph coming—perhaps the robe is a giveaway—and plot to kill him. The eldest son, Reuben, however, suggests that they not shed blood.

> So when Joseph came to his brothers, they stripped him of his robe, the long robe with sleeves that he wore; and they took him and threw him into a pit. (37:23–24a)

In the absence of Reuben, the brothers decide to sell the stripped Joseph to some Midianite slave traders. But now the absence of Joseph or his body must somehow be explained:

> Then they took Joseph's robe, slaughtered a goat, and dipped the robe in the blood. They had the long robe with sleeves taken to their father, and they said, "This we have found; see now whether it is your son's robe or not." He recognized it, and said, "It is my son's robe! A wild animal has devoured him; Joseph is without doubt torn to pieces." Then Jacob tore his garments, and put sackcloth on his loins, and mourned for his son many days. (37:31–34)

Three times we are told that the robe is "long" and "with sleeves." The first time it signals Joseph's status as beloved of his father. The last time it signals Joseph's death. What is this robe?

Oscar Wintermute observes that the description of the robe corresponds to the description of the garbing of the king's daughters in 2 Sam 13:18–19.[4] As it happens, this piece of sartorial evidence is found in the story of David's son Amnon raping Tamar, David's daughter. Tamar is reported to the reader as being "beautiful," which 13:1 says is why Amnon "fell in love with her." What follows is an attempted seduction in which Tamar resists, even suggesting that Amnon apply to David for Tamar's hand. But Amnon's impatience brooks no delay, and the result is a clear case of rape. The success of the rape does not, however, endear Tamar to Amnon: "Then Amnon was seized with a very great loathing for her" (13:15). Tamar, whose virginity has been taken by force, seems willing now to remain with Amnon as "his woman," but Amnon's loathing means that she is sent away, again over her protests. As she is dragged away from the scene of rape and loathing, we are informed:

---

4. O. S. Wintermute, "Joseph Son of Jacob," *Interpreter's Dictionary of the Bible* (ed. G. A. Buttrick; 4 vols.; Nashville: Abingdon, 1962), 2:981–86, esp. 982: "The question which then arises is, What is the significance of making a woman's garment for Joseph?" I am grateful to Jeanne Knepper, who first drew my attention to this remark, thereby setting me on the trail of the transgendering of Joseph. See *Shalom to You* (newsletter of Shalom Ministries) 9, no. 2 (February 2001): 1.

(Now she was wearing a long robe with sleeves; for this is how the virgin daughters of the king were clothed in earlier times.) So his servant put her out, and bolted the door after her. But Tamar put ashes on her head, and tore the long robe that she was wearing. (13:18–19a)

This is the only other reference in the Bible to the particular sort of garb that Joseph is identified as wearing. This apparently beautiful and luxurious garment that serves as a mark of distinction for the virgin daughters of the king is the same garment with which the patriarch vested his favored son. The parallels in the garment episodes are quite striking. Both play a role in the distinguishing of the wearer; both are worn by figures to whose beauty the reader is directed, and both wearers are assaulted by their brothers. Both garments become signs of mourning and violation. These multiple resonances of the long robe with sleeves prevent us from supposing that it is simply incidental that both Joseph and Tamar are depicted as wearing the same fashion statement.

But the dress is that of daughters; it is a woman's dress, or rather a girl's dress (the virgin daughters of the king), that Joseph's father gives him to mark him as specially loved. What are we to make of this curious case of transvestism?

One of the most interesting features of the commentaries that allow us to glimpse this transvestism is that they also seek to hide it from our eyes. Thus, rabbinic commentaries suggest that this garment is in any case not particular to girls but is generic for "children" (sons and daughters) of royalty.[5] Others emphasize what the text does not, that it is made of special material.[6] Wintermute himself, after drawing attention to the parallel to the dress of women, goes to considerable lengths to maintain that the garb of privileged male and females was basically indistinguishable.[7]

To a significant degree the motivation behind these attempts to disguise the dress may be an attempt to harmonize the story with Deut 22:5, which prohibits cross-dressing. We will have to return to this text in a bit. For now, it need only be said that a prohibition of cross-dressing entails at a minimum that the garments appropriate to male and female be noticeably different. Thus, neither the suggestion by Wintermute that they are the same for high-class males and females nor the suggestion of the rabbis to similar effect will work. It is clear that only Joseph of the brothers is dressed this way (thus, the garment is not something generally worn by males). And it is

5. Meir Zlotowitz, trans. and commentator, *Bereishis/Genesis: A New Translation with a Commentary Anthologized from Talmudic, Midrashic, and Rabbinic Sources* (overviews by Nosson Scherman; 1st ed.; 6 vols.; Brooklyn, NY: Mesorah Publications, 1977), 5:1617.

6. Ibid., citing Rashi, 5:1617.

7. Wintermute, "Joseph," 983.

quite clear that the daughters rather than the sons of royalty are dressed this way in 2 Samuel (thus it is not something worn by males in that period).

We seem to be left with the rather astonishing bit of news that Joseph is wearing ("classy") girls' clothes. If we foreground this understanding of the odd garment worn by Joseph, the story of the robe looks somewhat different. Joseph is introduced to us as a seventeen-year-old who is therefore entering into the roles of his older brothers: shepherding the flocks. This assimilation into a typical male role is, however, suspended by his father, who sets him apart on account of his special love for him. The narrator informs us that this special love has to do with Joseph being the "son of his old age." But this is not wholly satisfying to the attentive reader since there is, after all, a younger son, Benjamin, whose birth is the occasion of Rachel's death in childbirth. Thomas Mann assists the reader at this point by suggesting that Benjamin cannot be the favorite since he is the occasion for the death of the woman whom Jacob loves, and thus the favoritism must go to Joseph. We will later learn that Benjamin becomes the favorite of Joseph rather than Jacob. But for now, his baby brother is out of the picture. However, we will also subsequently learn that Joseph is distinguished by his great beauty (39:6). Is this a more plausible ground for Jacob's favor? In any case, as Joseph is poised between adolescence and adulthood, he is singled out and vested with a maiden's garment as a sign of the special affection of his father. He is, at least to this degree, transvested and thus transgendered. The remarkably lovely adolescent male is transgendered by the affection of a more powerful male.

The rage of the brothers is thus doubly motivated. Not only is the youth their father's favorite, but he is also deeply troubling for gender roles. Indeed, readers may well expect that the one to be most troubled by Joseph's place as favorite would be Reuben, the oldest. But as the story is told, Reuben is Joseph's defender. Hence, the gender trouble, rather than Jacob's favoring the younger son, may be much more to the foreground. This is emphasized by the way in which the narrative seems to lay the stress on the feminine garment as the pivot of the story. Thus, the feminine apparel bestowed upon Joseph is the sign of the older male's doting upon him. It is the immediate provocation of the brothers' hatred.[8] And this hatred has as its first object the stripping of Joseph; the removal of the infamous girl's

---

8. Westermann (*Genesis 37–50*) writes: "But it is not the father's predilection for Joseph that arouses the brothers' hatred; it is something else. Jacob presents Joseph with a distinctive garment; it is this that gives rise to open conflict" (37). "It is the garment of a princess. The garment then is not only a fine present from the father to his beloved son; it also sets Joseph apart from his brothers" (37). Somehow Westermann does not ask himself how the setting apart is connected to being vested with a princess's garment and how this then is the provocation of enmity. The words are all there. But it is as if the commentator is unconscious of what he is saying (37).

robe.[9] He is laid bare, revealed as not a girl but a boy; not different but the same. Hence, he is exposed to the elements, bare and alone, in the pit and without water. Finally, it the girlish dress that is stained in blood, the blood of the goat (the blood of rape? the blood of menstruation?) and presented, without explanation, to the doting father. It is Jacob who provides the explanation in his grief of the "wild beast" who has attacked and devoured the now consumed body of his beloved boy/girl. The resultant grief of Jacob is staggering; as its first expression he rips his own robe. Thus, in dishabille Jacob places rough sackcloth on his own genitalia, his own loins, as if his grief for the lovely boy has as its special site the phallus now drooping in lament.

Jacob/Israel has produced the queer Joseph, transvested him, and thereby transgendered him as a sign of his own masculine desire. And the progeny of Israel have engaged in the first instance of queer bashing.[10] This doubleness of attitude, which both creates the queer and bashes the queer, oddly anticipates what I believe to be the character of the relation of the biblical texts to queerness. For the texts, taken together, both incite homo-eroticism and will become the license for homophobia. But before explor-ing this fateful implication of the text, it is necessary first to see how the story of Joseph continues the thread of Joseph's queerness.

Joseph as (Wo)Man in a Man's World

The transgendering of Joseph is by no means restricted to Joseph's attire even if noticing this transvestism is necessary for raising the question of whether the transgendering occurs elsewhere and otherwise. If we take this clue, then we may begin to detect in the narrative other signs of transgen-dering at work.

In the first place, we may observe how the garb of Joseph not only sig-nals his special place in the affection of his father but also denotes a signifi-cant change in role vis à vis his brothers. The male role in the narrative of chapter 37 is clearly that of herding the flocks. This role had also character-ized Jacob in the household of his father-in-law as he sought to win the hand of Rachel. It is man's work. This now is also the work of Joseph's brothers. And it is the work that Joseph begins as he passes from adoles-cence to manhood (37:2). However, this movement into the masculine role

---

9. Westermann observes, "They strip him of the detested tunic." But he does not wonder, yet again, why the tunic is detested and what connection this might have to its feminine character (ibid., 41).

10. We should, however, point out that a parallel instance of something like queer bashing—involving strip-ping and abandonment as well as being handed over to foreigners (even slavers)—occurs in the prophetic trans-gendering texts that we have considered, most graphically, in Ezekiel.

of shepherding the flocks is interrupted, and the sign of its interruption is the investiture of Joseph with the long robe with sleeves. The point of such a garment is that it is precisely not appropriate to the work of a "real man," in the outdoors, with flocks. It is, instead, suggestive of domestic and even ornamental function. And indeed, it is with this bestowal of a robe that Joseph is taken from following the flocks and given the role of a kind of domestic overseer, a role that Joseph will assume throughout the story. Thus, Jacob/Israel sends Joseph to check on the brothers who are doing the men's work out at Shechem. It is in this connection that Joseph is seen from a distance by his brothers and made the subject of queer bashing.

This is by no means the end of the story. It serves as the transition to Egypt. But what is remarkable about Joseph's subsequent career is that he survives by being taken under the wing of a succession of more powerful males. He first comes to the attention of Potiphar, "the captain of the guard" (37:36). Following the intriguing intermission of the story of Judah and Tamar, we are returned to Joseph's initial career as one who "found favor" in the eyes of Potiphar (39:1–6) first as a kind of personal attendant and later as overseer. It is then that the reader's gaze is directed to Joseph's extraordinary beauty: "Now Joseph was handsome and good-looking" (39:6). This notice presumably serves to motivate the unwelcome attentions of Potiphar's wife even if we are entitled to wonder to what extent it will also explain the attention of Potiphar himself as well as subsequent male attentiveness to Joseph.

We will return to the episode with the wife of Potiphar, but first let us notice that Joseph is similarly "befriended" by more powerful males. When he winds up in prison, we read: "But the LORD was with Joseph and showed him steadfast love; he gave him favor in the sight of the chief jailer" (39:21). While we may suppose that finding favor *in the sight* of someone is but a metaphor, it also—like the similar phrase that indicates his relation to Potiphar (39:4) and even Potiphar's wife, who "cast her eyes" on Joseph (39:7)—is suggestive of erotic attraction. In the latter case, no doubt exists as to the connection between sight and sexual desire; should we dismiss this in the case of masculine vision? The metaphor occurs with similar effect in relation to Saul or Jonathan's attachment to David. Indeed, in this episode we are reminded of the David saga, for here we meet with a phrase that we have seen characterizing the relation between David and YHWH: "The LORD was with Joseph and showed him steadfast love" (39:21). We have already seen that YHWH's love for David was in no small part provoked by David's extraordinary beauty. Similarly, here no other motive is offered or seems plausible.

Joseph's career in jail lasts at least a couple of years. We are told that it was two years between his interpretation of the dreams of the baker and cup-bearer and his coming before Pharaoh, and he was seventeen when first introduced to us (37:2). Thus, his life as the favorite first of his father, next of Potiphar, and then of the jailer lasts for thirteen years (41:46). In this time he seems to do well on account of his benefactor, the chief jailer. In this, Joseph's experience seems not too unlike that of men in prison even today: survival depends upon a powerful male benefactor, who may exchange pro-tection for sexual favors.[11]

When Pharaoh summons Joseph to himself to undertake the interpreta-tion of a dream, he takes the precaution of presenting his notorious beauty to best advantage: "When he had shaved himself and changed his clothes, he came in before Pharaoh" (41:14). The combined result of Joseph's now mature beauty and his wisdom—both in the interpretation of the dream and his subsequent advice to Pharaoh—Joseph's being made once again the favorite of a more powerful male.

As at the beginning of his career as male "favorite," so also here at the summit of his success: the special status of Joseph is made clear by his being decoratively dressed by the man who favors him. "Removing his signet ring from his hand, Pharaoh put it on Joseph's hand; he arrayed him in garments of fine linen, and put a gold chain around his neck" (41:42).

Thus, it seems that at every phase of his career, Joseph is carried upon a wave of masculine desire. The consequence of this desire is the designation of Joseph as a kind of surrogate for the male, almost as a kind of wife substitute.

This point may be clarified somewhat if we have a look at the tale that stands at the end of the "historical" books of the Hebrew Bible, the story of Esther. The stories have in common that the character of YHWH plays vir-tually no active role in the unfolding of the plot. And both indicate how it is that a particular member of the people of God is instrumental in giving that people safe haven in an alien empire.[12] In the book of Esther the deci-sive role is played by Esther, who becomes the wife of the great king of Per-sia and is able to use her position to succor the Jews. In the case of Joseph's tale, he is the one who uses his position to gain refuge for his people. In the case of Esther, we are told, "The girl was fair and beautiful" (Esth 2:7). These terms recall the description of Joseph: "Now Joseph was handsome and good-looking" (Gen 39:6). Esther, who has been adopted by her cousin

---

11. For an intriguing study of this behavior, see Jacabo Schifter, *Macho Love: Sex Behind Bars in Central Amer-ica* (Binghampton, NY: Haworth Press, 2003).

12. "The similarity in content of the Book of Esther is probably to be explained from a conscious depen-dence of its author on this story," says Westermann (ibid., 26).

Mordecai (Esth 2:7), subsequently finds favor with another man, Hegai (2:8–9), the eunuch who has charge of the concubines (just as Joseph found favor with the eunuch Potiphar). Subsequently, she advances in the business of finding favor with more powerful men, eventually being brought to the attention of the great King Ahasuerus after a year of cosmetic treatment to enhance her already notable beauty. In consequence, she is made queen in place of Vashti and decorated with a crown (2:17). When the time comes to petition the king for her people, she again is described: "Esther put on her royal robes" with great effect: "she won his favor" (5:1, 2). In consequence of this, the king recalls Mordecai and causes him to be vested with "royal robes . . . , which the king has worn, and a horse that the king has ridden" (6:8). At the conclusion of this tale, "the king took off his signet ring, which he had taken from Haman, and gave it to Mordecai" (8:2). But the narrator explains, "So Esther set Mordecai over the house of Haman" (8:2). Somehow it is Esther who rules the scene by which Mordecai ascends. The ascent continues: "Mordecai went out from the presence of the king, wearing royal robes of blue and white, with a great golden crown and a mantle of fine linen and purple" (8:15). By now Mordecai has adopted the role of vizier to the great king, just as Joseph becomes the second in command of the Egyptian Empire.

By glancing at the book of Esther, we can see that the role of Joseph has now been distributed between two characters, Esther and Mordecai. Thus, the erotic attraction that sets everything in motion is attributed to Esther, while the governance of the empire is entrusted to Mordecai, albeit at Esther's behest. These stories serve as bookends for the history of Israel in relation to the empires. And in important respects, they seem to echo one another. But the effect of noticing this echoing is that the story of Joseph seems somewhat more erotically motivated than might otherwise appear.

Of course, the eroticism of the story of Esther is heterosexual and so may be taken for granted by the reader. But the erotic element in the story of Joseph is nearly hidden from view. It is made to appear directly only in the case of the curious episode of Potiphar's "wife." This tale is responsible for the Muslim tradition that Joseph was the most beautiful man God ever made. Nevertheless, as we have seen, the biblical narrative marks out other males for their beauty, generally as an explanation for how they find favor with YHWH (Saul, David) or at least are thought to find that favor (Absalom, Adonijah). In the case of Joseph, this beauty is made to be the explanation for the desire of Potiphar's wife for Joseph: "Now Joseph was handsome and good-looking. And after a time his master's wife cast her eyes on Joseph and said, 'Lie with me'" (Gen 39:6c–7). The circuit between the sight of Joseph's beauty and the desire to have sex with him could hardly be more direct. But how is this related to a possible homoeroticism?[13]

The ensuing story shows the perfidy of Potiphar's wife, just as the preceding narrative concerning Joseph had exposed the perfidy of his brothers. In both cases what is displayed is an article of clothing that Joseph is *not* wearing. The narrator fixes our attention on the flowing robe that Joseph is not wearing in the pit. And in the case of the episode with Potiphar's wife, she waves the flag of Joseph's garment that he had left in her hand as he fled her amorous advances (39:12). Not once but three times we are asked to behold the empty garment (39:12, 13, 15). Hence, we are invited to cast a sidelong glance at the lovely youth who flees naked, as in the first episode we are allowed only a furtive glance at the nude youth in the pit.

Thus, the obverse of the obsessive attention to the empty garment is the barely glimpsed nakedness of the beautiful young male. The story seems calculated to incite (at least mildly) the erotic interest of the reader. And what if this reader is male?[14] The reader is thus made to be complicit in the erotic attraction advertised of Joseph, both as splendidly draped and as dramatically undraped in the episodes that set the tone for what is to come. Likewise, Esther's beauty is made to be the pivot upon which her tale turns.

Is Joseph a Eunuch?

The story of Joseph's rise is to a significant degree the story of Joseph finding powerful male patrons who may be attracted to his beauty as well as to his other capacities. In this, he seems to echo or anticipate (depending on the chronological provenance of these stories) aspects of the story of David. He is also marked out as singularly beautiful, and his early career is determined by a series of relationships to more-powerful males, for whom he seems to function as a boy-toy. Yet throughout his saga David is a warrior among warriors and becomes a king. Joseph, on the other hand, always remains in a subordinate position as the male helpmeet of more conventionally masculine benefactors (father, military captain, jailer, pharaoh). To a certain degree this difference may reflect a difference in subcultural groups. The David saga seems to presuppose the conventions of a warrior society; the Joseph tale seems to presuppose a grouping of scribal and administrative

---

13. I have previously explored this connection between vision and desire as critical for an understanding of Mark 10:21. See Theodore W. Jennings Jr., *The Man Jesus Loved: Homoerotic Narratives from the New Testament* (Cleveland: Pilgrim, 2003), 105–9.

14. The flight of the nude youth in Genesis may be recalled in the flight of the nude youth in Mark 14:51–52, who also leaves the pursuer holding the linen and so to the reader's gaze offers his much-advertised nude body. See ibid., 109–14.

elites. The aspirations of the former may include that of becoming war-chief (king); the aspirations of the latter include rising to greater and greater administrative responsibilities under the suzerainty of men of a different station, class, and/or culture. The difference may also be related to a difference in the status of the people of God as a whole. In the David saga a certain independence seems presupposed; in the Joseph story it is the patronage of foreigners or of foreign empires that is most in focus. (This is another reason for the parallels between the Joseph story and that of Esther.)

Whether because of a different class location (administrator or warrior) or because of a different historical location (semi-independent people or client state), the question of gender is complicated. Compared to other classes or nations, the background of the Joseph story seems to entail a diminishment of masculinity and so a potential transgendering.

One of the ways such a destabilization of gender comes to expression in the world of the empire is the role of the eunuch. The eunuch plays an essential role in imperial households as one who can be trusted to serve the ruler without establishing a competing dynasty. In the story of Esther, eunuchs play a significant role.[15] What is often obscured in the Joseph story is the role of the eunuch there. Joseph's first Egyptian patron is a eunuch, although translators generally are inclined to substitute "officer/court official" in translating Potiphar's identification in the text as a eunuch (39:1 MT: saris, "eunuch"; LXX: eunouchos). The reason for this substitution probably lies in the puzzlement of translators concerning a eunuch who has a wife and is a military leader. These two markers of conventional masculine roles perhaps lead translators and interpreters to "correct" the term "eunuch" to that of "court official" since eunuchs did typically perform significant services in the court.[16] Of course, there is no reason to suppose that eunuchs were incapable of being warriors; after all, a great many imperial warriors were eunuchs.[17] But neither is having a wife incompatible with being a eunuch. Even in respect of sexual function, eunuchs were often

---

15. Thus, we encounter not only Hegai, whose advice she follows to win the king's favor (2:8–9, 15), but also Hathach, who serves as intermediary with Mordecai (4:5–17), as well as other named and unnamed eunuchs.

16. One wonders if having eunuchs as officials is also true for Egypt or only for Babylon or Persia. It is not necessarily the case that ancient Egypt, at least in the period represented by this narrative, did so employ eunuchs. A custom familiar to a later time and to other empires may simply be retrojected here. However, Frans Jonckheere in "L'Eunuque dans l'Égypte pharaonique," Revue d'Histoire des Sciences 7, no. 2 (April–June 1954): 139–55 = "Eunuchs in Pharaonic Egypt": http://www.well.com/user/aquarius/pharaonique.htm, claims that saris in Gen 39:1 is an Akkadian word that means "he who is at the head" (a secondary meaning that won out) and originally it also designated the emasculated individual (a meaning that is becoming obsolete). While he claims that this would indicate that Potiphar was not a eunuch in the conventional sense, this is not the conclusion reached by the Septuagint.

17. Illustrations come from a number of sources. In one that may have been familiar to compilers (at least) of this narrative, Cyrus the Great, so valorized in Israelite memory as the liberator of Israel from Babylonian exile,

notorious womanizers.[18] What eunuchs could not do is have progeny. Hence, they could not found lines of succession and use their position to advance them, possibly into competition with the ruler.

In hiding the gender ambiguity of Potiphar, translators may also be deflecting attention away from gender-troubling features of this narrative generally.

To focus this a bit more, we may ask to what extent Joseph himself functions as a eunuch. Throughout the narrative, his position certainly is as one who does not compete with other males for their position. In the story of his life with father and brothers, we may observe first that Joseph is most strongly contrasted with Reuben. Joseph is put in the dress of a princess or prospective bride; Reuben is clearly a competitor with the father, to the extent of having sex with the father's concubine (35:22; 49:4). Actually, the matter is somewhat more complicated. The object of Reuben's affections is not only his father's woman Bilhah. She is also the mother of two of his brothers (Dan and Naphtali) and the surrogate mother of Joseph and Benjamin (Bilhah, the "maid" of Rachel, was given as a concubine to Jacob; 30:3–8). Naturally, the story gives no indication of an awareness of the Levitical (and Deuteronomic) proscription of sex with the father's woman (see below). Had there been such an awareness, it would have been odd to wait several chapters before any sort of reproach (let alone punishment) is narrated (49:4). The point, however, is that Reuben, as the oldest son of Jacob (and firstborn of Leah), stands in decided contrast to Joseph, the oldest son of Rachel. Reuben is clearly marked as the competitor for the position of patriarch, whereas Joseph is decidedly feminized.

This feminization is continued in that Joseph is subsequently the trusted servant not of a patriarch but of a eunuch, Potiphar. In this tale the eroticism seems to be heterosexualized, but two elements count against that appearance. First, Joseph has no apparent desire for the woman who throws herself at him. He resists her attempted seduction, even rape. Indeed, the position seems to be that of gender reversal, with Potiphar's wife playing Amnon to Joseph's Tamar. To be sure, the narrator provides

---

is said by Xenophon to have preferred eunuchs as military commanders (*Cyropaedia* 7.60–65). For this reference I am grateful to Stephen O. Murray's *Homosexualities* (Chicago: University of Chicago Press, 2000), 303. The illustrious history of eunuchs as military commanders continues into late antiquity in the example of Narses, the famous general who served the emperor Justinian. See Kathryn M. Ringrose, "Living in the Shadows: Eunuchs and Gender in Byzantium," in *Third Sex, Third Gender: Beyond Sexual Dimorphism in Culture and History* (ed. Gilbert Herdt; New York: Zone Books, 1996), 97.

18. Kathryn Ringrose reports that men sometimes had themselves castrated "to have intercourse with women without fear of progeny" ("Living in the Shadows," 86). And Aline Rouselle tells of the reputation of (some) eunuchs for sexual profligacy, in her work *Porneia: On Desire and the Body in Late Antiquity* (trans. F. Pheasant; Oxford: Blackwell, 1988), 122–23.

Joseph with an anachronistic alibi: sleeping with another man's woman is a sin against God (39:9). But Joseph's resistance contrasts strongly with the actions of other males such as Reuben, David, and Amnon.

The attempted reheterosexualization of Joseph occurs again in relation to Pharaoh, who gives Joseph a wife, "Asenath, daughter of Potiphera, priest of On" (41:50). (Is the appearance here of the name Potiphera meant to remind us of Potiphar?[19]) From this wife Joseph has two sons, Ephraim and Manasseh (41:51–52). While these sons may assure the reader of Joseph's fulfillment of a conventionally masculine role, this comes to be unexpectedly undermined in the story as it unfolds.

As Jacob nears the end of his life, Joseph comes to him with his two sons. But Jacob informs Joseph:

> Therefore your two sons, who were born to you in the land of Egypt before I came to you in Egypt, are now mine; Ephraim and Manasseh shall be mine, just as Reuben and Simeon are. (48:5)

We are treated to a rather remarkable scene in which Israel/Jacob has the boys placed on his knees. They are then received from Jacob by Joseph, who in this case seems all the more like a wife (48:8–12). In a scene reminiscent of the tale of Jacob's youth, when he and his brother, Esau, were to receive the blessing of their father, Isaac, Jacob blesses the two boys as if he were their father. At the same time, he reverses the blessings of older and younger, as did his father (48:13–22). What, we may wonder, is going on in this scene? It seems clear that Joseph's paternity is being erased.[20] Jacob functions as the father in the place of Joseph. Quite dramatically, the sons born to Joseph become instead sons born to Jacob. Insofar as Joseph has any role, here it is that of "wife" of Jacob and "mother" of the two sons.[21] Like Rebekah his grandmother, he gives the sons over to Jacob to receive the blessings of the patriarch. It is as if Joseph has taken the place of Rachel, his mother. It is not for nothing, then, that Jacob invokes the fate of Rachel as partial explanation for his taking over the paternity of Joseph's sons (48:7).

The erasure of Joseph's paternity seems to characterize the perspectives of the eighth- and sixth-century prophets. For them, there are really only

---

19. Westermann points out that the two names are variations of the same (*Genesis 37–50*, 61).

20. In quite a different way this also happens to another Joseph, the "father" of Jesus and husband of Mary, who also dreams dreams and goes to Egypt. But in spite of being the connecting link to descent from the house of David, he is rather strikingly removed from the paternity of Jesus.

21. Do we hear overtones of this in Ps 77? "With your strong arm you redeemed your people, the descendants of Jacob and Joseph" (77:15). Either we have to do here only with the descendants of Ephraim and Manasseh (Joseph's "progeny"), or Joseph is being made into the "wife" of Jacob, and so in an odd way, the "mother" of all Jacob's sons, or both.

two comparable peoples: Judah and Ephraim (although Manasseh makes
an appearance as well). Both are regarded as sons of Jacob/Israel. When
the northern kingdom is addressed or spoken of, it is almost never as
"Joseph" but rather as either Jacob/Israel or as Ephraim. This is in some
contrast to other OT sources, especially those concerned with genealogical
matters, in which the name of Joseph does appear (e.g., Num 1:10; 13:11;
26:28). But at least for certain highly influential traditions, Joseph's paternity
virtually disappears from view. For all intents and purposes, he is made to be
as if a eunuch. Whether as eunuch or as surrogate wife to Jacob, Joseph
decidedly troubles the gender categories that circulate around the edges of
his story.

The Joseph Saga in Contrast to the Law

In our readings of narrative (and even prophetic) texts, we have been
noticing the seeming contrast between what we find in these stories and
what we might have expected to find if we took our view of sexual mores
from a consideration of legal texts. In the case of the Joseph story we have
been exploring, several provisions of the legal codes seem to be ignored,
such as those regarding cross-dressing and eunuchs. Even the legal views
regarding incest, especially with one's father's wife (Lev 18:8; 20:11,
requiring the death penalty for male and female; Deut 22:30[22]), seem to
have been suspended or ignored in the case of Reuben's sexual escapade
with his father's concubine.[23]

Transvestism
    The transvesting of Joseph seems to run counter to the (later) legal code
in Deut 22:5, which proscribes cross-dressing. We thus may pay some attention to this curious law, which is not repeated in any of the other legal
codes of Israel:

> A woman shall not wear a man's apparel, nor shall a man put on a woman's
> garment; for whoever does such things is abhorrent to the LORD your God.

---

22. We may notice a certain progression in these laws, starting from the rather restricted formulation of Deut
22:30, speaking against marrying one's father's wife and explaining that it would be a violation of the father's
rights. Next, Lev 18:8 suggests that acting in this way is "uncovering the nakedness of your father." Then Lev
20:11 maintains that both parties to the deed should be put to death (although the punishment is identical for
any sort of adultery whatever).

23. Reuben's escapade seems to have been emulated by at least one member of the early Christian community; see 1 Cor 5:1–5. Paul seems curiously unaware of the precedents for this action in Israelite (the case of
Reuben) as well as pagan (the story of Phaedrus, not to mention Oedipus) tradition.

The provision is intriguing for three reasons: it is not repeated in other legal codes of Israel, it starts with the woman, and it has the oddity of invoking the idea of abomination.

We may first notice that the provision seems to be rather oddly located in the body of law within which it is found. The verses that immediately precede and follow this saying have a quite different character. They have to do with obligations to care for the neighbor's possessions (vv. 1–4), the importance of putting a parapet on one's roof so that no one would fall from it (v. 8), and even a prohibition against taking a mother bird together with her young (vv. 6–7). In this context the provision about cross-dressing seems arbitrarily inserted.

The material with which it might seem to more naturally belong is that of the provisions of verses 9–11:

> You shall not sow your vineyard with a second kind of seed, or the whole yield will have to be forfeited. . . . You shall not plow with an ox and a donkey yoked together. You shall not wear clothes made of wool and linen woven together.

These laws seem to be aimed at some mixing of kinds that might plausibly be linked to the mixing involved in cross-dressing. Even here, however, there are problems. In the parallel formulation of Lev 19:19, the provision concerning plowing with ox and donkey yoked together is dropped in favor of a prohibition of crossbreeding animals. Of greater interest, however, is that the prohibition of cross-dressing does not appear there or anywhere in Leviticus. What does link the prohibition of cross-dressing to certain of the other provisions of Leviticus, however, is the notice that it is "an abomination to the LORD your God" (RSV), a formulation that seems most at home in the priestly codes gathered in Leviticus.

The point of this review of the context of the prohibition of cross-dressing is to suggest that it has a quite marginal position even in the legal traditions of Israel and appears as a rather late and misplaced insertion into the legal code in which it is found. It is scarcely surprising, then, that it has no role in the apparent consciousness of the putative author(s) of the Joseph narrative. The supposition that cross-dressing or even transgendering is inconceivable in the history or traditions of Israel because of the existence of such a legal formulation is simply absurd. Yet commentators commonly invoke this law to rule out the suggestion of cross-dressing in the Joseph story or of transgendering in the prophetic material we earlier discussed. This same attitude may have prevented subsequent generations either of cross-dressers or of transgendered folk generally from recognizing themselves in the biblical narrative.

Eunuchs

Something similar happens with respect to that other category that seems to destabilize gender, that of the eunuch. The legal provision sometimes invoked here is also from Deuteronomy:

> No one whose testicles are crushed or whose penis is cut off shall be admitted to the assembly of the LORD. (23:1)

Directly following this legal provision is one prohibiting also any Moabite or even tenth-generation descendent of a Moabite from being part of "the assembly of the LORD" (23:3). Both rules offer us an even more direct way of seeing the incompatibility of legal traditions with narrative and prophetic traditions. With respect to the exclusion of descendants of Moabites, we would obviously have to exclude David himself from the assembly since he is a third-generation descendent of the Moabitess Ruth, and thus the first several generations of kings of Judah would be excluded. With respect to the exclusion of eunuchs, it is clear that the oracle of Isaiah near the end of the prophetic tradition undoes that provision without referring to it. This may be because it was unknown at that stage or because it was being specifically contested (Isa 56:3–5; cf. Wis 3:14).

Fortunately, Nancy Wilson has already made the biblical material on eunuchs the subject of an extensive treatment in *Our Tribe*.[24] I have dealt with some of those texts as well in my discussion of Jesus' odd saying in Matthew concerning the three kinds of eunuchs, so there is no need to repeat any of that analysis here.[25]

In any case, I am not suggesting that Joseph was a literal eunuch but rather that he fulfills something of the function of a eunuch. This appears in his relationship to more-powerful males who entrust him with managerial responsibility, and in how his character seems to disrupt gender binarism (either male or female), as the ancient category of the eunuch also often did.

---

24. Nancy Wilson, *Our Tribe: Queer Folks, God, Jesus, and the Bible* (San Francisco: HarperSanFrancisco, 1995). In addition to the interesting use of "eunuch" as a generic term for "queer folk," Wilson offers a list of biblical texts on eunuchs (281–85). Kathryn Ringrose gives a synopsis of a twelfth-century text, *Defense of Eunuchs* by Theophylaktos, in her "Living in the Shadows," 102–7.

25. Jennings, *Man Jesus Loved*, ch. 8. Matthew Kuefler's excellent study of the eunuch in antiquity and early Christianity merits serious attention: *The Manly Eunuch: Masculinity, Gender Ambiguity, and Christian Ideology in Late Antiquity* (Chicago: University of Chicago Press, 2001).

Neither the prohibition of cross-dressing nor the provision concerning eunuchs can tell us much about the attitudes of ancient Israel on these matters. In both cases what we might have deduced about Israel from a scrutiny of legal texts is confounded by what we discover upon examination of the much more plentiful narrative and prophetic texts.

The difficulty is that Christians and perhaps especially Protestant Christians have a pronounced tendency to take legal texts as providing a privileged perspective upon ancient Israel. We do this in spite of their relatively marginal status in the whole corpus that we call the OT. Why should this be so? It has to do, I believe, with the way Protestants in particular, especially given a particular reading of Romans, have been inclined to regard "Judaism," ancient and contemporary, as a religion of the law. This general characterization has produced a privileging of legal texts as uniquely qualified to give us information about Israel's thought world. Then we may regard narrative texts that seem to be ignorant of these legal provisions as simply "primitive" relative to the law. If we discover disharmonious elements, we are tempted simply to level them out in order to present a unified picture of the thought world of the texts. Or we try to place them along a time line of what is more or less developed relative to the controlling instance of what counts as evidence for the perspective of "the OT" view.

The point is that we cannot take the mere appearance of legal provisions in law codes of uncertain date and provenance as a substitute for a reading of other texts. These other passages may offer quite surprisingly different perspectives on the attitudes to be found in texts (and levels of texts) that also go to make up the astonishingly vibrant multiplicity that we term the Bible.

Joseph, In Between

The strange figure of Joseph as a male in female clothing, as a patriarch deprived of progeny, as always exercising authority that can never be his own or correspond to his own "identity"—this figure makes for a strange impression. In a number of ways he is an in-between figure, a status that corresponds to his somewhat transgendered position in the narrative.

We meet him first as a son in daughter's clothing, as one whose privileged place within the family places him outside the company of brothers, as one whose role is suddenly changed from one entering manhood to one who will forever be at the margins of manhood.

This initial in-betweenness, signaled by the robe that covers him completely, continues in the narrative development. He is a slave who rules a household, a prisoner who rules a prison, an immigrant who rules an empire. His authority is always borrowed from another: a father, a captain, a jailer, a pharaoh. These others are recognizable types of masculinity, but Joseph's masculinity is derivative, never his own.

Even Joseph's "ethnicity" is strangely ambivalent. As one taken to Egypt (by Midianites or Ishmaelites; 37:28, 36), he is a stranger in that land. His positions are always to a certain extent undermined or underlined by this difference from those among whom he labors, at least in Egypt. But this also reacts upon his relation to his "own," to his brothers. For not only do they expel him from the family cohort of brothers, but also he is strange to them. In the narrative much depends on them not recognizing him, on him being taken for what he also is, a man of great and unpredictable power in the land of Egypt. He is one of them, and yet he is also decidedly not one of them.

And this is still true at the end of the story, when all has been revealed. For now he is the father of sons who are, however, Egyptian. They are born of the daughter of an Egyptian priest and the administrator of the Egyptian Empire. How are they to be regarded as still somehow "Hebrew"? This dilemma is resolved, but at the cost of making Jacob their legal father; and Joseph, what is he then? This in-betweeness is characteristic of another element of the story that we have not examined, Joseph as dream master. As one who seems utterly at home in the world of dreams, Joseph is decidedly odd. His liminality with respect to gender role is echoed in his liminality in the division of waking and sleeping, of night and day. For him, the shadowy dreams that come in the night are as clear as daylight. The interpretation of dreams, Freud will later declare, is the royal road to understanding the unconscious. But for Joseph, they disclose a future as fixed as if it were the past. The uncanniness of his at-homeness in what is *unheimlich* marks him off from other men as surely as his strange transgendering of dress and role. Hence, we may say that the transvesting and transgendering of Joseph are not accidents in the narrative or simply fortuitous or extraneous to the plot. Rather, they are pieces of the whole as it develops.

What I am suggesting here is that Joseph's queerness with respect to gender anticipates and echoes his liminality in respect to the most basic divisions of life: class, ethnicity, day/night, present/future. In this the character of Joseph is not unlike what we discover cross-culturally about "intermediate gender" types generally.[26]

---

26. Excellent essays on the phenomenon of transgendering from historical and anthropological perspectives are gathered together in Julia Epstein and Kristina Straub's *Body Guards: The Cultural Politics of Gender Ambiguity* (New York: Routledge, 1991) and in Herdt's *Third Sex, Third Gender.* The relation between gender liminality and religious liminality in North American *berdache* (two-spirit) phenomena is explored by Walter Williams, *The Spirit and the Flesh: Sexual Diversity in American Indian Culture* (Boston: Beacon, 1986), esp. 17–43.

Social and Historical Location

How does such a story come to be written? In what cultural context is it at home? Scholars have been in some doubt about where to place this story in the development of Israel. Some have suggested that it arises in the time of Solomon, as a way to reflect on the change from family- and clan-based society and to one determined by the administrative structures of kingship and bureaucracy. Solomon has an Egyptian wife and thus may bring Israel into contact with Egyptian customs. This may explain the positive fascination with Egypt articulated in this story. Others have maintained that it may derive from a somewhat later time, the time of Jeroboam and the conflicted view of kingship and the Davidic line that characterized the northern kingdom. But there are other candidates for other times when Israel, or Judah, found itself seeking succor from the Egyptians when threatened with more deadly neighbors to the north. Even at the end of the story about Israel's nationhood, we have the exile of Jeremiah and others not in Babylon but in Egypt (Jer 42–44).

Even though little of certainty can be established about the time frame for the development of this story or "novella," it does seem to depend on quite a different world from that in which we encounter the tales of David or the stories of the first prophets. The world is now decidedly more settled, and the task is to accommodate to this new cultural world, in which administrators and bureaucrats exercise real power, even if in the name of another.

From our perspective, what is most important is that the story of Joseph does seem to reflect a subculture of petty officials associated with the court, who may find in Egypt a fitting analogy for the ideal of managerial ethos. This may come at a time when, in comparison to other roles and other subcultures within the same epoch, the managerial class is transgendered relative to more traditional masculine roles. Yet if so, this transgendering is not here a simply negative feature. It has its compensations after all. One may thereby in this strange new world be able to provide for one's family and clan in ways that mere shepherds or soldiers are unable to do. Of course, there is another name for this from a quite different perspective: patronage or even corruption.

Those who are marginal to traditional gender roles and to traditional families have not infrequently been known to claim in defense of their marginalized status that they are thereby enabled to confer advantages upon their families. From transgendered prostitutes in Mexico to eunuchs in royal courts, the family that despises the transgendered person may also have to rely on the one they despise to keep the wolf of hunger from the door.[27] The story of Joseph may indeed be one in which they recognize themselves.

We have discussed how Israel is transgendered in certain prophetic narrativizations of the relation between YHWH and Israel. In doing so, we have had occasion to wonder whether there might be any further general social phenomena of transgendering that would make these oracles seem more at home in the life of the people of Israel. In the story of Joseph we have found an example of transgendering that may indicate a supportive context for the imagination of transgendering in the life and stories of the people of Israel. Transgendering is a complex phenomenon, or perhaps better, a whole set of phenomena. I am reminded of the complexity that emerges in a recent ethnographic study by Don Kulick. He found that Brazilian *travestis* use hormones and silicone to alter their bodies and scorn those who merely cross-dress. At the same, time they regard as insane someone who undergoes sex-change surgery. Clearly, there are significant differences even in a single culture, and we are far from knowing how to map the diverse forms of transgendering that may be at work in the biblical texts we have been considering, from cultures and epochs so far removed from our own.

It does seem clear, however, that transgendering in story and oracle is by no means unknown in Israel, in spite of the also-clear presence of a homoeroticism that does not entail anything like transgendering. However, it is the felt risk of demasculinizing the men of Israel that, I will argue, stands behind the emergence of legal proscriptions not only of transgendering but also of other forms of male same-sex eroticism. To that issue we must next turn.

---

27. For the strongly ambivalent relationship between transgendered prostitutes and their families in modern Mexico, see Annick Prieur, *Mema's House: On Transvestites, Queens, and Machos* (Chicago: University of Chicago Press, 1998), esp. 42–57. Something similar seems also to be true of travesti prostitutes in Brazil; see Don Kulick's *Travesti: Sex, Gender, and Culture among Brazilian Transgendered Prostitutes* (Chicago: University of Chicago Press, 1998), esp. 178–81.

PART FOUR

Questions

In the final part of this study of homoeroticism in the literature of ancient Israel, I turn to a consideration of three issues that have been just below the surface of the inquiry until now. These issues place the discussions thus far into wider frames of reference.

Given the proliferation of traces of homoerotic relationships in the literature of ancient Israel, how are we to understand the emergence of a prohibition against at least some forms of male homoeroticism in the latest version of Israel's legal codes? In Lev 18 and 20 the prohibitions of some sort of male same-sex practice have long served to characterize the whole of biblical tradition as "homophobic." The result of our study thus far is to suggest that such a prohibition must be seen not as representative of Hebrew Bible attitudes toward same-sex activity but rather as an anomaly. Here I rehearse the ways in which much of what we encounter in the narratives we have considered is irreconcilable with Israel's law codes. Then I attempt to show that precisely the proliferation of forms of homoeroticism at which we have looked actually helps to clarify the aim of, and the motivation for, this prohibition. Thus, not only is the prohibition anomalous; it is also explicable precisely *as* anomalous from the point of view that has emerged from this study.

To this point the material we have interrogated has been concerned with male same-sex eroticism. This is partly determined by the androcentric character of the materials in question but also by the problematic of a relationship between a divinity represented as a male character in these narratives and his male adherents. In chapter 11 I seek to raise the question of the place of female homoeroticism in this literature. I suggest that there is some evidence for a certain "priority" for "lesbian" relationships not only in the literature of ancient Israel but also in that of Greece and Rome. What is of significance here, however, is not mere chronological priority but also the way in which female homoeroticism, particularly as discernible in traces left behind in the book of Ruth, serves to indicate the interiority of relationships of desire, delight, and long-term faithfulness. This enables us to read elements of homoeroticism in the stories with which our study began. At the end of our discussion of transgendered Israel, we raised the question of female same-sex relationships as a further permutation of transgendering imagination working in the prophetic tradition. We wondered how this might impact the understanding of the divine. In the case of Ruth, we discover the way in which love between two women actually serves as a stand-in for, and a model of, the steadfast love that may otherwise be attributed to the divinity.

At several points in the discussion, we have observed the relationship between various aspects of homoeroticism in this literature to what we find represented in ancient Greece, long believed to be the home or origin of the acceptance of certain forms of at least male same-sex eroticism. In chapter 12 we turn to confront this relationship more directly. When we do so, it emerges that the evidence for significant same-sex eroticism in Israel actually precedes the evidence for Greece, in some cases by several centuries. Hence, it appears that ancient Israel may have more of a claim to be a cultural home to same-sex eroticism than does ancient Greece.

This puts in question some of the most widely held presuppositions about these two cultures.

It is appropriate that this sort of study end with questions rather than with answers. Thus, in place of a conclusion I will offer a sort of theological postscript (by way of a reflection on Moses and, especially, Jacob) that suggests what all this might mean when thought about in relation to (Christian) theology.

10. *The Question of the Law*

IT HAS BECOME A NEARLY UNIVERSAL COMMONPLACE of biblical inter-pretation that the Bible and the religion it reflects or produces, biblical reli-gion as it is sometimes called, is virulently homophobic. Thereby we are led to believe that eroticism between males or between females is either com-pletely unknown or vigorously opposed by these texts and by the religion to which they are supposed to testify. Indeed, this seems to be one charac-terization of these texts upon which both homophobic and antihomopho-bic readers can agree.

If this characterization were "true," then the readings I have been pursuing in these pages would be unthinkable. But let us suppose that the readings I have undertaken suggest that Israel was not anomalously homo-phobic, that it was as worldly wise about same-sex as it is about cross-sex desire and behavior. What issues would then arise? We would first have to make clear to what extent these legal provisions regarding sexual practices are anomalous with respect to the materials we have been considering. Then with some care we would have to attend to the interpretation of these texts with a view to understanding what it is precisely that they pro-hibit. In this task we must first attend to the traditional interpretation that wrestles with an apparent prohibition of the role of phallic aggressor in same-sex sexual practices. We will see that this set of interpretations falls into difficulties that can only be resolved by supposing that what is really in

199

view here is the desire to be penetrated. This in turn will link up with the texts that we have been considering, which, I contend, actually solicit or incite the bottom's desire. I will then suggest that this desire is interdicted in legal texts under pressure from a fear of cultural and colonial penetration.

Law and Narrative

If one asks for the textual evidence supporting the characterization of Israel as homophobic, we are directed to two kinds of texts: the narrative concerning Sodom of Gen 19, and the legal proscriptions of male same-sex behavior in Lev 18 and 20. The Sodom narrative, it is now generally recognized, is an indicator, at most, of attitudes toward gang rape as an especially extreme example of the opposite of hospitality to the stranger. It is no more indicative of attitudes toward same-sex eroticism than the stories of the rape of Dinah or the rape of the concubine in Judg 19 are indicative of attitudes toward heterosexual eroticism.

We are then left with Leviticus, which alone among Israel's legal codes makes reference to something like same-sex behavior. It is generally supposed that these texts count male same-sex practices as abominable; it is alleged that this view characterizes the perspective of ancient Israel and of Judaism, or at least of the law. It is therefore worth recalling that of all the many legal codes to be found incorporated into the Scriptures of Israel, in only one of these law codes is there anything remotely touching upon the subject of male same-sex eroticism. In a fine discussion of these texts, Saul Olyan reports: "They are the only such laws in the Hebrew Bible; there is absolutely nothing analogous to them in other Israelite legal collections mediated to us, though their uniqueness has not been generally acknowledged by scholars."[1] And he points out that this uniqueness does not hold with respect to other laws in Leviticus generally or to the laws in these very chapters. This serves to highlight the importance of the issue of how these laws come to have a place in Leviticus, since other (and earlier) legal traditions seem to have felt no interest in legislating against these activities.

Before we attempt to analyze these texts, it is important for us to remind ourselves of something we have found throughout our reading of the Hebrew Bible: narrative (and prophetic) texts either contest such codes or are ignorant of them. If we restrict ourselves only to those legal codes that the narratives we have read seem to violate, we will still have an impressive array.

---

1. Saul M. Olyan, "'And with a Male You Shall Not Lie the Lying Down of a Woman': On the Meaning and Significance of Leviticus 18:22 and 20:13," *Journal of the History of Sexuality* 5, no. 2 (1994): 179–206, esp. 181.

In the story of Joseph that we discussed in chapter 9, for example, we have seen the depiction of Reuben's incest with his father's wife (Gen 35:22), something clearly proscribed by Deut 22:30 and Lev 18:8. But while the editor of the tale may have disapproved strongly of this action (cf. Gen 49:4), there is no indication of the severity suggested by the legal code of Lev 20:11, which requires the death penalty for both male and female. We have also seen the evident transvestism of the youthful Joseph (Gen 37:3), which shows no knowledge of the Deuteronomic prohibition (Deut 22:5). And we have also seen that the narrative of Joseph, like that of Esther and even Jeremiah, seems not to be aware of the strong bias against eunuchs that characterizes the legal codes (Deut 23:1), if not the perspective of the prophets generally (cf. Isa 56:4–5).

In the case of the prophetic oracles that transgender Israel and/or Judah, we have seen several features in the quasi-narrative development of this image that are at considerable variance with what might be understood to be the attitude of ancient Israel if we consulted only the legal codes. Of course, we are confronted in any case with a manifest transgendering of male subjects. And this transgendering, as we have seen, not only functions to depict the promiscuity of Israel and Judah but also to depict the appropriate or desired relation of these subjects to their very male divinity (they are to be his devoted "women"). But this is not all. We are also asked to imagine YHWH taking sisters as wives, as in the imagining of Israel and Judah (and even Sodom) as sisters. In this there is no apparent awareness of the horror evinced by Leviticus concerning such an arrangement (Lev 18:18).[2]

In the David saga we have encountered a number of elements that show that the narrator either was not aware of or chose to ignore legal provisions. We have seen this with respect to the laws concerning adultery, as in the case of David and Bathsheba. While Leviticus may require the death penalty for such an affair (20:10), the narrative focuses not on the adultery itself but upon the betrayal of the other man (Uriah; 2 Sam 11–12). In the case of the narrative concerning Amnon, we have also seen that the prohibition of marriage or sexual relations with one's sister (Lev 20:17) seems not to be invoked. The narrator leads the reader to believe that Amnon should simply have asked David for the hand of David's daughter in marriage rather than engaging in a rape and then rejecting her (2 Sam 13:13).[3]

---

2. In discussion of these passages, I also referred to the case of Jacob marrying sisters, which similarly shows no knowledge of the prohibition of Lev 18:18.

3. A further illustration of a possible violation of this provision of Leviticus is Abraham's marriage to Sarah, who is his half-sister (Gen 20:12).

These are only a few of the instances that could be cited to show that from the standpoint of narrative and prophetic texts, the proscriptions of legal codes are largely irrelevant for attempting to understand the perspectives of Israel on sexual matters. In all of these cases—and they are only a few of those that might be cited—we see that it would be impossible to deduce the plots of narrative from the provisions of legal codes. What the law prohibits is regularly flaunted in the narratives.

This is true not only of the so-called "ritual" law but also of what seems to be the "moral" law, even assuming that it would be possible to make such a distinction.

The point of this review is only to notice that whatever may be prohibited by Lev 18 and 20, it would be folly to suppose that this would provide a reliable indication of the attitudes toward "homosexuality" in the texts of ancient Israel. Proscriptions in legal codes cannot be taken without further ado as reliable indices of attitudes toward sexual behavior in other parts of the Hebrew Bible, still less of the attitudes or practices of the people of ancient Israel (whether preexilic, exilic, or even postexilic).

This is all the more so of quite late texts such as what is arguably the latest legal code of Israel, the so-called Holiness Code (Lev 17–26); unlike all other legal codes in Israel, it contains what is often interpreted as a prohibition of male homosexual behavior.

Yet whatever the meaning of the prohibition, it is remarkable that an apparently late and quite isolated formulation should be allowed like a magical abracadabra to make disappear all the material from many different sources that yields itself to a queer reading. The question of how these texts come to play such a prominent role belongs to a different project, the investigation of the construction of homophobic discourse. Here our task is rather more limited. It is to suggest an interpretation of these proscriptions and to place them within the context of the homoerotic reading of Hebrew Bible texts that has so far been proposed here.

The Prohibition

What exactly do these texts from Leviticus actually prohibit? They are often cited and sometimes even quoted. Our first step is to examine the verses themselves, something surprisingly seldom done by those who cite or even quote the texts. As is often the case, texts frequently cited or quoted are usually assumed to mean what we want them to mean. But this is rather often a misleading supposition. The best way to figure out what a text is driving at is not to cite it or even quote it but to attend to it carefully, with genuine curiosity.

So what then is going on here? We read in the NRSV:

You shall not lie with a male as with a woman; it is an abomination. (18:22)

If a man lies with a male as with a woman, both of them have committed an abomination; they shall be put to death; their blood is upon them. (20:13)

These are the texts. What are we to make of them?

The Question of Abomination

Previous commentators have noticed that the term "abomination," which occurs in both verses, is highly suggestive of cultic concerns.[4] The reason is that in Hebrew the term *to'evah* (abomination) occurs primarily in contexts that have idolatry or deviant cultic practices in view. Here in Leviticus, it occurs only in these two chapters. Outside of Leviticus, it is most common in Ezekiel and in Deuteronomy. In both of these chapters of Leviticus there is, in addition to a consideration of incest taboos, also the question of the sacrifice or dedication of children or seed to "Molech." In Lev 18:21 this immediately precedes the prohibition of a man lying with a male as with a female. In contrast, the sacrifice/dedication to Molech is the lead concern in 20:1–5 and is followed by warnings against consulting mediums and wizards.

In Ezekiel (where the term *to'evah* appears most frequently) as well as in Jeremiah and Deuteronomy, it occurs regularly in connection with idolatry and is mentioned in connection with child sacrifice (e.g., Ezek 16:36). It is also used in connection with the *qedeshim* (e.g., 1 Kgs 14:24). The association with cultic practices generally and with the *qedeshim* particularly has led many to suppose that at least at some stage in the development of this prohibition, it was concerned with the issue of "male cultic prostitution." Thus, it would serve as the Levitical equivalent of the prohibition of such activity in Deut 23:17–18.[5]

This would also help to make sense of the way in which both chapters of Leviticus refer to the practices of the Canaanites (18:3; 20:23). We know nothing of Canaanite sexual practices generally, but we do know that they were associated, at least in the minds of the authors of Israel's history, with fertility cults and cultic sexual practices (or at least the use of *qedeshim*).

4. This is the focus of John Boswell's interpretation of the texts. See *Christianity, Social Tolerance, and Homosexuality* (Chicago: University of Chicago Press, 1980), 100–102.
5. This is the view of Tom Horner, *Jonathan Loved David* (Philadelphia: Westminster, 1978), 71–85, and Boswell, *Christianity*, 101.

We know little about the sexual mores of the Canaanites. But we do know something at least about the Egyptians. And one thing about the Egyptians that we know is that they seem to have disapproved of same-sex relations among males. Hence, the initial reference to "not do as they do in the land of Egypt" (18:3) cannot be plausibly connected to same-sex practices among males as a typical Egyptian "vice." Here the writer/compiler could have in mind the incest provisions (pharaohs typically had their sisters as their consorts) or (less likely in Egypt) cultic fertility practices.

In short, critical scholars argue, considerations of cultic associations, as well as the reference to Egypt and Canaan, all point us away from a blanket prohibition of same-sex acts among males and toward a particular kind of act: that earlier discussed in relation to the *qedeshim* (ch. 7).

In spite of the plausibility of this interpretation, it has been increasingly questioned, even by antihomophobic readers and scholars. The ground for this doubt primarily has to do with the scope of the term *to'evah*. This term may be deployed in contexts where no cultic issue appears to be at stake. It may be used, for example, in contexts where it is simply a question of crossing boundaries or mixing categories.[6]

If we are not to restrict the scope of the prohibition to cultic activities that are imagined to involve some sort of ritual sexuality, then we seem to be left with noncultic sexual acts that involve males. In our discussion of the texts, it is first important to see that what is involved is some sort of sexual practice and then to see what sort of sexual practice may be involved.

Sex Acts

What is in view seems to be two related things. First is "lying with." We may take this to refer to a sexual act. That is indeed the way the verb often works, as, for example, in the case of Lot's daughters: "Come, let us make our father drink wine, and we will lie with him, so that we may preserve offspring through our father" (Gen 19:32). The verb generally and widely occurs with this meaning. In this way it is rather like, though less puzzling to the uninitiated than, the English expression "to sleep with."

The context of the law seems to confirm this. It occurs in a series of laws that seem to govern sexual relationships, although the metaphor in most of the other laws is not "lie with" but the perhaps older metaphor

6. See, for example, David F. Greenberg, *The Construction of Homosexuality* (Chicago: University of Chicago Press, 1988), 195–96, with 195n58 supplying a list of texts where *to'evah* is used without cultic associations. Olyan, "With a Male," 195, agrees with Greenberg, as does Martin Samuel Cohen, "The Biblical Prohibition of Homosexual Intercourse," *Journal of Homosexuality* 19, no. 4 (1990): 3–20.

"uncover the nakedness of." Saul used the latter metaphor in his tirade at Jonathan for his relationship with David (1 Sam 20:30).

Thus far, then, we have "A male shall not lie with [have sex with] a male." And that is what many suppose to be prohibited here. But that is not what the text in fact says. What is prohibited, it seems, is not just any "lying with a male" but a lying with a male that is the sort of "lying with" (sex) that a male has with a female, or is like the "lying down of a female."[7]

What is that supposed to mean? Of course, many simply pass over this in a rush, supposing that it is not a particular sort of "lying with" between males (as the "lying with" of a male with a female) but any kind of lying with (any kind of sex). If that's what the text means, it could have easily said so. After all, the verb is generally intelligible. And the text does not seem to feel it necessary to say with respect to relationships with animals: "You shall not lie with a beast as with a female." Nor does it tell the woman not to lie with an animal with the sort of sex (lying with) that she has with a male. The prohibition of sex with an animal can simply say "no sex with an animal (no lying with them)" and leave it at that. But with respect to males, this is obviously not enough. A special kind of lying with is what is prohibited.

This idiom is typically understood to mean that a male should not lie with a male in the way in which he lies with a female. Although I shall argue that this is fundamentally misleading, we must attend to this possibility with some care since it has such an important place in many commentaries.

Accordingly, what would it mean for a male to have sex with another male "as with a female"? It certainly is not the sort of "lying with" that a male can only have with a female: vaginal intercourse. For a male cannot have vaginal intercourse with a male. At the literal level the text prohibits an impossibility. Yet again, this is the only literal kind of sex that is specific to male and female. With respect to everything else, it is all equally possible.

Some commentators have supposed that what is meant here is anal intercourse between males. An initial difficulty here is that anal intercourse is something equally possible between male and female and between male and male. Why should this be termed the "lying with" that is appropriate with a female? Anal intercourse between male and female is about the only reliable means of birth control known to antiquity and remains the only readily available means in many societies today. Does this mean that anal intercourse is typical of male and female (and good there), but is therefore

---

7. The most detailed discussion of this metaphor is to be found in the helpful article by Olyan, "With a Male."

(as appropriate to male and female) prohibited between male and male? This is what the text would have to mean if it meant anal intercourse.

Many sodomy laws have supposed that Leviticus prohibits anal intercourse between male and female, or between male and male. This has been explained as a prohibition of nonprocreative sex. However, the statutes of Leviticus appear to have no such concern. Many of the sexual relationships that are prohibited (incest) are procreative. And there is no prohibition of nonprocreative sex between male and female known to the Bible (or to rabbinic tradition, for that matter).[8]

Feminization of the Male

There is another possibility that is not usually considered. It is that the law prohibits sexually using a male as an ersatz or imitation female. On this view what is interdicted is the feminizing of the male partner. Thus, in cases of male phallic aggression against other males, what is at stake is the "reduction" of the male to the position of the female. This was regularly recognized in antiquity as a danger lurking at the edges of male-male erotic relationships. There was always the possibility of the sex act degrading the partner, demasculinizing the partner. And the reason for this was that it was rather common to use sex in this aggressive way to humiliate one's foes. The example of the relationship between Seth and Horus, which we have cited from Egyptian tradition,[9] is only one salient illustration of this possibility.

As it stands, does this text forbid a certain type of male sex with males, the kind that uses the male as a female and so feminizes the male? If so, then it certainly does identify a practice that we also know from the stories of Sodom and Gibeah, of attempted male phallic aggression against males (Gen 19; Judg 19). If this is what the text prohibits, then it surely is not in contradiction to the story of David and Saul or David and Jonathan. In this view, it does not prohibit male same-sex relationships where these are the expression of desire or delight, which desires and delights in the maleness of the partner. It prohibits relationships where the maleness of the partner is not the object of delight but is an obstacle to be overcome in order to lie with the male "as with a female."

This interpretation would also help to make clear another feature of the text. While it is concerned with the sexuality of females, it is not concerned with same-sex activity between females. If the text were truly worried about same-sex activity as a problem, it would seem natural to forbid this

---

8. A fine discussion of the impossibility of explaining these laws by reference to the issue of procreation is in Cohen, "Prohibition," 5 and 5n5.

9. In connection with the romance of David and YHWH; see chapter 3.

among women, just as bestiality is equally forbidden to men and to women.[10] But if the issue is the sort of phallic aggression that makes the male into an ersatz female, then same-sex behavior between women understandably does not come into view.

There is another consideration that further supports this interpretation. The prohibition is found in the context of a series of prohibitions of sexual activity that expose another person to the violation of their honor or standing. Thus, the uncovering of the nakedness of "your father's wife" uncovers your father's nakedness; it exposes him to the loss of honor or to shame. But that is precisely what phallic aggression does in denying the maleness of the sexual partner. And this is something that other forms of same-sex behavior do not do and generally take significant precautions not to do.

Finally, we may observe that if the law meant to prohibit same-sex relationships, generally it would not make sense to append this prohibition to a series of laws that begins by apparently prohibiting males from having sexual relations with their fathers (18:7).[11] If all same-sex relationships are prohibited, why a special prohibition of this one? And if this one is covered by the prohibition of lying with a male as with a female, then why is it said that lying with one's father is forbidden because it exposes one's mother's nakedness? Why not simply say, because it is lying with another male (as with a female)? The reason is, I think, rather simple. Sexual relations with one's father is *not* lying with a male as with a female (for it is sex with one's father precisely as father and not as a substitute for a female). Yet it is still forbidden because it exposes the sexual partner of one's father, who is also one's mother.

Careful attention to the text thus suggests that what may be at stake here (if we take as our starting point the perspective of the penetrator) is not same-sex relations as such but precisely those that are an attack on the maleness of the male partner.

On this reading, whatever the text prohibits, it does not prohibit much of what would ordinarily be involved in same-sex relationships. But if that is true, it turns out that same-sex relationships as such are nowhere prohibited in biblical literature and are in fact regularly affirmed and celebrated. What the Bible prohibits is simply the use of sex to do violence to another person.

---

10. This is also a problem with Olyan's contention that the problem has to do with anal intercourse mixing two polluting substances, semen and excrement ("With a Male," 202–4). This would surely be at least as much of a problem in heterosexual anal intercourse, which the codes do not proscribe.

11. Many commentators avoid this problem by supposing that in this case the idiom "uncover the nakedness of" does not refer to a specifically sexual act. This stratagem, however, is forced. In Lev 18:6–19 the idiom occurs fourteen times in full form and another dozen times in a derivative (because it is so-and-so's nakedness)—all in fourteen verses. It is the worst form of ad hoc exegesis to suppose that in one occurrence of the term, and the lead occurrence at that, something else is meant than what it means in every other occurrence.

That is where we might leave the matter. But this discussion has taken the position, regularly presupposed by commentators, that the prohibition is addressed to those who penetrate other males. This is the way many restrictions of same-sex practice were formulated in antiquity. But is this really what is going on here?

Don't Be Penetrated

Most commentators simply assume that anal penetration is what is at stake in this prohibition. Saul Olyan has produced a convincing argument for this interpretation in his analysis of the parallel expression "the lying with of a male."[12] This idiom is used to designate a virgin who has not experienced "the lying with of a male."[13]

Olyan argues not only that what is in view is insertive sex and therefore (as the only possibility for this among males) anal penetration. But he also maintains (as the previous argument has also done) that the law is addressed to the would-be penetrator. This is also the view of subsequent rabbinic commentary. Nevertheless, it is important to give attention to the possibility that what is specifically prohibited here is being penetrated by another male.

Hence, the idiom would mean: Don't lie with a male as if *you* were a female. This would make sense of a number of otherwise puzzling features of the text. First, it enables us to take into account that the term "lie with" may be used of either the male or the female in reference to cross-sex practice (see Gen 39:7, 12; 2 Sam 13:11). Thus, the specification here of a prohibition addressed to males against lying with another male would specify "not in the way a woman does," not as the insertee in intercourse.

Understanding the prohibition in this way clears up how it is that the text shows no interest, for example, in cross-sex anal intercourse. For whether in anal or vaginal intercourse, the female partner is the one penetrated, and so is the one who has sex "in the way of a woman." The text is concerned only when the male has sex in this way, that is, as being penetrated—in this case necessarily anally.

If the term *to'evah* (abomination) is to be understood in a general sense as the mixing of categories or the crossing of boundaries, then what would be in view here is crossing the boundary of gender role expectation. But the penetrator does not do this. He remains in the "typically male position." The one who is penetrated performs the mixing of categories. It is he who

---

12. Olyan, "With a Male," 183–86.
13. Ibid., citing Num 31:17–18, 35; Judg 21:11–12.

acts as a female and so confuses the social categories that Leviticus (and not only Leviticus) is concerned to enforce.

In this case we have to do not with the moral equivalent of rape but with the moral equivalent of, say, cross-dressing. The law of Lev 18:22 is concerned only with the one who voluntarily submits to being penetrated or actually solicits that penetration. The prohibition of Lev 20:13 includes the penetrator as the (secondary) collaborator in this subversion of boundaries.

This would also help to clarify another aspect of the text observed by Olyan, that unlike other comparable laws in the ancient Near East or classical antiquity, this law seems formulated without regard to the status of the object of penetration. Many comparable laws say something like "Don't penetrate a male who is an adult, or free, or compatriot, or neighbor."[14] Here the prohibition seems to ignore lines of status. But this is exactly what one would expect if the law were addressed not to the would-be penetrator but to the would-be penetratee. The law is addressed not to slaves or foreigners or youths, but to free adult males. And these are the very ones who are generally off-limits with respect to being penetrated in the comparable texts from other societies. That is, the status of the penetrator never licenses the penetration of precisely the sort of males who are addressed by this law code.

The law, as thus understood, would also comport well with the kind of gender consciousness of other Hebrew Bible texts such as the law of Deut 22:5, against cross-dressing, or the suggestion that gender role reversal is a decided misfortune (in 2 Sam 3:29). From the standpoint of a highly gender-conscious society, the willing acceptance of the "feminine" role in sexual intercourse would self-evidently be "abominable," regardless of the views concerning same-sex eroticism in general. This is all the more likely since the law of Deut 22:5 uses the same notion of *to'evah* to apply to the gender mixing involved in cross-dressing. Hence, putting on the other gender's clothes is the moral equivalent of a male assuming the other gender's role in sex.

Confirmation of this interpretation of the Levitical prohibition comes from Philo's book *On the Special Laws.* Philo's task in this commentary on the legal codes of Israel is to show that they are not arcane but rather enlightened legislation, which a Hellenistic audience may receive with approbation. In his commentary Philo first singles out the activity of the "passive" partner in a homoerotic relationship. He writes that this "is a matter of boasting not only to the active but [also] to the passive partners, who

---

14. For example, the Middle Assyrian laws (A.20) prohibit a man from lying with his neighbor (*ANET*, 181), while the Hittite laws prohibit a man from sexually violating his son (*ANET*, 196).

habituate themselves to endure the disease of effemination" (3.37). After a description of the use of cosmetics and fragrances, he asserts, "These persons are rightly judged worthy of death by those who obey the law" (3.38). Only subsequently will he also apply the same law to the active partner: "And the lover of such may be assured that he is subject to the same penalty" (3.39). Philo returns to vent his indignation about those who effeminize themselves (3.40–42).[15] What is of greatest concern for Philo is not the feminizing of the other, which serves as a way of condemning the "active" or insertive partner, but the feminizing of oneself in order to lure the attentions of the "masculine" or active partner. The prohibition is addressed to the male subject who desires to be penetrated by the male and only then to the active male who collaborates in this design.

The View from the Bottom

We have seen that the prohibition in Leviticus directs itself to males who desire to be penetrated by other males and, subsequently, to the males who collaborate with this desire. What is still lacking is to inquire whether the desire to be penetrated itself is rooted in the religious imaginarium of Israel. I will be suggesting that there is, in the religion of Israel (and to a significant degree the same would be true of monotheism generally), a pronounced incitement for males to desire the dominant male. What this means is that what Leviticus prohibits, the biblical tradition more generally also incites.

In his landmark study *God's Phallus and Other Problems for Men and Monotheism*, Howard Eilberg-Schwartz notices that the development of a strong affective relation between a male deity and a male devotee is already homosocial and homoerotic. It is homosocial because it involves two male subjects; it is homoerotic because it involves a strong affective component. We may add that the specific eroticism involved is that of the erotic or sexual submission of the human partner to the divine. The more intensely felt this relationship, the more the solicitation of an erotic submission to the divine. And the more the masculinity or maleness of the partners is emphasized, the more likely a specifically homosexual component comes to the fore.

In developing his thesis, Eilberg-Schwartz pays particular attention to the accounts of "sightings" of YHWH, which in his view betray an uneasy aversion of the gaze from the loins, the genitals, and so the penis/phallus of

God. In his interpretation, this uneasiness is rooted in the implicit homo-eroticism of the encounter and so stirs up warding-off gestures calculated to diminish the threat of the homosexualization of this relationship.

But on what grounds should the homosexualization of this relationship be a problem? Eilberg-Schwartz supposes that this is because of the inter-diction of father-son incest in which the son is the agent or active subject of the incest, a prohibition inscribed in Israel's law codes and the probable sub-ject matter of the incident of Noah and Ham (Gen 9). But we are left to wonder why it is that Israel should be the site of this odd prohibition. Recourse to psychoanalytic theory does not help here. For if this were to function as an explanation, it would tell us why such a prohibition is uni-versal, not why it appears precisely here in the law codes of Israel.

The answer to this question rather lies, I believe, in the character of the erotic desire that the religious perspective of Israel, at least in many of its expressions, incites or solicits. That is precisely the desire of the man to be erotically or sexually the object of another male's erotic or sexual attraction. In other words, it is the desire of the bottom for the top.

This is quite different from the way in which homoerotic desire is gen-erally construed, especially in the other societies of antiquity about which we have much information. In Greece and Rome and perhaps in others as well, the preoccupation has to do with the desire of the top for the bottom, the desire of the *erastēs* (lover) for the *eromenos* (beloved). In this discourse, at least in terms of its dominant features, it is the *erastēs*, the penetrating male, who is the subject or agent of desire. But not so, I am arguing, in a monotheistic, androcentric faith/culture. Here the desiring subject is precisely the would-be beloved, *eromenos*, or bottom.

This is already evident from the very structure of monotheism when both divinity and the deity's devotee are figured as decidedly male. But the argument here is not only structural; it also is amply attested by the very texts we have examined in the course of this study. Perhaps the most vibrant example is that of David, who may serve as exemplar here. As we have seen, David is ideal bottom not only for Saul (and Jonathan and Achish) but also for Adonai. Moreover, David's role as the beloved of more-powerful males is directly related to his being the beloved of Adonai. It is his steadfastness in love, as for Saul, in spite of the latter's repeated attempts upon his life, that serves to demonstrate in the narrative how it is that David may also be the ideal beloved of YHWH. It is as if his relationship to Saul (as well as to Jonathan) teaches David how to be a proper beloved. The story gives no hint that his relation to Saul or Jonathan conflicts with his relation to YHWH. These relations do not conflict with, but rather complement, the relation with Adonai. After all, it is because YHWH has looked on him with favor that David is brought to the attention of Saul (and then of Jonathan). Conversely, it is because of David's relations with Saul and Jonathan that he becomes the man who is able to deal with YHWH, to tame his ferocious lover and teach him, as it were, the character of steadfast love.

We have noticed that with respect to the homoeroticism of the David narrative as well as that of the Former Prophets from Samuel to Elijah and Elisha, the homoerotic relations do not result in what might be properly termed the feminization of the beloved. David, like the boy-companions of Saul and Jonathan, is and remains the decidedly male companion of the more powerful lover. This remains true of the prophets. Samuel is not feminized by his relation with Adonai but rather becomes the center of the phallic potency of YHWH. The boys who are raised by Elijah and Elisha are not only brought to life; they also become "potent."

Only in the case of Israel being transgendered can we speak of something like a feminization. But even here a certain caution must be observed. As we have seen, interpreters of the transgendering metaphor in the Prophets have often simply assumed that this is to have a shaming effect upon the male readers, who are expected to identify with/as Israel or Judah. But this shaming applies to the adulterous or promiscuous behavior of transgendered Israel, not to the transgendered subject as such. For even or especially as transgendered, the idealized Israel/Judah is envisioned as returning the steadfast love of YHWH. Israel still relates to YHWH as if Israel were female (though clearly male).

What does seem to emerge from these texts, then, is a remarkable picture of homoerotic relations that privileges (for human males) the role of the one who is penetrated. What the texts exemplify in their ideal male subjects is not the penetrator so idealized in Rome or taken for granted in Greece, but the role of the bottom.

If this is so, we can gain some perspective on the relation of the Leviticus prohibition to the biblical traditions that we have been considering. There is indeed in a fundamental respect a matching up of perspective. In the case of the narrative tradition, we have what amounts to something like an incitement of the bottom's desire and a privileging of the bottom as desiring subject. It is precisely this desire that the Levitical prohibitions interdict. In both narrative and legal code, it is the bottom, the penetratee, who is primarily addressed. In this matter, Israel is distinct from the better-known examples of Greece and Rome. But it is also clear how it could happen that in Israel, unlike in other cultures known to us, a prohibition of taking the position of bottom is addressed to adult free males. It is precisely because so much conspires to make it almost self-evident that this would be the "temptation" of those who are the male adorers or devotees of a masculine divinity who is figured as in some way their "Lover."

What the legal texts prohibit is not this relation to the divinity, who in any case has begun to markedly recede into transcendence and so is no longer quite the vibrant, potent, masculine force of the sagas or even the prophetic narratives. What is interdicted is the seeking of this relation with other human males. This itself may owe to a certain progression from the prophetic figuring of the rivals for Israel's affections. The new rivals are not other male divinities but other human males: the masculine empires of Assyria or Babylon or even of Egypt. Israel turns his erotic attentions to these (human) males instead of to the Great Male, to whom his love was first pledged (or in some other way owed).

It is a further step, though an intelligible one, to suppose that the turning to one's male neighbor, not an empire but an actual individual male, for the satisfaction of erotic desire may come into conflict with devotion to YHWH. As we have seen, erotic practices among males in Israel are not understood this way at all in the narrative traditions. Nor are the prophets who transgender Israel concerned to accuse him of promiscuity and even adultery with the great powers. But the imagery is available for use in this way, and the linking of same-sex erotic practices to the customs of the foreigners (Canaanites and Egypt) serves as a kind of bridge in this direction.

Nevertheless, it really is the association of same-sex interhuman practices with collaboration with, or cultural penetration by, foreign cultures that seems to me to make this last step really thinkable.

The Fear of Colonial Penetration

We may point out that the concern for being penetrated comports well with the suggestion that Israel is to avoid cultural contamination (penetration) by foreign cultures, which the law itself names as the Egyptians and the Canaanites (Lev 18:3). The whole worldview of Leviticus is one that suggests the fear of assimilating to the mores of other nations, societies, and cultures. Mary Douglas has observed, "When rituals express anxiety about the body's orifices, the sociological counterpart of this anxiety is a care to protect the political and cultural unity of a minority group."[16]

It is precisely this connection linking several concerns—for group boundaries (expressed everywhere in Leviticus), for gender role reversal (in

16. Margaret Mary Douglas, *Purity and Danger* (London: Routledge & Kegan Paul, 1966), 124.

the proscriptions), and about cultural and social threat—that leads us to the question of the way in which the laws of Leviticus came into being.

There are, I believe, two related explanations: (1) the cultural influence of Persian (especially Zoroastrian) religious concerns on the priestly world-view, with its emphasis on purity; and (2) the need to mobilize a defense against the cultural imperialism of Hellenism following the conquests of Alexander the Great (326 BCE).

After the Babylonian exile (586–538), the former leadership cadres of Judea and Jerusalem were permitted to return under the colonial administration of the Persian emperor. This process was gradual and extended over several generations (from 538–358). In the early stages of this, the returned exiles began to build the second temple (ca. 515) and started the immense work of compiling what we now have as the Prime Testament. This process continued through the time of the writing of Daniel, which occurred after 164. Most of the literature of the Apocrypha was produced even later. Although little is known about this period of Israel's history (especially from 520 to 170), it appears to be the period of greatest literary productivity.

During this time the book of Leviticus took its final shape. This shaping may have taken place in the Persian period (530–326), or at the latest in the early Hellenistic period (after 326 but before 150). Since Ezra was regarded as a foremost student of the law and his work was done under Artaxerxes (404–358), it is most unlikely that the Torah had taken final form before his work was completed. The Pentateuch must have taken final shape before the division between the Jews and the Samaritans since the latter accept the Pentateuch as the Law of Moses. But while many scholars have supposed that this schism took place rather soon after the return from exile, others place the division as late as the second century BCE, well after the Alexandrian conquest.[17] Thus, it is quite possible that it comes to its final form after the Macedonian conquest, in the period of Greek hegemony, and it may even be as late as the Hasmonean period (from about 160 BCE).[18]

The primary religious influence from the Persian period was the Zoroastrian religion. From this tradition Israel adopted many of the themes of apocalypse (the final battle between good and evil, the resurrection of the dead, the final judgment, the views of angels and demons, and so on). Hence, we know that Zoroastrian ideas influenced the development of Israel's religion. Among the most important ideas of Zoroastrianism was the

---

17. See Greenberg, *Construction*, 192n45.
18. Niels Peter Lemche, in his intriguing essay "The Old Testament—A Hellenistic Book?" *Scandinavian Journal of the Old Testament* 7, no. 2 (1993): 163–93, has argued that virtually the whole of the OT may be attributed to the Hellenistic period. Whatever the merits of that discussion, for my purposes it is enough to suggest that at least some of this literature, including certain legal formulations, may derive from this period.

emphasis on rigid notions of purity and the focus on the body as the locus for the struggle for that purity. In Leviticus, many ideas concerning purity and pollution seem to reflect Persian/Zoroastrian influence.[19]

Within this context, Zoroastrianism developed an absolute prohibition of male same-sex activity. This prohibition takes the form of a prohibition almost identical in form to what we find in Leviticus, including the death penalty of Lev 20:13.

The prohibition, as cited by Horner,[20] is as follows:

> Ahura Mazda answered: the man that lies with mankind as a man lies with womankind, or as a woman lies with womankind, is the man that is a Daeva [demon]; this is the man that is a worshiper of the Daevas, that is the male paramour of the Daevas, that is a she Daeva; . . . so is he, whether he has lain with mankind as mankind, or as womankind.

And Horner comments:

> A footnote on the same page in this translation[21] says that the guilty "may be killed by anyone without an order from the Dastur."

The Zoroastrian text seems to substantiate the proposal that the Leviticus text should be understood as initially concerned with the willing assumption of the passive, or insertee, position in same-sex anal intercourse. The conclusion of the Zoroastrian law moves from the condemnation of the passive partner to a condemnation of both partners, just as Lev 20:13 (but not 18:22) does. The Zoroastrian addition of the death penalty similarly corresponds to the direction of 20:13.

Therefore, we seem to have a parallel progression from the condemnation of the willing acceptance of anal penetration, to the condemnation of both parties, to the insistence on the death penalty.

The imposition of the death penalty, which does not appear in Lev 18, makes sense in the context of Zoroastrianism's war to the death against the demons that invade the body with pollution. Hence, the death penalty for same-sex activity prescribed by the *Vendidad* may well be the origin for the imposition of the death penalty for this and other "crimes" in Lev 20.

---

19. Greenberg, *Construction*, 192, observes: "The period of ritual impurity after childbirth is exactly the same in both. This could hardly be coincidence."

20. Horner, *Jonathan*, 78.

21. *The Zend-Avesta*, part 1, *The VendÔdad*, in *Sacred Books of the East*, vol. 4 (trans. James Darmeteter; ed. F. Max Müller; Oxford: Clarendon, 1880; repr. Delhi: Motilal Banarsidass, 1965), 101–2.

Concerning this death penalty, there is no record that Judaism, either in the Second Temple period or in nearly two millennia following the temple's destruction, has ever imposed the death penalty for same-sex behavior.[22] Although the text comes from Judaism, only Christians have applied it! The apparently extreme homophobia of Lev 20:13 remains only symbolic in Judaism's history. But it becomes terribly real in the Christianity of the late Middle Ages and in the Protestantism of the early modern (Enlightenment!) period.

Does the Zoroastrian view influence the view of Leviticus? Unfortunately, we know almost as little about the redaction process that produces the basic texts of Zoroastrianism as we do of the production of Leviticus. However, Greenberg reports that the earliest text of Zoroastrianism does not condemn same-sex practices, but the *Vendidad* does. This text he ascribes to the period following the conquest of Persia by Alexander. If the *Vendidad* comes from the Parthian period (in Persia, 247 BCE–228 CE), as seems quite possible, then it would correspond to the late Second Temple period of Judaism.

It seems possible that Zoroastrian ideas influenced the production of Leviticus and especially the prohibition of same-sex activity. But on what grounds would this have come to seem so compelling an idea in Judaism, with its previously much more relaxed attitude?

To understand how the prohibition of male same-sex behavior came to have the form of Lev 20:13, it may be helpful to suggest how this also may have happened in Zoroastrianism.

Here it is useful to recall the suggestion of Herodotus, writing in the fifth century BCE, who says that the Persian ruling classes freely adopted customs from other cultures. In this context he suggests that they have adopted pederasty from the Greeks (*Histories* 1.135).

For our purposes it does not matter whether Herodotus or his Persian informants are correct about the origin of the Persian practice of pederasty. But it does matter that the Persians thought this was the origin of the practice and that it was relatively widespread among the ruling elites. This in itself would be enough to suggest how popular Zoroastrianism (as opposed to the culture of the court) could develop an antipathy to these practices. But this would be greatly exacerbated as Greece became a more militant and threatening rival and finally became (through Alexander) a conquering power, threatening cultural hegemony. Thus, Greenberg attributes the

---

22. "We have no record of a death sentence for this crime being carried out under Jewish auspices," writes Bernard J. Bamberger in *Leviticus* (vol. 3 of *The Torah: A Modern Commentary*; New York: Union of American Hebrew Congregations, 1979), 189.

Vendidad's extreme preoccupation with purity and pollution to a "response to foreign conquest and domination," specifically that of Hellenistic cultural hegemony.[23] Hence, if Zoroastrianism had an earlier prohibition against same-sex activity even before the Alexandrian conquest, that prohibition itself may have been a defensive reaction against Greek ideas.

The Zoroastrian precedent may have commended itself to the authors of the Holiness Code when they faced similar problems of cultural contamination or penetration following the Alexandrian conquest and the threat represented by this cultural invasion. One of the most obvious features of this cultural expansion was the institutionalization and valorization of same-sex relationships. We do know that this cultural imperialism does eventually produce a strong reaction in Israel in the second century (the Maccabean revolt). A part of the reason for that reaction had to do with the importation of the gymnasium (around 174 BCE), which was the privileged site of institutionalized same-sex (and cross-generational) erotic relationships (1 Macc 1:14; 2 Macc 4:12).

As a way of distinguishing itself as sharply as possible from cultural contamination by the culturally aggressive Hellenistic world, the blanket prohibition of same-sex activity may have commended itself to some already strongly influenced by Persian ideas of purity.

We have, then, the following possible sequence of events. In the period of the First Temple, there is widespread acceptance of same-sex as well as cross-sex activity. There is little interest in the detailed supervision of personal life and more in the question of justice and mercy as social matters. The only concern detectable about sexuality generally is either when this runs afoul of property rights (adultery) or when it is a matter of violation of other people's honor (and perhaps incest taboos).

The concern with the centralization of the cult as a part of the centralization of the Israelite state does produce a concern with the *qedeshim*, but this is so popular an institution that it proves impossible to eradicate during the time of the First Temple. Moreover, the prophets show little interest in this question.

Following the exile to Babylon of Judea's religious and political elites and their return under Persian cultural and political hegemony, Israel begins to consolidate its traditions. In this period Leviticus takes shape with its concern for ritual purity. Either directly (following the Alexandrian conquest) or indirectly (as a result of Persia's preoccupation with Greek cultural influence), Judea's leaders adopt a basically defensive posture

---

23. Greenberg, *Construction*, 189.

relative to Greek cultural imperialism and so develop a prohibition of male same-sex sexual practices.[24] Given the persistence of Greek (and later Roman) cultural (and often military) threat, this prohibition comes to seem increasingly self-evident. The commonsense interpretation of the David saga is relegated to those who are attracted to the Hellenistic and Gentile world.[25]

Conclusion

It is one of the most curious features of biblical interpretation that two badly misunderstood verses from a late legal code should serve to character-ize an entire and otherwise polyphonous tradition as condemning same-sex eroticism and sexuality with particular ferocity. As a result the common sense of the tradition has been that Judaism is especially hostile to same-sex erotic practices and that in this way it is to be distinguished from the nations with which it came into contact. So successful has this interpretive tradition become that it has been accepted almost without question both by those who oppose and by those who celebrate same-sex eroticism. With respect to this issue, at least these two verses have been made to stand in the place of an entire biblical corpus.

What I have attempted to demonstrate, however, is that these prohibi-tions do not represent or reflect the range of perspectives that may be encountered in biblical literature. Indeed, so far from demonstrating the implicit homophobia of biblical traditions, they in fact offer testimony to the very homoeroticism they seem to interdict. They become intelligible precisely in a context in which homoeroticism is not only present but actu-ally incited or provoked by the traditions themselves. The laws interdict what the tradition incites; the laws prohibit what the narratives provoke.

This becomes especially clear when we recognize that the narratives we have considered in this study reflect and incite a particular kind of homoeroticism—the desire of the male to be sexually possessed by another male. I have termed this the desire of the bottom. It is the representation

24. This is a process that may be observed in the modern period as well. It is not uncommon for cultures that feel themselves under threat of imperializing cultural penetration to also maintain that male same-sex sexual practices are an especially noxious feature of the alien culture. Thus, contemporary Arab cultures regularly deny their own rather rich traditions of male same-sex eroticism in order to maintain that this is a feature of the Western culture by which they feel threatened. Similarly, Africanist opposition to Western cultural imperialism often takes the form of denying that same-sex eroticism was ever a feature of African cultures.

25. We may catch a glimpse of those who favor this Hellenistic approach and who may for that reason have appropriated the homoerotic traditions of Israel in the Hellenizers of 1 Maccabees who solicited the building of a gymnasium (1 Macc 1:11–14; 2 Macc 4:9–15). Unfortunately, the views of those associated with Jason are not recorded, but we have seen that there is ample support in biblical narrative for the program of adopting Greek ways associated with the building of a gymnasium, the leading institution of Greek-style pederasty.

and valorization of this subject position that distinguishes the homoeroticism of Israelite traditions from the styles of homoerotic desire more familiar to us from ancient Greece and Rome.

In the narratives related to the David saga, we have encountered the valorization of a character who is the erotic object of attraction for a succession of more-powerful males. It is precisely this that makes David the very type of one who is beloved of YHWH. It likewise is what makes David the one for whose sake YHWH remains loyal with steadfast love to the people whom David represents.

It was noticing how this dynamic works that led us to wonder about the relationship to YHWH enacted by what we termed YHWH's male groupies. These include not only the mysterious *qedeshim* but also the *bene-hanebi'im* and particularly the figures of Samuel and Saul, Elijah and Elisha.

And we have seen the later prophets employing this erotic structuring of the relation between YHWH and Israel in a series of remarkable representations of a transgendered Israel/Judah. This transgendering serves not only to admonish Israel/Judah for her/his promiscuity but also to invite the (male) people of God to imagine themselves as the faithful objects of YHWH's amorous attentions.

I have suggested that the particular structure of Israelite religion—a male deity with male adorers—has, at least in part, fueled the valorization of the subject position of the one who desires to be sexually possessed by another male. If this is true, then homoeroticism, while perhaps present in all cultures, is incited in an especially intense way by biblical traditions. That these traditions should come to be associated with, and even characterized by, the condemnation of homosexuality is one of the great ironies of history.

That the prohibition should be invented in the first place may have been due not only to a fear of being overcome by another more powerful culture. It may also be due to an internalization of that culture's norms, characterized by a disavowal of the desire of the male beloved for the male lover. How that may have happened and progressed to the point that the prohibition of male same-sex desire and practice comes to seem the self-evident character of the tradition must be the subject of another study. Such a project would take us beyond the canonical texts of Israel.

In any case, what seems to have happened is that the prohibition has come to serve to silence the provocation of homoerotic desire, and the interdiction has come to obscure the incitement of homoerotic desire. This conflict plays itself out in the energy generated by contemporary discussions of homosexuality in the religious traditions that derive from these biblical texts, and most dramatically today in Christianity. Only by removing from these prohibitions their power to hide and deny the eroticism to which they nevertheless testify can we hope to find ways to defuse the violence of this conflict.

11. The Question of Lesbian Priority

THE NARRATIVE MATERIAL we have considered thus far has been concerned with the erotic relationships evidenced between males in the Hebrew Bible. But is there no evidence for what we may term lesbian erotic relationships in this library of antiquity? Here I argue not only that we do have evidence of this sort of relationship depicted in these narratives, but also that it is even possible to identify a certain priority to female same-sex relationships in this material. Indeed, I wonder whether female same-sex relationships do not play an essential role in the transformation of male same-sex relationships. The latter change from those barely distinguishable from rape to those that seem to entail a structure more like that of lovers, characterized by desire, delight, and a certain faithfulness.

There is some evidence from antiquity that lesbian relationships do have a certain priority relative to male same-sex relationships, although this evidence is seldom noticed. The most famous example is that of Sappho, whose love poetry to her female beloveds was a paradigm not only for same-sex love poetry but also for poetry generally in the world of ancient Greece. Although her work was exceptionally well known in antiquity and has been acknowledged as influential ever since, what has been less often noticed is that her poetry may precede the evidence for male pederasty by several decades.

It is generally agreed that evidence for pederastic relations in Greece does not exist prior to about 630 BCE. It is only after this time that evidence begins to emerge of the valorization of such relationships. This is true both for physical remains, such as representations painted on pottery, and for literary traces. This date, however, is not certain. It simply marks the outside limit for the possible dating of evidence suggested by a significant change in the styles of pottery (from geometric to representational) and in the poetic evidence. The earliest poetic reference to cross-generational same-sex relations comes in the treatment of the tale of Zeus and Ganymede, which begins to be retold in ways that suggest sexual or erotic elements. Hence, Percy supposes that there is some evidence of this in the Homeric *Hymn to Aphrodite*, which he supposes was being recast around 600 BCE.[1] However, the dating of this revision is quite uncertain. The first datable literary source for imagining this relationship as homoerotic comes from the work of Ibycus, a poet who flourished around 530 BCE.[2] Most of the evidence relating to Greek-style pederasty comes more than a century later, when it seems that the Homeric tale of the friendship of Achilles and Patroclus begins to be reimagined as erotic in character.

Therefore, the earliest sure date for a representation of cross-generational, same-sex erotic attachment between males in Greece is about 530 BCE. Surprisingly, this is a full half-century after the composition of the poetry of Sappho, who flourished around 588. This poetry, which was revered by (male) intellectuals of the Greek-speaking world for a millennium, including (in the latter part of this period) Christian writers, was also known for its celebration of the love of a woman for her younger female students and admirers.[3] Indeed, the island on which she made her home and where she developed a sort of academy for young women has given its name (Lesbos) to female same-sex eroticism.

Nothing like certainty is possible when we are dealing with the fragmentary evidence that remains to us from antiquity. There is a great deal that has been lost, including most of Sappho's own poetry, and other evidence is often ambiguous in the extreme. However, there are here at least grounds for the hypothesis that female same-sex eroticism may exert a significant influence on the development of male same-sex eroticism. And this

1. William Armstrong Percy III, *Pederasty and Pedagogy in Archaic Greece* (Urbana: University of Illinois Press, 1996), 38.

2. Ibid., 39, citing K. J. Dover, *Greek Homosexuality* (New York: Vintage, 1978), 197.

3. For a useful discussion of Sappho and her reception by antiquity, see Bernadette Brooten, *Love between Women: Early Christian Responses to Female Homoeroticism* (Chicago: University of Chicago Press, 1996), 30–41.

may be especially so where elements of erotic attachment and strong feelings of desire and so on come to the fore. After all, the reputation of Sappho
as the greatest of Greek poets ensures that the language she develops as a
poet to express strong desire for and attachment to a younger person of the
same sex will have great influence. It indeed shapes the way subsequent
writers (and readers) express their own attachments and desire. That is, after
all, what great poets do.

Bacchae in Rome

This is not the only case in which the description of female same-sex relations seems to precede the development of male same-sex relations. If we
turn our attention from Greece to Rome, we may catch sight of a quite different example, this time from Livy's account of the transformation of the
followers of Dionysus (Bacchus) from an all-female group to one that
includes Roman males.

The cult of Dionysus seems to have involved homosociality among
women in classical Greece, and this may have continued to be true in
ancient Rome as this cult was imported under the name of Bacchus.
Some writers, such as Christine Downing,[4] have pointed to evidence that
male same-sex eroticism was a prominent feature of this Roman cult,
pointing to Livy's description of this as evidence. Yet what emerges from
attention to Livy's account is the supposition that female same-sex eroticism generates a certain imitation on the part of males.

The evidence for this transition is found in Livy's account of the discovery and suppression of a Bacchanalian plot or conspiracy in Rome around
the year 186 BCE.[5] (Livy, *History of Rome* 39.8–19). The story is launched
when a freedwoman prostitute, Hispala Fecenia, who had an adolescent
youth as a kind of kept boy, seeks to prevent her lover from being initiated
into Bacchic mysteries by his mother and stepfather. She seeks to scare him
away from this initiation by telling him that it will mean that his virtue
would be violently attacked under cover of the singing of a choir and the
beating of loud drums. He would then have not only to endure but also to
perform these "disgraceful practices."

Eventually this story comes to the attention of a consul, who launches an
investigation. The result is that about seven thousand Romans are condemned

---

4. Christine Downing, *Myths and Mysteries of Same-Sex Love* (New York: Continuum, 1989), 163. In this connection she cites Walter Burkert, *Greek Religion* (trans. J. Raffan; Cambridge: Harvard University Press, 1985),
109, citing Livy, *History of Rome* 39.

5. Livy, *The History of Rome* 38–39, in *Livy*, vol. 11, *Books 38–39* (trans. E. T. Sage; Loeb Classical Library;
Cambridge: Harvard University Press, 1936), 240–75.

as participants in this secret society; many of them, perhaps most (at least of the males), are executed.

The story of how this group came to be formed is of some interest. It is said to have been brought to Rome from Etruria, spreading "like the contagion of a pestilence" (39.9.1). According to Hispala's confession to the consul, the rites have originally been confined to women, but Paculla Annia as priestess has changed this by initiating her sons and holding the rites at night and with greater frequency. Finally, over the previous two years, only adolescents under the age of twenty have been initiated (39.13.9). Hispala maintains that now "there were more lustful practices among men than among women. If any were disinclined to endure abuse or reluctant to commit crime, they were sacrificed as victims" (39.13.11). In keeping with what we have seen of the connection with "prophetic" behavior (in part 2), Hispala tells the consul: "Men, as if insane, with fanatical tossings of their bodies, would utter prophecies" (39.13.12). In his report to the people, the consul maintains that there are many thousands of adherents to this cabal; "a great part of them are women, and they are the source of the mischief" (39.15.9). The consul maintains that this cabal is the source of all crime in Rome and that it has the goal of controlling the state (39.16.3). The panic produced by the consul's depiction of a vast underground criminal conspiracy results in officials sealing the city and neighbors and friends denouncing each other, with the result that thousands were indeed arrested and a great many executed.

In sorting out the features of this group, the difficulty is exacerbated by the McCarthyite witch-hunt rhetoric with which the ever credulous and patriotic Livy recounts it. What does stand out is that the movement, beginning with the female groups so regularly associated with the Bacchanalia, apparently did evolve in such a way as to include males. It is supposed that the predictable result of the incorporation of males into orgiastic mysteries is that they engage in same-sex behavior, which then is characterized as the rape of adolescent free males. The latter become perpetrators of the same sorts of sex acts on others as well as innumerable other crimes.

It is a classic sex panic. But it tells us little that is reliable about same-sex behavior among males in the context of the Bacchanalia or of Dionysian ecstasy. It does, however, offer a tantalizing hint of female homosociality serving as a precursor to and impetus for male homoerotic behavior. Hence, for both ancient Greece and ancient Rome, there is some indication that lesbian relations precede and serve as a model for male same-sex relationships.

This may leave us wondering whether the homosociality (and possible homoeroticism) of Israelite women after the incident of Jephthah's daughter contributes, through a process of imitation and adaptation, to the formation of homoerotic bands among Israelite males particularly devoted to YHWH. Let us see how this might work.

Jephthah's Daughter

The tale of Jephthah takes up the whole of Judg 11 and seems to divide itself into three acts. The first part of the story hinges on Jephthah's illegitimacy as the son of Gilead since his mother is a prostitute. Gilead also has sons with his wife, and these drive Jephthah away after Gilead's death to prevent him from sharing in (or, as the eldest son, having the lion's share of) Gilead's inheritance.

Jephthah becomes a notorious and apparently effective bandit leader in the hills of Tob. But when the Ammonites make war on the Israelites, the elders of Gilead beseech him to be their war-leader. After making them beg (he reminds them of the way he has been treated in the past), Jephthah makes a pact with them "before the LORD at Mizpah" (11:11).

The middle part of the story concerns Jephthah's recounting of the mighty deeds of YHWH to the Ammonite king in an attempt to make him back off from his attack. This is a kind of homiletical interlude.

The third part of the story begins as the first part ends, with a vow made by Jephthah to YHWH. In this case he vows that he will sacrifice to YHWH the first member of his household who comes to meet him.[6] This vow, so far from rousing the ire of YHWH, actually seems to provide Jephthah with the military success he has hoped for.

The result, however, is tragic; the first member of his household to meet him after his great victory is his daughter, his only child, who comes to meet him "with timbrels and with dancing" (11:34). A vow is a vow, especially one made "before the face of YHWH." To his credit Jephthah is distraught at this turn of events (unlike, for example, Abraham, of whom no such reaction is reported under similar circumstances). It is his daughter who consoles him by piously exclaiming:

> My father, if you have opened your mouth to the LORD, do to me according to what has gone out of your mouth, now that the LORD has given you vengeance against your enemies, the Ammonites. (11:36)

---

6. The question of human sacrifice in ancient Israel is one that requires a good deal of investigation. This is but one of many places where the saga materials make it clear that the sacrifice, especially of sons, to YHWH had been widespread in Israel, something that later authors are at pains to explain was a mistake.

But she also asks for a temporary reprieve:

> Let this thing be done for me: Grant me two months, so that I may go
> and wander on the mountains, and bewail my virginity, my companions
> and I. (11:37)

Jephthah agrees, and his daughter goes out into the mountain wilderness with her companions for two months to "bewail [her] virginity." When
she does return, the text informs us that Jephthah performed his vow (but
averting the reader's gaze from the grisly act of turning his daughter into a
burnt offering). Instead, what the text focuses on is the aftermath:

> So there arose an Israelite custom that for four days every year the daughters
> of Israel would go out to lament the daughter of Jephthah the Gileadite.
> (11:39–40)

What we have here, it would seem, is the etiology of a custom of long
duration in Israel. In this practice the (young?) women of Israel leave
behind their normal lives in order to wander in the mountain wilderness
and to recall the fate of one who was dedicated/sacrificed to YHWH.

This custom certainly suggests a form of female homosociality far from
the supervision of the patriarchal household. Do they reenact the daughter's
dance with timbrels and other instruments in the wild places? Do they
rejoice in the solace of one another's company as they lament the costs of
belonging to a world ruled by the strange customs of males and their
implacable male deity?

The modern reader may be put in mind of the contemporary
women's music festivals, where women find in one another the strength
to endure for another year the indignities of an androcentric world (and
the courage to transform that world). But in the ancient world, the parallel to the Dionysian maenads seems strong. In either case the possibility of
female homoeroticism as an expression of deep emotion and intimate
bonding cannot be ruled out. The writer assures us that Jephthah's daughter "had never slept with a man" even after the two months in the mountains. But the writer does not tell us how women found means to give
one another solace in the wilderness as they faced the coming death of
their friend.

The fleeting glance afforded us by this narrative of same-sex bands
singing and lamenting in the wilderness may seem a precursor to the bands
of wandering prophets that we have encountered in the saga materials

relating to Samuel and Saul, Elijah and Elisha. Again, there is some indication that the female groups may even precede and so perhaps influence the development of the all-male groups associated with YHWH.

The Story of Ruth and Naomi

The allusion in Judges to the solace that women may find with and from one another in temporary escape from the constraints of patriarchal structures prepares us for a quite different narrative. In it the bonds uniting women to one another take a quite different and far more definite form. It is the story of the love between Ruth and Naomi.

The story of Ruth and Naomi serves not only as an ancestral prelude to the story of David but also as an essential, if surprising, counterpoint to that saga. The story of David appears to be above all a story for and about men celebrating the adventures and exploits of men among men, in which women play only subordinate and minor roles. The story of Ruth and Naomi is the reverse of this field, focusing as it does on the struggles and the exploits of women in which even the principal male character, Boaz, is reduced to being the mechanism for securing the well-being of an enterprising partnership of women.

The Ruth-Naomi and David-Jonathan stories are also linked together thematically; they both deal with persons of the same gender loving one another. Because of the passionate romance that characterizes the relationships depicted, and the deep feeling and undying loyalty of the love narrated, these two stories have regularly served as models not only of same-sex but also of cross-sex friendship and lifelong loyalty.

The portion of the story that has been most often quoted comes early, after the reader has been told that Naomi has accompanied her husband and two sons to Moab on account of a famine in the land of Judah. As immigrant aliens in Moab, they apparently find hospitality. They settle there for several years, and Naomi's two sons find wives among the Moabites. Her husband has died, however, and soon her sons die as well. Hearing that the famine has passed in her own land, Naomi resolves to return, a lonely and bitter woman, in hopes of finding some kinsfolk to ease her last years. Her Moabitess daughters-in-law have apparently come to love Naomi and resolve to accompany her, themselves to be immigrant aliens in her land, as Naomi has been in theirs. Naomi argues that to do this would be tantamount to never marrying again. Orpah allows herself, reluctantly, to be persuaded, but "Ruth clung to her" (1:14). Naomi tries again to convince her to stay in Moab, but Ruth replies:

Entreat me not to leave you or to return from following after you; for
where you go I will go, and where you lodge I will lodge; your people shall
be my people, and your God my God; where you die I will die, and there
will I be buried. May the LORD do so to me and more also if even death
parts me from you. (1:16–17 RSV)

With good reason this declaration has been taken as a staple of wedding
ceremonies. It goes even beyond the "till death do us part" of the wedding
pledge to declare an unalterable commitment and permanent loyalty. Nowhere else in the Bible and scarcely in any literature do we find a more
affecting exhibition of love and loyalty.

Yet it is the declaration of one woman to another. It is the declaration of same-sex love that has become the model and expression of cross-
sex marriage.

Nor is this simply fortuitous or arbitrary. The text itself makes the reader
think of heterosexual conjugality.[7] The verb translated as "clung" (*dabaq*) in
the assertion that Ruth clung to Naomi (1:14) is the same verb used in Gen
2:24 to articulate the mystery of (hetero)sexual union:

Therefore a man leaves his father and mother and cleaves to his wife, and
they become one flesh. (RSV)

The extravagance of desire and delight, which the author of Genesis has
attributed to the relationship between male and female, becomes articulated
in the words of Ruth. Her "cleaving" breaks into speech with this declaration in such a way that it gives voice as well to the longing and loyalty that
struggle for speech between persons of the opposite sex.[8]

Moreover, the content of her speaking makes clear that Ruth, like the
man in Genesis, is leaving hearth and home in order to embark upon this
new relationship. This is underscored by the words of Boaz to Ruth when
he meets her in the field and tells her that he knows all she has done for the
sake of Naomi, including leaving "your father and mother and your native
land" (2:11).

---

7. For many of the following suggestions, I am indebted to the essay "The Book of Ruth: Idyllic Revisionism," in Ilana Pardes, *Countertraditions in the Bible: A Feminist Approach* (Cambridge: Harvard University Press,
1992), 98–117.

8. Tod Linafelt's commentary on Ruth in T. Linafelt and T. K. Beal, *Ruth and Esther* (Berit Olam; ed. D. W.
Cotter et al. Collegeville, MN: Liturgical Press, 1999), also points this out. He concludes: "It is likely that the
author is evoking intentionally the language of marriage in an attempt to express the intensification of the
relationship between Ruth and Naomi" (15). Linafelt, however, never explicitly suggests the homoerotics of
this relationship.

Finally, we have heard from Naomi that the choice her daughters-in-law have contemplated, which Ruth has subsequently actually made, is one that almost surely replaces marriage (1:13).

In a number of ways, then, the story insistently portrays the relationship between Ruth and Naomi as comparable to marriage and as an embodiment of it.

Nevertheless, this is not the end of the story. Ruth will eventually remarry, this time to Boaz. But this marriage is clearly not a relinquishing of the relationship to Naomi but a way of sheltering that relationship and of giving it security. Ruth and Naomi become coconspirators in snaring the wealthy Boaz. Indeed, Naomi gives Ruth precise instructions for an act of brazen seduction. She is to go onto the threshing floor after all are asleep and crawl under the cloak blanketing Boaz, uncovering his "feet" (3:4). Linafelt points out that here "feet" is likely a euphemism for genitalia and thus implies a fairly direct seduction.[9] When he discovers Ruth snuggling up to his bared flesh, he agrees to cover her so as to hide her (or rather, them) from the eyes of the other men. He appears delighted that she has tried to seduce him, an old man, rather than the young bucks on the floor (3:10). Hence, he decides on a way to prevent Ruth from being exposed as a shameless hussy so that he can marry her and have this beauty for himself.[10]

The plots all work out. Boaz acquires Ruth for a wife, and they produce an heir who is David's grandfather. But the fulfillment of this design is itself more than a little strange. It is not only that the whole thing is arranged by women in order to find security for the love that binds them to one another. The way the wording of the conspiracy works is also that Naomi, in telling Ruth what to do, says that she herself will do it (cf. 3:1). Thus, where we read "you," the Hebrew often reads "I."[11] It is as if in some fundamental way Ruth and Naomi are already "one flesh" (e.g., 3:3–4).

Moreover, the birth of Obed should, in patriarchal culture, mean that Ruth has given a son to Boaz. But the text makes clear that the son is born to Naomi. This is, at least, the view of the women of the village, who exclaim, "A son has been born to Naomi" (4:17). In an odd way the text makes Naomi both the mother (for she becomes the nurse of the infant; v. 16) and the father (for it is to her that the son is born). This merging and

---

9. Ibid., 49; cf. Exod 4:25; Isa 6:2; 7:20. As Linafelt (50) also points out, Fewell and Gunn have made the connection to the ruse employed by Tamar to become pregnant by Judah (Gen 38). See Danna Nolan Fewell and David Miller Gunn, *Compromising Redemption: Relating Characters in the Book of Ruth* (Louisville: Westminster/John Knox, 1990), 78.

10. The spreading of the cloak (3:9) and Boaz's vow (3:11) roughly correspond to the action of Ezek 16:8 save that in the case of Ruth it is she who has taken the initiative.

11. For a more detailed analysis of this grammatical mixing, see Pardes, *Countertraditions*, 104–5.

shifting of gender mirrors what has happened earlier in the case of Ruth. Though younger, she leaves mother and father and cleaves to Naomi as Genesis says the man cleaves to the woman.[12]

So interpreted, the story may help us to see how the love of women for one another has managed to survive and even thrive under conditions of patriarchy and heterosexism. The obligations of the patriarchal structure are in fact complied with: Boaz has a son.[13] But by this means the women find a shelter within which their love for one another can flourish. It is, after all, this love—the love of these two women for one another—that is the entire motivating force for the plot that unfolds; that is the romantic heart of this short story.

It is difficult to imagine how any tale from antiquity could have been more explicit in dealing with "women loving women" or with what is more prosaically termed a lesbian relationship. Yet, of course, men like Boaz have no clue about what is going on. He doesn't know that he spent the night not only with Ruth but also with her coconspirator. Boaz is pleased to be chosen over younger, more attractive mates, never suspecting the motive of economic security. He thinks a son has been born to him, but the village women know better; they know that Ruth has succeeded in giving Naomi a son. Boaz doesn't even name the son; the women do that for him. Boaz gets a son and more land and so never suspects what was and is going on.

Perhaps the story helps us see how literature produced for and by the beneficiaries of patriarchy scarcely ever notices the love affairs among women going on all around them. How could such a text have been produced? Could it have really been written with an eye to undermining the pretensions of patriarchy and heterosexism? Does the story actually flaunt conventions in the way I have suggested?

The narrative is remarkable in several ways and does seem calculated to overturn a number of conventions. In the first place, its central character, Ruth, is specifically and repeatedly identified as a Moabitess. No less than five times she is called "Ruth the Moabitess" (RSV: 1:22; 2:2, 21; 4:5; 4:10; cf. 1:4; 2:6). And there are at least eight other references to Moab as the land of her origin. Thirteen times the story underscores not only that Ruth is an immigrant alien in Israel but also that she is of the people of Moab. This is

---

12. Linafelt notices considerable gender bending going on in the story. For example, he suggests that in Ruth's initial experience in the field, she is doing harvesting while the men are drawing water (*Ruth*, 35). At the end of the story (4:12), it is Ruth who will provide "seed" to Boaz rather than the reverse (77).

13. Ruth 4 oddly echoes the instructions concerning levirate marriage in Deut 5:5–10. However, in Deuteronomy the sandal is taken from the man's foot in order to shame him, whereas in Ruth the man removes his own sandal to relinquish his claim on Naomi's inheritance.

especially striking given the assertion of Deut 23:3–6 that all descendants of a Moabite are cut off "even to the tenth generation." Not only would Ruth be affected by this curse but also David, the fourth generation from Ruth and Boaz, and the Davidic line until the curse ran out!

The repeated references to Ruth's nationality seem to constitute a protest against at least some of the legal traditions articulated in Deuteronomy. It is like the opposition between Isaiah and Deuteronomy regarding eunuchs, in which Deuteronomy casts them out of the land of Israel while Isaiah speaks of their specific inclusion (see ch. 9).

The story of Ruth is connected to another story that we have had occasion to consider before in connection with the *qedeshim*, that of Tamar and Judah. At the conclusion of the story of Ruth, the chorus of villagers chants to Boaz:

> May your house be like the house of Perez, whom Tamar bore to Judah, because of the children that the LORD will give you by this young woman. (4:12 RSV)

And the tale concludes with a recital of the "descendants of Perez," which continues the line from Tamar to David (4:18–22). Matthew repeats this genealogy (with the single addition of providing Boaz not only with a father (Salmon) but also with a mother: Rahab, the hospitable whore of Jericho.

The story of Ruth, like that of Tamar, is a story of how women manage to manipulate men in order to acquire what they need in order not only to survive but also to thrive.

The connection with Moab prepares us for a story that will stand in tension with legal traditions in Israel.[14] The connection with Tamar prepares us for a story of the adventures of women negotiating the hostile territory of heterosexist patriarchy.

We have concentrated on the relationships among the characters and the securing of a hospitable environment for the flourishing of the love between Ruth and Naomi. But there is another dimension to the text that should also be noticed: the transformation of Naomi. At the beginning of the text, she is rather like Job. Her husband and sons have died, and she is reduced to returning as a beggar to Judah. Her words are bitter concerning her plight, and she does not hesitate to blame God for her situation. She tells her daughters-in-law: "It is exceedingly bitter to me for your sake that

14. Linafelt also points out that the repeated references to Moab also suggest "illicit sexuality" (*Ruth*, 27). He identifies a number of parallels in terminology between the account of Ruth's seduction of Boaz and the seduction of Lot by his daughters (52).

the hand of the LORD has gone forth against me" (1:13 RSV). When she arrives home, she says:

> Do not call me Naomi [Pleasant], call me Mara [Bitter], for the Almighty has dealt very bitterly with me. I went away full, and the LORD has brought me back empty. Why call me Naomi, when the LORD has afflicted me and the Almighty has brought calamity upon me? (1:20–21 RSV)

Nevertheless, by the end of the story, there is rejoicing for Naomi; the women say she has "a son" and moreover a "daughter-in-law who loves you, who is [worth] more to you than seven sons" (4:15, 17). Naomi's faith has been restored and her life redeemed. This too God has done. But God has done this precisely through the love of one woman for another.[15] The story of Ruth is a story of redemption. It is the story of how women loving women is itself an instrument of blessing and redemption. For this it is appropriate also, as the village women insist, to declare, "Blessed be the LORD" (4:14).[16]

To be sure, in our own day the story of women loving women takes other forms. Often it takes the form not of finding shelter within the structures of heterosexism and patriarchy but of an exodus from these structures. But like the love of Ruth for Naomi, it often enough rejoices in the birth and care of children. It still echoes, at least as well as other relationships, the passionate and enduring words of commitment found on the lips of Ruth. And it still serves to assuage the bitterness of life so that even those who have experienced this bitterness come to have cause to bless the Lord.

This beautiful and strange story of the love of two women for one another and of how that love both survives and flourishes is the prelude to the story of David. Perhaps it is only because it was connected to David in this way that so subversive a story could have been retained in the canon of literature sacred to Judaism and to Christianity.

But that it is the prelude to the story of David also means that the story of Ruth incites us to read the story of David in its light. This means to attend even more closely to the astonishing fact that the saga

---

15. Linafelt reports that traditional commentaries emphasize God at work behind the scenes of this story, which they then make into a homily upon divine providence. However, he declares: "If there is someone acting throughout the story from behind the scenes or in the shadows, we must conclude that it is Ruth" (*Ruth*, 78). However, Naomi also takes her turn to work behind the scenes in her instructions to Ruth concerning Boaz. Hence, what takes the place of God's work is the steadfast love between these two women.

16. Fewell and Gunn observe the way in which Ruth in particular is "a redeemer in her own right" (*Compromising Redemption*, 105). In addition, the act of YHWH, the *khesed* of YHWH, is to be found not in something that comes from outside but from the action of the characters, especially the love of these women for one another (103–5).

of young David is the story of the vicissitudes of love when men love one another.

While the story of Ruth chronologically precedes the story of David, it may not have been written before the Davidic sagas took shape. It may indeed have been written in part to link previously existing versions of our books of Judges and Samuel.[17] If this is true, then in written form the complex love stories of 1 and 2 Samuel would have preceded the love story of Ruth and Naomi. Hence, this story of women loving one another would not have the chronological priority of influence we have suspected in the cases of Sappho in Greece, the Bacchanalia in Rome, or possibly the sojourn of the daughters of Israel in commemoration of Jephthah. The priority here would be of a different character, one oddly signaled by its placement as a prelude to the story of David.

For this story gives us a more interior view of the relationships of love and loyalty between persons of the same sex. In the case of the David saga, it is necessary to tease out traces of this kind of relationship. But these traces seem more emotionally compelling when seen in the light of the love between Ruth and Naomi. When we read this story, we are prepared to notice the extravagant loyalty that comes to be expressed between David and Jonathan, for example, and thereby to see how other relationships in that saga are lit up by the light of complex and conflicting loves and loyalties.

The story of Ruth and Naomi serves to depict what it means to have steadfast love, what it means to "cleave to one another," what it means to be knit together as one soul. It shows what it means for the love of two persons of the same sex to love one another in ways that "surpass" the more structured heterosexual relationships within patriarchal culture. David says that Jonathan's love to him was "wonderful, [sur]passing the love of women" (2 Sam 1:26). One can imagine what this means by thinking what it would mean for Ruth or Naomi to say that their love for one another surpasses the love of/for men (such as Boaz). Thus, a kind of canonical priority works to provide a certain interpretive priority in the sense of helping the reader to grasp what comes next.

But there is also another sense in which we can say that this story of love between two women has a certain priority. It has to do with the way in which the theme of *khesed* (steadfast love) comes to expression here. We have seen that this term is associated with the sort of love that comes into

---

17. For a brief discussion of the dating of the book, see Linafelt, *Ruth*, xviii. He supposes that it may have been written about the time of the Babylonian exile, which would make it contemporaneous with Sappho. Since most of Sappho's poetry is lost, such dating would make this story the earliest testimony to female same-sex love so far identified in history.

being between David and YHWH; it becomes the identifying character of
YHWH in relating to Israel, "for David's sake" (see ch. 3). But we have also
seen that David's relation to YHWH—a relation that elicits this steadfast
love on the part of the formerly arbitrary and tyrannical deity depicted in
the early part of the narrative—is itself dependent upon David's training in
steadfast love in his relationships to his human lovers. All of this, we may
now say, is grounded in the narrative depiction of what steadfastness in
love really means as it comes to expression in the tale of Ruth and Naomi.
We have seen that this steadfast love is what stands in for the beneficent
care of YHWH. If God is in the story at all, God is there as their love for
one another.

And this brings us back to the suggestion I made at the end of the discussion of the transgendering of Israel. I observed that it was not only Israel
that could be transgendered; at the end of the process evident in prophetic
speech, YHWH also was coming to be transgendered. In that connection
I wondered whether there might be grounds for imagining the love of
YHWH for the people to be like the love of two women for one another.
The story of love between Ruth and Naomi not only shows us this love,
producing what otherwise YHWH's love is said to provide: seed, sons, and
security. This story also shows this love in such a way as to invite us to
reimagine the divine beyond and over against the ways associated with God
the father, god the warrior, god the law, god the husband, and all the other
ways in which the imaging of God has been held captive to an androcentric
world of discourse.

Ironically, it is by attending to the role of homoeroticism in these narratives, a homoeroticism that seems to exclude women, that we come to the
recognition that female homoeroticism may have the most to teach us
about the relationships we have been considering.

12. The Question
of Israel
and Greece

ONE OF THE COMMONPLACE ASSUMPTIONS and assertions that governs our perception of antiquity is that ancient Israel is the source of homophobia while classical Greece is the home of a more accepting attitude toward homosexuality. The rereading of Hebrew Bible narrative texts that we have undertaken in these pages casts considerable doubt on this assumption, or at least the first part of the assumption, that Israel is the source of homophobia, that same-sex eroticism was unknown there or universally condemned.

So entrenched has this view become on the part of both homophobic and homophilic readers that the readings I have proposed may seem positively bizarre. Yet I believe that reading these narratives from the standpoint of a gay-affirmative hermeneutic or interpretive strategy actually serves to make these narratives more rather than less intelligible, more rather than less accessible. I suppose that the narratives seen from this perspective make significantly more sense both internally (they hang together better) and in terms of our own contemporary understanding and appropriation of them. I do not suppose that the readings here proposed will be immediately adopted. Too many long-standing prejudices concerning these texts and the attitudes they are imagined to reflect are brought into question for any reappraisal of them and their significance to be either easy or quick. This is true not only because of the reign of something like homophobia but also because of the long-standing historical typology that casts Israel as the origin of homophobia for both gay and straight readers. In this chapter I suggest some consequences that follow for our understanding of antiquity and the rise and fall of same-sex relations.

It is difficult to imagine a more firmly entrenched view of the difference between ancient Greece and ancient Israel than one that ascribes an open tolerance for homoerotic relations to Greece and an abhorrence of them to Israel. However, if the readings of Hebrew biblical narratives as proposed in this book are at all persuasive, then it clearly seems that the ascription of homophobia to ancient Israel is at least a gross simplification and, more likely, a complete distortion of the evidence. For we have seen that the narratives of the Hebrew Bible lend themselves to a queer reading.

In part, this is nothing more than identifying the extraordinarily diverse heteroeroticism evident in Hebrew Bible narrative and extending into the domain of what is now called "homosexuality." With many others, we recognize the eroticism of the stories of Samson and Delilah, and David and Bathsheba (or David and the Schunammite maiden), the erotic poetry of the Song of Solomon, together with the presence of heroic prostitutes (Rahab and Tamar), the multiple wives of patriarchs and kings, the incest of Lot and his daughters, and of Amnon and Tamar, and much more. These accounts fill the pages of the Hebrew Bible with a diverse and insistent eroticism quite at odds with what have become the norms of heterosexuality in the modern period. Hence, it should scarcely be surprising that we also discover within this erotic panorama a multitude of similarly diverse representations of same-sex eroticism. What may have been evident to earlier generations of readers is that, so far as rape is concerned, the peoples described in the Hebrew Bible seem to have been equal-opportunity offenders. Males and females seem indiscriminately to be (potential) victims of violent assault, as the stories of Sodom and Gibeah remind us. But closer reading of the narratives shows a far greater diversity of same-sex practice than one limited to occasions of stranger gang rape, just as heteroeroticism in the Hebrew Bible extends far beyond the episodes of gang rape in which females are the victims.

Thus, we have encountered tales of a warrior culture in which many of the primary affectional relationships appear to be between warrior-heroes and their younger companions in derring-do. And we have seen this come to expression in the tangled relationships that bind together David and Saul and Jonathan. We have also encountered bands of males who seem to be subject to erotic trances in relation to their hypermasculine divinity, prophets who awaken boys to life and sexual potency by something very like sexual initiation, as well as the mysterious *qedeshim*, or holy ones. We have also encountered the transgendering of Israel, who is made into a promiscuous or faithful wife of the warrior God, and the transgendering of Joseph, a liminal figure.

This profusion of homoerotic types or tropes is already quite different from the rather staid representation of institutionalized pederasty in ancient Greece, so familiar to modern readers. While in Hebrew literature we don't find clear evidence of the institutionalization of same-sex relations and especially not in the rather restricted conventions of Athenian-style pederasty, we do find evidence of a rather diverse set of expressions of male same-sex attractions and practices. Hence, the difference between Greece and Israel appears not to lie in something so simple as the prohomosexuality of Greece and the antihomosexuality of Israel. Rather, the difference appears to be more that between a relatively restricted form of acceptable same-sex practice (classical pederasty) and a rather more diverse proliferation of kinds of same-sex practice and relationships reflected in the literature of ancient Israel.

This is true as well for the evidence that remains of female same-sex relationships. In both cultures the evidence is rather slender, given the preoccupations of androcentric and patriarchal cultures. The lack of attention may also permit a somewhat greater diversity to appear in both cultures. The anxiety that surrounds the institutional forms of pederasty in Greece is not reflected in a similar anxiety about forms of female same-sex behavior. Hence, we receive illustrations of structures like pederasty (in Plutarch's description of ancient Sparta as well as the love poetry produced by Sappho). We hear of Dionysian bands of women, who take to the wilderness in what are at least imagined by their contemporaries to be orgiastic periods of abandonment. In ancient Israel we have encountered the phenomena of women taking to the wilderness to escape the confines of male-centered society, the queen Vashti choosing the company of women over the rewards of patriarchy, and most strikingly the first full-fledged romance of women inscribed in the story of Ruth and Naomi.

The literature of ancient Israel is like that of ancient Greece in letting us catch glimpses of female same-sex eroticism in a variety of styles. The most striking difference appears to be that a similarly wide range of behaviors and relationships is present for males in Israel, though not in Greece.

The differences that appear from this somewhat synchronic perspective, however, are magnified if we move to a more diachronic perspective, looking at the emergence of accounts of same-sex relationships. There is

no literary evidence of pederastic relationships in connection with the
literature of Greece before about 630 BCE[1] and perhaps not until 530. Following this time the Homeric tales as well as the stories of the gods begin
to be interpreted in accordance with the institutions of pederasty. The
preponderance of literary evidence for pederasty in Greece comes from
much later, in the fifth and fourth centuries BCE.

If we compare this to what we know or suspect about the emergence of
Israelite literature, what do we find? The emergence of Greek pederasty
comes a century after the fall of Samaria and is just getting underway at the
time of the Babylonian destruction of Jerusalem in 586. Of the material we
have considered in our queer reading of the Hebrew Bible, the transgendering of Israel in prophetic narrative renditions of Israel's history may be the
easiest to date. The earliest of these is Hosea, who writes before the fall of
Samaria to the Assyrians (722) and so predates Greek pederasty by well over
a century, perhaps as much as two centuries. The oracles of Jeremiah that
also depict an erotic relation between YHWH and Israel and Judah come
from about the same time that the first attempts to ascribe a homoerotic
adventure to Zeus appear in Greece.[2] But Jeremiah is only developing what
had already been a well-known trope in Israel.

When we come to the narrative material itself, it is far more difficult to
be sure of a way of dating. The events associated with David's relation to Saul
and Jonathan probably precede 1000 BCE, but exactly when they begin to
take written form is less clear. If, as many suppose, the Davidic saga takes initial shape during the reign of Solomon, say around 930 BCE, then we would
have homoerotic themes coming to rather clear expression about three centuries before this happens in Greece. During this period from the eleventh
till the eighth or even seventh century, Greece was in what is sometimes
called the "dark ages." Just as Greece was emerging from its dark ages, Israel
was disappearing as a national entity, to become a province of Babylon, Persia, and the Hellenistic Empire launched by Alexandrian conquest. The saga
materials in the books of Samuel date from the tenth century, with a possible date for redaction of these same sagas in the seventh century. In any case,
the homoerotic aspects of this saga material—including the love triangle of
David, Saul, and Jonathan; the narratives of Samuel's night visitor and Saul's

---

1. In a careful study William Armstrong Percy III has shown rather convincingly that this is the time in which
pederasty comes to be institutionalized in Greece. See his *Pederasty and Pedagogy in Archaic Greece* (Urbana: University of Illinois Press, 1996), 48–49.

2. Percy attributes the beginning of this process to the Homeric "Hymn to Aphrodite," which he supposes
"crystallizes" about 600 BCE (ibid., 38). But he also cites with approval Dover's suggestion that a "homosexual" rendering of this relationship first appears in the poem of Ibycus, ca. 530 (ibid., 39). Cf. K. J. Dover, *Greek
Homosexuality* (New York: Vintage, 1978), 197.

erotic possession in "prophetic frenzy"; and finally the erotic character of YHWH's relation to these characters—all predate the emergence of homo-erotic themes in Greek literature in the following century.

The narratives at which we have looked in 1 and 2 Kings may have been edited in the time of Josiah (about 630) but almost surely include material that is much earlier, especially that concerning the adventures of Elijah and Elisha. This material is most likely appropriated from northern-kingdom traditions that much predated the fall of Samaria in 722. Again, if this mate-rial comes from before the fall of Samaria, then it too predates, by more than a century and perhaps two centuries, the appearance of homoerotic themes in Greek literature (around 530 BCE).

We don't know how the much-vexed question of the successive redactions of Israel's history might be solved. In any case, it appears that the primary materials—telling of the warrior love of the Davidic saga and of YHWH's male groupies—all come from a time between one and three cen-turies before any literary evidence of same-sex erotic relationships in ancient Greece. Thus, Greek-style pederasty appears to be significantly later than the same-sex eroticism that we have encountered in the Hebrew Bible.

What are we to make of this? If my suggested readings of this material have any merit, then not only are accounts of Israelite same-sex relation-ships more diverse than the better-known examples of Greek and especially Athenian pederasty. They are also significantly earlier. This certainly over-turns some of the most widespread prejudices about the relation between Greek and Israelite cultures with respect to the question of the place of homoeroticism in either.

One explanation for both the diversity and the priority of Israelite same-sex eroticism is the difference in Israelite religion compared to Greek religion(s). In discussing relationships among warriors—found above all in sagas concerning David and prominently including the relationship between YHWH and David—we found important differences between the depiction of the Greek gods and the depiction of YHWH. The most important difference is that the gods of the Greeks constitute an entire soci-ety largely independent of the society of humans; they are as distinct from people as the life of a royal court is from a peasant village. In this situation the Greek gods interfere rather sporadically in the lives of mortals, and only occasionally is this intervention of an erotic character. In the early period the erotic adventures of deities with mortals take the form of occasional episodes of heterosexual affairs. Indeed, before the mid-seventh century BCE, the Greek gods seem to be preeminently heterosexual in character, whether with divine consorts or with the rarer forays among the mortals in search of erotic adventures with the opposite sex.[3] Only in the sixth century do we begin to hear of male gods taking on younger male companions in ways that reflect the emergence of pederastic culture among the Greeks.

But YHWH is different from this society of Greek gods. He generally appears as a warrior-bachelor whose basic interest is in mortals, especially the people of Israel. Largely bereft of divine companionship and interests, he seems to occupy himself with the affairs of his beloved people. Among these YHWH finds friends and companions such as Abraham and Moses. Among them he finds more erotically charged relationships such as those with Saul and David, or even with Israel as a whole.

This difference of Adonai being for the most part a bachelor divinity[4] may account for the earliness of homoerotic themes in the literature concerned with this deity and his people, and also for the diversity of forms taken by the homoeroticism of this literature.

YHWH is represented as a male divinity whose human adherents are also most frequently represented as male. This may give homoeroticism a certain prominence in the literature of this people that might otherwise be lacking in other cultures. While I suppose homoeroticism to be ubiquitous in human experience, I do not suppose that it is always present in the same forms or that it will everywhere have the same cultural importance. What may give homoeroticism a certain importance in Israelite literature is precisely the male-male relationship highlighted in the relationship between the people and their deity.

But this may also be related to the variety of same-sex eroticism in Israelite culture. The great variety of forms that a relationship to the deity may take, and the variety of cultural arenas that this relationship may permeate and structure—these would result in a variety of forms that the erotic imagining of this relationship might take. It may take one form (the Davidic) among those who basically adhere to a warrior ethos, and quite another where what is in question is the role of ecstatic holy men. It may take yet another form among devotees of cultic rites (*qedeshim*, and still another among those who are a subaltern managerial elite (as in the case of Joseph).

---

3. The only example of something of this sort in Israelite literature would be the adventures of the "sons of the gods," who seek wives among the daughters of men (Gen 6:2). As in the case of the Greeks, the ones born to these unions of gods and mortals "were the heroes that were of old, warriors of renown" (6:4). These warriors are linked to the "Nephilim," giants also known to Num 13:33; cf. Deut 2:10–11.

4. I leave aside the question of the attempts to provide YHWH with a female consort and the role this may have played in certain aspects of early and late Israelite religion. The narratives with which we are concerned in this essay show little interest in this particular variation.

An already existing set of human erotic arrangements and experiences may be used to make sense of or to represent the relationship between the deity and his devotees. Or perhaps the erotic potency of the god helps to provoke or create the space for the elaboration of interhuman erotic practices. We suppose that it matters little which of these directions of influence is more true. The point rather would be that these are correlative, mutually reinforcing, and variously affecting one another. The Greeks and others could officially divide their attentions among a variety of gods. Unlike them, the Israelites seemed to have felt the need to relate themselves to one god or to integrate their different ways of being religious around a divine figure imagined as, in some way, the same. As we have seen, the worship of Baal, so often contrasted with the worship of YHWH, may often have seemed to be the worship of the same god under different cultural or subcultural conditions.

The consequence of this analysis would be that Israel's relation to God decisively shapes same-sex eroticism in Israel. This may be interpreted as a reciprocal relationship, with cultural forms of homoeroticism shaping the experience of the divine while the experience with the divine in turn shapes and underlines and even incites same-sex eroticism in the culture.

In any case, it would appear that same-sex eroticism in Israel is inseparably connected to Israel's Yahwism. It is no extraneous import but something deeply and inextricably embedded in the religion of Israel.

Accordingly, it is by no means necessary to look outside Israel for the origin of its homoeroticism. However, it is also the case that Israel did not invent homoeroticism. I have already suggested that this may be a pervasive feature of human experience, requiring no more explanation than heteroeroticism. However, it is also true that various cultural factors play important roles in shaping erotic experience and practice, and in evaluating certain practices as obligatory, permissible, prohibited, and so on. It is precisely the henotheism of Israel that provides a favorable climate for the development of homoerotic themes.

Added to this is the rather frank attitude that seems to be taken quite generally toward all forms of eroticism in the literature of Israel. As I mentioned at the beginning of this discussion, the literature of ancient Israel is characterized by an eclectic eroticism. The tales of Lot and his daughters, the rapes attempted in Sodom and Gibeah, the rape of Dinah or of Tamar, the ruse of an earlier Tamar that produces progeny for Judah, the role of Rahab the prostitute in the conquest of Canaan, David and Bathsheba, Samson and Delilah, the Song of Songs, and so on—all make clear that this literature is by no means prudish when it comes to the varieties of erotic experience. These accounts may also be seen to provide a favorable climate for considering same-sex eroticism among the varieties of human experience and sexual practice. The erotophobia of modern Bible readers cannot be ascribed to or derived from the biblical materials they pretend to study.

There is, however, one way in which erotophobia and also homophobia have been ascribed to this literature. It is by supposing that the law codes of Israel may be taken to be the first and last word on the subject of sex and the Bible. We have seen that such a perspective makes nonsense of much of this literature.

We have also observed that even with respect to law codes, it is only in the very latest of Israel's law codes, the so-called Holiness Code of Leviticus, that we find anything like a proscription of (some) homosexual practices. While I must reserve an exploration of the emergence of homophobia to a subsequent study, it is worthwhile to recognize that the Leviticus proscriptions are likely no earlier than the fourth century BCE. Hence, they do not predate the homophobic program of Plato's *Laws*! I am not suggesting that Plato's proposal to legally abolish the custom of pederasty influences the legislation of Leviticus. I am only suggesting that homophobia is at least as old (and perhaps more influential) in Greece as in Israel.

I do not suppose that Israel's openness to same-sex eroticism requires an explanation in terms of derivation from some other culture (Egyptian and Canaanite; Lev 18:3), as the legal codes imply. Yet I do suppose that other and earlier cultures gave expression to same-sex eroticism in ways that may have influenced how Israel inscribed erotic attachments within its literature. Exploring these possible connections would be the subject of a host of studies. Here I will only offer three preliminary hypotheses.

First, the most notable story of love between two males is the Gilgamesh epic of Babylon, celebrating the love of Gilgamesh for Enkidu.[5] It is by no means impossible that this powerful love story had some impact on the development of the somewhat later saga of David or the significantly later homoerotic interpretation in the epic of Homer.

Second, some have supposed that the seafaring peoples of Crete were the source for valorizing pederasty among the Greeks. Plato and even Aristotle accepted this view. Peoples from the same area but an earlier culture were those against whom the heroes of the Davidic saga struggled, as the Philistines. David is even said to have been the lieutenant of a commander of the Philistines, one Achish. Has a Minoan or Mycenaean cultural acceptance of same-sex relationships entered into Israel in this way? In his summary of

---

5. An excellent study of this epic can be found in Neal Walls's *Desire, Discord, and Death: Approaches to Ancient Near Eastern Myth* (Boston: American Schools of Oriental Research, 2001).

the evidence concerning pederasty, Percy has maintained that no institutionalized pederasty can be attributed to earlier cultures of Crete. But that is a somewhat different question. What is in question is not the precise institution of Greek pederasty but an acceptance of same-sex eroticism, which might inspire heroic lovers and their subordinate companions in Israel. Then, in a quite different way, it might develop the antecedent conditions for Greek pederasty.

A third intriguing possibility has to do with Egypt's brief flirtation with monotheism under the heretic pharaoh Akhenaton (1379–1362 BCE). Israel's literature has always pointed to Egypt as involved in its origins. The first patriarch, Abraham, is said to have spent time in Egypt, and his grandson Jacob/Israel found refuge there due to the influence of his son Joseph. A rather less benign view of Egypt is associated with the story of the liberation of the enslaved peoples of Egypt under Moses. Some have wondered whether Moses, despite his opposition to the current pharaoh, had somehow been influenced by the ideas of the heretic Akhenaton. From the perspective of this study, what makes this interesting is that there is also evidence, though not perhaps as clear-cut as one might like, that Akhenaton's adoration of the one god was also somehow associated with his alleged relationship with a younger male. The latter became his consort after the death or displacement of the fabled Nefertiti. Hence, there may be here an anticipation of the relationship between a male devotee with a male (and single) god, something also related to male same-sex relationships.

All of this is speculative at best. It simply shows that there are avenues for further exploration. I do not suppose that these are the only possible avenues of exploration, nor that any one of these will prove to be in any way explanatory of the variety of same-sex erotic relationships that we have noticed in this study. It is only to suggest that the depictions of same-sex eroticism that we find in the literature of Israel need not have developed in a cultural vacuum even if there are a number of ways in which Israel's depictions of this eroticism may be rather distinctive.

Epilogue

JACOB'S WOUND

At several points in this rereading of Hebrew Bible narratives that lend themselves to a homoerotic interpretation, we have encountered episodes depicting the divine relating to the human not only in sexual or erotic terms but also in terms that suggest something like rape. This may be most graphically depicted in the scenes attendant upon the ark of YHWH falling into the hands of the Philistines. This is true both with respect to what happens to Dagon, who is found facedown before YHWH, and to the Philistines themselves, who seem to bear the mark of anal rape. It also seems to lie behind the depiction of Saul's last encounter with the phallic potency of YHWH, an encounter that leaves him stunned and naked upon the hillside. But it is also found in the complaint of Jeremiah that he has been seduced or perhaps even raped by YHWH, and in the graphic depiction from Ezekiel of YHWH's discovery of the maiden Israel in the desert.

To be sure, this is only one aspect of the examined narratives that may provoke distaste on the part of contemporary readers. We have also looked at stories that suggest something like what in modern times might be classified as "statutory rape." These stories involve possible sexual encounters between adult and juvenile males, not only in the resuscitation narratives concerning Elijah and Elisha but also in the call narrative of the young Samuel. And we have also seen phenomena that have sometimes been classified as prostitution in the case of the *qedeshim* and promiscuity in the case of YHWH's conflicted affairs with Saul and David.

The point of rehearsing these stories is not to suggest that the erotic adventures attributed to Israel's anthropomorphic deity may serve as somehow exemplary, as models for emulation or as legitimation for patterns of practice. The extraordinary heteroeroticism of the sagas and epics of Hebrew narrative is not generally deployed in order to legitimate adultery or rape or incest or even polygamy. Nor does the role of Israel's divinity necessarily function as a role model otherwise. The text places the ferocity of YHWH's relationship to Saul, for example, within the same narrative frame as YHWH's demand that Israel's enemies be massacred down to the last woman and child. This surely is not something that Jews, Christians, or Muslims normally take as a proper paradigm for warfare, even against those who are all too often described as evil.

The point of looking at these narratives as I have suggested, therefore, is not to take the God figure as in all ways a paradigm for human behavior, or even as a disclosure or unveiling of the true character of this God. It is rather to take into account something that is illuminated against the backdrop of this undeniable ferocity: the transformation of the divine in the experience of Israel. A consideration of the most aggressive features of divine behavior toward those singled out for divine attention also discloses great distance between episodes suggesting practices of sexual aggression such as rape and practices that may mediate more mutual forms of erotically charged relationships. Only by taking seriously the more ferocious and violent features of the tradition may we be led to appreciate the vast difference that separates these features from the attempts to depict relationships of mutuality and steadfast love that emerge against this more lurid background.

To bring these questions into focus, I first want to ponder two narratives that have so far not been discussed: the assault on Moses and the earlier divine assault on Jacob.

The Attack on Moses

Much of Eilberg-Schwartz's groundbreaking book *God's Phallus* focused on the relationship between Moses and YHWH and especially on the question of the sighting or not of the divine genitalia.[1] I will not go over

---

1. H. Eilberg-Schwartz, *God's Phallus and Other Problems for Men and Monotheism* (Boston: Beacon, 1994).

that material here. Instead, I want to focus on a single episode to which he also refers, the episode of the divine attack on Moses.

The odd episode that I will comment on follows the divine revelation to Moses, a revelation of the divine name (YHWH) and of the divine purpose (to deliver the Hebrew people from bondage in Pharaoh's Egypt; Exod 3–4). At first Moses engages in a series of attempts to get out of the divine commission, excuses rebuffed by YHWH, who becomes increasingly irritated at Moses' recalcitrance. YHWH's designation of Aaron as Moses' spokesperson seems to solve his questions, and Moses obtains permission from his father-in-law, Jethro, to return to Egypt with his wife, Zipporah, and sons. We have previously heard that Moses has taken Zipporah as his wife and that they have one son, Gershom (2:22); later we will learn of a second son, Eliezer (4:20; 18:3–4).

With his new family acquired in the desert, Moses sets out to return to Egypt in order to fulfill the commission YHWH has entrusted to him. It is then that we read the following episode:

> On the way, at a place where they spent the night, the LORD met him and tried to kill him. But Zipporah took a flint and cut off her son's foreskin, and touched Moses' feet with it, and said, "Truly you are a bridegroom of blood to me!" So he [YHWH] let him [Moses] alone. It was then she said, "A bridegroom of blood by circumcision." (Exod 4:24–26)

How are we to account for this strange episode that seems so unconnected either with what goes before or what follows?

The story has been justifiably puzzling to most commentators. Why should YHWH set upon Moses with apparently murderous intent at the very moment when Moses is undertaking the commission with which YHWH has entrusted him and to which YHWH has committed himself? This commission leads to the very event that lends the book of Exodus its name.

Beyond this quite sufficiently startling attack is the no less astonishing way in which it is averted. Why is it Zipporah, Moses' wife, who intervenes here? Why not, for example, Aaron? And what does a bloody penis have to do with forcing an apparently enraged YHWH to back off?

Let's begin with the blood, for to this Zipporah's words draw our attention. Twice she calls Moses a "bridegroom of blood" (vv. 25, 26). Somehow it is the blood that is meant to signify that Moses belongs to her (her bridegroom) and that therefore YHWH has no right to Moses' person. The application of blood tells the murderous divinity: "He is mine; you can't have him!"

The phrasing of this is quite odd. It suggests that Moses belongs either to his wife or to YHWH. It is a question of possession, even perhaps a question of whose bride/bridegroom Moses is.

That a question above all of sexual possession is involved here is not only suggested by Zipporah's words that claim Moses as her own. It is also suggested by the application of blood. First, what blood, and where does it come from? It comes from Gershom, more specifically, from Gershom's penis. The text also suggests that the blood is applied to Moses' penis; "feet" sometimes substitutes for "penis" in Hebrew narrative (cf. Ruth 3:4; Isa 6:2; 7:20). Hence, Moses' penis is touched by the bloody foreskin of Gershom's penis, and this somehow signifies that Moses belongs to Zipporah and that YHWH has no right to his body.

How might this work? If we focus first on the bloody penis of Moses, which is where Zipporah's words direct our (and YHWH's) attention, then we might ask how blood on one's penis suggests that one belongs not to YHWH but to a woman. There are two ways in which this might be true. On the one hand, it may represent the blood signifying that the woman with whom the male has had intercourse was a virgin and that the relationship with her has actually been consummated. In many cultures blood on the bedclothes has been the ritual sign of the bride's prior virginity and the consummation of the marriage (cf. Deut 22:13–21). And Zipporah's words seem to point us in this direction since she calls Moses her bridegroom, as if they have only just been married, have only just now consummated their relationship. But the plausibility of such a subterfuge founders on the presence of the son of Moses' and Zipporah's long-since consummated union. It is, after all, his blood that is proffered here. Is Adonai supposed to be ignorant of this?

A second possibility is that blood on the man's penis comes from intercourse with a menstruating woman and somehow renders him ritually impure. There are plenty of indications from the law codes of Israel suggesting that contact with menstrual blood renders one "unclean" (e.g., Lev 15:19–31). But to be "ritually unclean" means only that one is not an appropriate object for the favorable attention of the divine. Indeed, Leviticus even suggests that contamination from menstrual blood could defile the tabernacle and force YHWH to desert his people and let them "die in their uncleanness" (15:31). In that case a few drops of blood on Moses' penis could plausibly make that divinity back off from further contact and so from contamination. (We should recognize, however, the inconvenience for this view that if indeed Moses has had intercourse with Zipporah during her menstrual period, the law of Lev 20:18 would require that they be "cut off from their people").[2]

The blood on Moses' penis could have the desired effect of protecting Moses from YHWH's assault if the blood came in either of these ways from Zipporah herself (as a token of former virginity or as menstruation). But though Zipporah acquires and applies the blood, she is not herself the (ultimate) source of the blood. Instead, the blood comes from their firstborn, the son born to Moses and Zipporah, the firstfruit of the consummation of their relationship. Moreover, it comes from the boy's penis, the penis that is the result of that consummation.

If circumcision may be understood as a way of indicating that a man's sex belongs to YHWH, here the meaning of the act is reversed to signify that Moses' sex belongs to Zipporah rather than to YHWH. The circumcision that is performed here is not a cultic act but an anticultic act. It occurs in an emergency rather than as part of a ritual, and it aims to render Moses unfit for YHWH's attentions rather than fit for them.

I don't suppose that I have solved the problems of this episode. It remains irreducibly puzzling. But I have suggested that what is going on here is that Zipporah has acted in such a way as to claim Moses for herself and to avert the claim of YHWH to Moses. Moreover, we have seen that this claim has to do with the claim to Moses' sexuality. Thus, the assault on Moses appears to have been a kind of attempted rape, a violent sexual assault. It is this violent sexual assault that is averted by the claim of Zipporah upon Moses' sexuality.

This by no means is the end of the relationship between YHWH and Moses. It is not even the end of what seems to be an intimate and even erotic relationship between them. After all, Moses will be recalled as one who has a uniquely intimate relationship with God, whom he sees not only face-to-face (Exod 33:11; Deut 34:10) but also mouth-to-mouth (Num 12:8 KJV/MT). The result of this intimacy will be that Moses' very skin is transformed and that he goes about veiled like a woman (Exod 34:29–35; cf. 2 Cor 3:12–18). Other traditions will deny that he has a face-to-face encounter with God but say that he is given to see, not the divine front/face, but the divine buttocks (Exod 33:20–23). All of this is quite odd, to be sure.[3] But what is important for our purposes here is that an erotic

2. This would be yet another indication of the noncommensurability of legal codes and narrative traditions. As we shall see, this incommensurability obtains regardless of whether the narratives deal with events prior to or following the narrated giving of the law.

3. For further reflection on the puzzling aspects of these accounts, see ibid., 64–73.

relationship seeming to begin as a kind of attempted rape ends instead with something far more consensual and as something that comes to be marked by faithfulness.

We do not hear directly of YHWH's steadfast love of Israel for the sake of his love for Moses (as we have repeatedly in the case of David). Nonetheless, we do find within the Moses sagas an acclamation of God as one "abounding in steadfast love [*khesed*] and faithfulness, keeping steadfast love for the thousandth generation" (Exod 34:6–7).

The Assault on Jacob (Gen 32:22–32)

The story of YHWH's unprovoked assault on Moses is a quite different story concerning the ancestor of those whom Moses is commissioned to liberate—the patriarch Jacob. Unlike the story of the assault on Moses, Jacob's encounter with God is better known because it has lent itself to all sorts of edifying reflections on "wrestling with God" as a metaphor for intense spiritual experience. As a consequence, the oddity and, specifically, the erotic suggestiveness of the episode have been largely suppressed.

The story occurs as Jacob is returning to the land from which he has set out in search of a wife after having acquired through trickery the inheritance of his elder brother, Esau (Gen 27–28). The difficulty, as Jacob perceives it, is that of dealing with Esau upon his return with wives, concubines, children, and cattle. Accordingly, he sets out to appease Esau's imagined wrath. To do so, he sends ahead droves of livestock and servants with the instruction to each caravan, when it meets with Esau, to greet him and say that they are a present from Jacob to Esau (32:13–21). During the night he sends "his two wives, his two maids, and his eleven children" across "the ford of the Jabbok" (32:22–23).

Jacob is left alone at the boundary indicated by the ford of Jabbok, the boundary between what will become the land of Jacob/Israel and what is outside. While he is in this liminal space, neither inside nor outside the land that will bear his name, we are told: "A man wrestled with him until daybreak" (32:24). Who is this mysterious "man," and what is the character of this wrestling? One gains the impression of a titanic struggle; the one who has accosted Jacob in the dark struggles with him all through the night until daybreak. Jacob has outwitted his father, Isaac, and his brother, Esau, to steal the firstborn's inheritance. He has outlasted his uncle Laban to gain the hand of Rachel and secure a huge share of the livestock. Now he is shown as one who seems capable of overpowering this mysterious stranger who has assaulted him in the night. First we are told: "When the man saw that he did not prevail against Jacob, he struck him on the hip socket" (32:25). Even this "low blow" and the (permanent?) injury that results does not succeed in overcoming Jacob.

As the night begins to give way to day, the mysterious attacker pleads to be released from Jacob's grip. It appears that the coming of day is something of a danger to this power that lurks at the boundary, much as in more recent legend the vampire must escape the coming of the sun's rays. Thus far we suppose we may have to do with some sort of demon or demigod that breaks out at night in the boundary places. In spite of Jacob's prowess in fending off the attack of this strange power, Jacob nevertheless seems to suppose that the one with whom he has been wrestling is no ordinary being but one capable of giving him a "blessing." When he demands one as the price for releasing his grip, the attacker asks his name. The consequence is that one who has been called Jacob (the supplanter) is now called Israel (God strives), which the story interprets to mean "one who strives with God."

In the course of a long-night wrestling bout, the mysterious partner of Jacob has been transformed from a man to a being with mysterious and uncanny power, now to be disclosed as "God." Indeed, it is this last identity that will stick, at least as far as this narrative (and its doublet) is concerned. The place where this night attack occurs is renamed by Jacob (who has been renamed "Israel") as Peniel, "the face of God." And Jacob explains this name: "For I have seen God face to face, and yet my life is preserved" (32:30).

What has begun as an unknown assailant's assault in the night has become the intimacy of face-to-face encounter with none other than God.[4] The tradition that Jacob's assailant was an angel derives not from Genesis but from Hosea. His oracle seems to conflate the Peniel and Bethel traditions from Genesis and to move between identifying the assailant as an angel or as God, an ambiguity present in the Genesis story of Abraham's encounter with the messengers/God at Mamre (Gen 18). The oracle of Hosea is as follows:

> The LORD has an indictment against Judah,
>   and will punish Jacob according to his ways,
>   and repay him according to his deeds.
> In the womb he tried to supplant his brother,
>   and in his manhood he strove with God.

---

4. The Jacob tradition thus anticipates two features that we also found in the Moses saga: a nighttime assault by YHWH and a relationship that is transfigured as a "face-to-face."

He strove with the angel and prevailed,
  he wept and sought his favor;
He met him at Bethel,
  and there he spoke with him. (Hos 12:2–4)

Striving with God and striving with an angel/messenger are here in parallel, just as the preceding lines placed Jacob's ways and deeds into parallel as
that in accordance with which Jacob will be punished or repaid. The ambiguity of the story is also expressed in the juxtaposition of Jacob's prevailing
with weeping and beseeching ("he wept and sought his favor"). But just
who is doing the weeping? Who is doing the beseeching? Who will grant
favor? If we compare Hosea's version to that of Gen 32, we would have to
say that it is the divine being who does the beseeching: "Let me go, for the
day is breaking" (32:26). Yet Jacob refuses this plea "unless you bless me." So
is it Jacob who seeks favor, while the divine being pleads for release? Who
then does the weeping? Is it the divine being (angel or God)? Or is it Jacob?
Hosea's poetic compression leaves the subject of these clauses undecidable.

What is clear is that Hosea retains the sense that Jacob is the one who
prevails over his divine assailant. And it is this that will be responsible for
the way subsequent tradition tends to substitute the angel for God. How
could it be fitting to say that Israel "prevails" in his struggle with/against
God? At the end of this reflection on the story of Jacob, we will return to
this question.

Certain elements of the Gen 32 account will be repeated in Gen 35, but
missing all the interesting legendary details. The doublet is found the next
time that Jacob is noticed crossing back into the land that will bear his name:
"God appeared to Jacob again when he came from Paddan-aram, and he
blessed him. God said to him, 'Your name is Jacob; no longer shall you be
called Jacob, but Israel shall be your name.' So he was called Israel" (35:9–10).
It is precisely this apparent doublet of the first story that throws into relief the
more bizarre aspects of the first story of Jacob's renaming. Missing in the second account are the elements of attack or assault, the sense of violent and
titanic struggle, the contest of wills over name and blessing, and the wound.
It is precisely the elements expurgated from the second account that make
the first story so interesting, not only for the queer reading that I am proposing but also for any of the many uses to which this story has been put to
illumine the struggle of people with God. Put another way, it is the homoerotic features of the story that make it provocative of insight for the life of
faith. Without these elements the encounter between Jacob and YHWH
seems capable of producing only an exegetical yawn.

If we return to that first story, we see that it is more than Jacob's name that is changed. Despite his successful grappling with his attacker, he is not the man he was before the encounter. He has been struck in the vicinity of the hip socket, and now he limps, the public sign of his private wound. Where is this wound? What is its nature? The text refers to the place where the leg joins the hip and thus may turn the reader's gaze to the outside of the leg joint. Is this what is meant here?

The story concludes by noticing that thereafter and "to this day the Israelites do not eat the thigh muscle that is on the hip socket, because he struck Jacob on the hip socket at the thigh muscle" (32:32). Subsequent rabbinic commentators identify the locus of the crippling blow as the sciatic nerve, the largest nerve on the human (and mammalian) body.[5] On the human it runs the length of the back of the upper leg after descending from under the buttocks. It issues from the hip bones at the notch located near the rectal cavity. The prohibition of eating the nerve is practicable because it is so readily identifiable, being about as big around as the small finger. In wrestling, a particularly violent grip at the base of the buttocks could strain or damage this nerve, resulting in serious injury. The same would be true of a violent sexual assault.

In the parallel story of Gen 35, the wounding of Jacob by YHWH disappears, only to be replaced with another wound: the death in childbirth of his beloved Rachel. It is the end of Jacob's activity as a progenitor. He will sire no more sons. Indeed, Jacob—the prime mover in earlier parts of the sagas recounted in Genesis—begins to fade into the background, to become not the agent of the tales but the one upon whom events act. Despite the blessing he bears, he retires into wounded grief. It is as if his story is consummated in the fateful encounter with the savage deity, from whom he has wrested a blessing. He limps away from the face of God, less a victorious hero than a man of sorrow. Broken, yet still the medium through whom the blessing of the divine flows to succeeding generations. The prophet Jeremiah will recall this encounter: "When Israel sought for rest, the LORD appeared to him long ago. I have loved you with an everlasting love" (Jer 31:2c–3 NRSV n). Once more, the assault at night is renarrated as the origin of an everlasting love.

The mystery and ambiguity of the tale of Jacob's encounter with God is captured in the massive alabaster statue created by Jacob Epstein called *Jacob and the Angel*. The statue was regarded as scandalous when first exhibited in England in 1940, for it unmistakably exudes enormous erotic

5. For a review of the main sources and views in this literature, see William T. Miller, *Mysterious Encounters at Mamre and Jabbok* (Brown Judaic Studies 50; Chico, CA: Scholars Press, 1984), 97–117.

power.[6] Moreover, it expresses the eroticism in a remarkable way. While many other artistic representations focus on the struggle itself (in ways reminiscent of Greco-Roman depictions of nude wrestling matches), the work by Epstein seems to represent more the aftermath of the struggle. The colossal nude Jacob seems to relax into the supporting embrace of the colossal nude divinity as in the aftermath of a passionate embrace. Jacob seems to "go limp" in the arms of his savage yet tender lover. The artist conveys Jacob's (going) limp as the mark of spent passion.

These two tales that I have read are filled with many mysteries. But the reason I have focused on them here, at the end of this book, is that they both suggest something of the ferocity of the divine being who attacks even the men he has chosen. They show that these attacks are later transmuted into relationships characterized as steadfast love. In each case we can detect the signs of a more or less submerged eroticism. By themselves these stories (and the eroticism at which they hint) remain puzzling and ambiguous. They serve only as a sort of ambiguous prelude to the more extended narratives to which we have given more attention in this study. But they anticipate a pattern in the erotic narratives in the Hebrew Bible that we have considered. The pattern is one of a ferocity that becomes, over time, something else: the story of God's steadfast love for his chosen ones, whether David or the people who take their name from the one who was assaulted and blessed at the ford of the Jabbok.

Jacob's Wound

In important respects we may characterize our entire study of "homoerotic narrative in the literature of ancient Israel" as a tracing of Jacob's wound. The narratives upon which we have focused most attention are stories of those who have lived in the light and shadow of a passionate, and indeed erotic, encounter with Jacob's most intimate adversary. The name that Jacob receives from this passion is one that is carried by the people who take his new name, Israel, and who as well, perhaps, inherit the wound of this passion. At least, that is what this study has suggested. The homoeroticism prefigured in Jacob's intimate grappling with God is a homoeroticism that will be disseminated across the traditions that bear his name.

---

6. Jacob Epstein's statue *Jacob and the Angel* (1940–41) is displayed on the cover of this book and held by the Tate Gallery (London): http://www.tate.org.uk/servlet/ViewWork?workid=21761.

The Dissemination of Homoeroticism

The narrative materials that we have examined in this study seem rife with eroticism of all kinds. And within this multiform eroticism we have found notable examples of homoeroticism as well. We have identified the "warrior eroticism" that seems to permeate the sagas concerned with David and his many lovers, an eroticism that drives the plot of his complex relation to Saul and Jonathan. We have noticed the eroticism that seems to play a role in the careers of the first prophets, Samuel and Saul, Elijah and Elisha, and to be at work among the *bene-hanebi'im* and perhaps the *qedeshim* as well; they are channels and agents of erotic possession. Unlike these instances of homoeroticism, we have also encountered a homoeroticism that seems to entail the transgendering of the beloved male in the story of Joseph.

But the homoeroticism among the male descendents of Jacob is unintelligible apart from the homoeroticism of the relation between these males and their male deity. It seems impossible to decide whether the relation between David and YHWH, for example, is figured as homoerotic because of the antecedent familiarity of the field of warrior homoeroticism, which then serves to structure the story world within which YHWH also is a character. Or, on the other hand, does the homoerotic structure of a relation between a male hero and a male deity serve to produce a cultural world within which male homoeroticism can flourish? Or, perhaps more likely, is there a mutually reinforcing or mirroring effect to be discerned here in which cultural assumptions affect the depiction of the relationship to God while that relationship itself functions to highlight and foster the homoerotic relations that it both echoes and incites?

Similar questions can be asked about the homoerotic features of the careers of the early prophets. On the one hand, the activity of these prophets seems to include elements of homoerotic possession, a sort of erotic power that can bring the dead back to life or overwhelm their followers with erotic energy. Or are they simply channels of the erotic initiative or force field that emanates from the hypermasculinity of the deity they worship and on whose behalf they act?

Finally, we may wonder at the readiness of the writing prophets to depict Israel as a (faithless) bride to his/her God. Is this an analogy that is already "ready to hand" because of Israel's cultural experience with transgendered male subjects like Joseph? Or does Israel—at least for a time and because of the implications of the prophetic metaphor for the relation between Israel and God—become hospitable to the experience of (some) Israelite males being transgendered? Or, again, are we to discern here a mutually reinforcing effect in which each side of this equation (man to man, man to God) mirrors and provokes the other?

In any case, the homoeroticism of the narrative traditions of ancient Israel seem to both disseminate and clarify the hints of the story of Jacob's encounter with the mysterious and uncanny stranger at the ford of the Jabbok. For we recall that this partner in passionate embrace is figured both as a man and as God.

Wounded Patriarchy

We have observed that this encounter marks Jacob with a wound that leaves him limping. How are we to understand this wound and what it suggests about the narratives we have studied? The wound is a wound at the heart of patriarchy, the very patriarchy that will come to be (mis)recognized as the defining characteristic of "Israel." For Israel is a father, indeed, the father of all the tribes of Israel. Yet the rule of this father is at best ambivalent. For he is, on the one hand, one who struggles and indeed prevails against God and is thus a truly titanic figure. Yet he is also one who bears the wound of homoerotic passion. This wound makes itself felt in his odd relation to his son Joseph, whom he transgenders with a fine robe, whom he seems to supplant as father of Manasseh and Ephraim, yet upon whom he must be wholly dependent for refuge in the land of Egypt. In Jacob's name patriarchy is not demolished, but it is rendered oddly unstable, limping (rather than striding) toward an uncertain future—a patriarchy always already subverted from within.[7]

Perhaps the most dramatic expression of this wounding of patriarchy is the way in which, beginning with Hosea, Jacob/Israel may be understood not only as the one who has prevailed against God (or the angel) but also as one who is transgendered to become the adulterous bride of this same YHWH. On the one hand, he is the great patriarch who contends with and even prevails against the divine. On the other hand, he is the one who becomes the feminine counterpart of this same God.

Hence, the patriarchal traditions of Israel are always already undermined from within. They bear the mark of Jacob's wound—and, perhaps, of the attempt to disguise or suture this wound, to erase or heal it.

Subsequent rabbinic commentary will read the assertion of Gen 33:18, that Jacob later arrived at Shechem "safely," and propose that it should be

7. The wound is a wound at the inception of the law as well. For this is what it means that Moses is one who bears the mark, and indeed the text does not hesitate to suggest the feminizing mark (the veil), of an intimate encounter with Israel's God. The Torah itself, ascribed to Moses, is grammatically feminine. Hence, whatever psychoanalytic theory may say about the law as masculine, as "name of the father" or "phallus" and so on, Hebrew grammar carries the suggestion of a very different gendering of the law.

understood as "whole" or "hale." This suggests to them that Jacob's wound was healed by the arrival of daybreak after his struggle. In this way the mark of Jacob's struggle will be erased. But why this erasure? Why the need to suture this wound in or by the light of day?

It may be that this wound is sutured precisely in the proscriptions of same-sex erotic practice in the Leviticus Holiness Code. We have seen that these proscriptions are anomalous, not only because it is here alone among the collections of legal materials in the Hebrew Bible that we encounter a prohibition of some same-sex practice. It is also anomalous because these proscriptions interdict what seems to empower the very narratives of this same "law." Hence, here the law itself seems to become an anomaly, an exception to the narrative law or the narrated law of these texts. The pattern (law in that sense) of the narrative materials at which we have looked reflects homoerotic attachment both as determinative of the relation between Israel and YHWH and as commonplace among the male actors within Israel. If so, then the legal texts seem to stand outside and over against the "law" of the narrative.

One way of accounting for this, in addition to the ways that we indicated in the discussion of Leviticus itself, is that the legal codes come to cover over the wound that is the passion of God for Israel, and the passion of Israel for God. The legal texts serve as a kind of alibi, pointing the reader away from what is happening before her eyes.

In this way they may attempt to reinscribe a masculinity and patriarchy that are deeply destabilized from within. And this they do above all by interdicting the desire to take up the very position of alleged femininity in relation to the erotic advances of (another) male that the narrative traditions reflect and incite.

But the price paid by thus covering over the wound, by this alleged or feigned healing of the wound, is that something else may be lost, the blessing that is carried by the one who is wounded.

Empowered Beloved (Blessing)

This wound is the wound inflicted by the violence of a passion for God, for a God whose own passion is figured first as an assault in the night and later as a love that endures "forever."

It is not only a wound or a mere vulnerability. It is also, and most importantly, a blessing. It is the blessing of a name that marks one as subject to the divine favor and everlasting love. We have seen that Jeremiah's reference to this story ascribes to Jacob's encounter with YHWH the inception of an "everlasting love." But our reading of the David saga has made it quite evident that the lifelong affair between David and YHWH is regularly recalled as the ground of YHWH's faithful love not only toward David and his descendents or house but also, extending through this line, to Israel as a whole. Similarly, this love, even when tested to the limit by Israel's unfaithfulness and YHWH's jealous rage, is reinstated through Israel's suffering and YHWH's compassion, with the consequence that YHWH promises never again to allow rage to overwhelm his love for Israel. It is the woundedness of Israel that may serve to incite YHWH to repent of his fury and to wed himself forever and unconditionally to Israel.

The homoeroticism of Israel's relation to his "LORD" is one that not only makes Israel vulnerable to the wound of homoerotic passion but also makes Israel the bearer of the divine blessing. This is not just true of the extreme case of Israel's dereliction or abandonment in the struggle with the great political powers, but is also prefigured in the stories of homoerotic passion that precede the prophetic transgendering of Israel. For we recognized that David becomes a king precisely as the one marked by this passion. Homoerotic passion is what makes him what he is, the true king of Israel.

In our rereading of narratives from the Bible, we also had occasion to notice a third style of homoeroticism in connection with what we termed there "YHWH's male groupies." To be sure, the evidence for this type of relationship is more ambiguous, less definite, and more diffuse than relations between warriors and their companions as discerned in the David stories, or than the prophets' transgendering of Israel. Nevertheless, in some of these stories we have noticed hints of a kind of erotic possession of the prophet and, in some of them, the way in which this erotic possession is, in a certain way, transitive. In the case of Samuel, for example, if he is possessed by Adonai's erotic potency, this does not reduce him to an object of lust but actually empowers him to become YHWH's mighty prophet. The overpowering becomes empowering. Similarly, the lads who are the beneficiaries of Elijah's and Elisha's erotic potency are not overpowered or captured by this erotic power but are empowered, made alive.

We are all aware of ways in which erotic power may work to deprive the other of their agency, of their own subjectivity, of their own power. This has too often been the effect of erotic possession by the other. But in these stories we may glimpse a different operation of erotic power, one that makes alive, one that does not destroy the other (as rape) but instead releases the potentiality, the strength, the power of the other.

Divine Passion

In the story as recounted in Gen 32, we pointed out that Jacob was described as contending with and even gaining a sort of victory over his antagonist, an antagonist first depicted as a "man" but subsequently recognized as "God." And we commented that for subsequent tradition the difficult notion that Jacob/Israel may have overcome God served to alter the identity of Jacob's antagonist from God to an angel or messenger. But if we are right in seeing in this story an anticipation of narratives like those of the David saga or the prophets' transgendering of Israel, then it may become clear how Jacob/Israel does indeed overcome his ferocious Lover. For it is precisely through the "passion" of Jacob and Moses, of David and Israel itself, that the divine lover is transfigured from one who assaults his privileged "victims" to one whose loyalty lasts from generation to generation. Therefore, the contending with Adonai and even the victory over YHWH that is attributed to Jacob/Israel are attested in our narratives as a whole.

Accordingly, one way of trying to make sense of the range of erotic potentialities deployed in biblical narrative is to take seriously the possibility to which I have repeatedly referred: the divine character reshaped by interaction with human characters. In the case of David, we have noticed how the phallic aggression of Adonai is reshaped into what the text calls steadfast love by the skillful and patient strategies of David, who had been well schooled in the ways of love in relation to other more powerful males. And in the Prophets we have seen how the divine jealousy that has taken such ferocious form in his outraged response to his transgendered beloved is transformed into pity and compassion and covenant. This would mean that crucially important theological themes are produced through reflection on the divine human relationship imagined as erotic, and indeed homoerotic, in character. Let us see how this may be so.

We have already noticed that the story of David and YHWH is in part a story of the taming of YHWH, who first appears as something of a phallic bully, ready to burst into testosteronic rage. In the course of David's relation with this deity, however, the latter seems won over to a permanent condition of commitment to David, his house, and indeed Israel as a whole. The theme of God's steadfast love is forged out of the homoerotic bond with David. In the story world as we have reread it, it appears that David's ability to woo and tame his divine lover is to a significant degree derived from his lifelong apprenticeship as the beloved of more powerful males. David's homoerotic experience with Saul and Jonathan (and Achish perhaps) makes his steadfastness as beloved come to serve as a paradigm for YHWH's steadfast love for him (and thence for David's people).

Therefore, not only is homoeroticism a training ground for relationship to the divine (or at least to this particular divinity), but the resultant homo-erotic relation to the divine also transforms the divine partner in the relationship in crucially important ways. From the bloodthirsty, arbitrary, and unpredictable tyrant whom we encounter early in 1 Samuel, YHWH is transformed through his love for David and the history of that love. He is changed into the YHWH whose faithfulness can be counted on even when the ardor of first love has cooled. Even when the one who has wooed him has died, YHWH remains faithful to David's people "for David's sake."

A quite different picture emerges when we focus our attention on the prophetic depiction of the relation of YHWH to a transgendered Israel. Now it is not Adonai's fickleness that is in view, but Israel's. Their faithlessness to their Great Lover is brought to expression in these narrative allegories. But more happens—the justified rage of that lover at Israel's infidelities also comes to expression as the prophets wrestle with the horror of Israel's and Judah's fate in the cockpit of Near Eastern power politics. What emerges from this tale of horror is a deity awakened to compassion by the sufferings of his unfaithful but somehow still beloved Israel. In consequence, the iron justice of divine judgment is tempered by mercy that flows from compassion. YHWH repents of his rage even though it was "just." For from now on, justice must be tempered by mercy, by grace. Indeed, it may even be that mercy or compassion becomes the new name for and reality of justice. Or as Paul will say, justice comes as and through grace.

This is a hard-won view whether we attribute the change to YHWH or to Israel's understanding of YHWH. But without it, it is impossible to imagine the attractiveness of biblical religion or the God whose worship is solicited by these testimonies. Yet precisely this perspective is importantly shaped by, and in the crucible of, something like a homoerotic attachment between Israel and his God, a homoeroticism that, as we have repeatedly seen, is reflected in the homoeroticism of Israelite culture generally.

The idea that the divine, or at least this divine, is transformed by erotic attachment to another may at first seem more odd than it is. We all know that we are transformed by intense erotic experiences and relationships. But theology has often supposed that God is beyond all that. Under the impress of certain forms of Greek philosophizing, God has often come to be thought of as literally unchanging, unaffected by relationships to human beings, and certainly beyond erotic relationships.

In the late modern era there have been a number of attempts to suggest that the divine may also be rethought relationally, as in some way affected and even to a certain extent changed by relationships to the world, to human history, to human suffering. Some who have moved in this direction have been influenced by Whiteheadian metaphysics. But others have recognized that the crucial paradigm for this view in Christianity is the doctrine of the incarnation and atonement and most important the theological reflection on the cross.

To be sure, the heritage of Greek metaphysics as appropriated for Christian theological reflection made it quite difficult to imagine how the divine could be changed and yet remain divine. Hence, there has always been a certain reticence in putting forward notions of radical or fundamental transformation of the divine through the Christ event, even though there have always been attempts to speak of the love or compassion of God as if these are not mere metaphors.

For religious reasons it often becomes necessary for us to speak of the transformation of the divine in Christian faith. So we often foreground themes we have seen emerging in the exploration of the erotic relationships between persons of the same gender and between Israel and God. It is common for us to affirm that God commits Godself to "us" on account of God's commitment to Christ. We affirm that through the cross God's justice is turned to compassion for humanity (or whatever part of humanity is deemed to be included in the event of salvation). But these are the very themes that emerge from Israel's experience with the divine, an experience often rooted in homoeroticism.

Indeed, it may even appear that the passion of Christ is also prefigured here in a way making clear that it is firmly rooted in the traditions of ancient Israel. This is not a replacement or a supersession but a kind of culmination. After all, Christians maintain that this latter passion results in the inclusion of the Gentiles, the nations, in the steadfast love of the one whose mercy endures forever. Jacob/Israel becomes, as foretold, both wounded and blessed, and the source of blessing for humanity as a whole.

The repudiation of homoerotic passion that has come to characterize the traditions that derive from this literature (Judaism, Christianity, and Islam) may thus be seen not only as obscuring important ingredients within that literature but also as cutting the very nerve of the passion in and through which these narratives may be healing for humanity as such. How it happens that traditions so deeply implicated in homoerotic passion have become the legitimation of homophobia is a question that our study does not answer but renders more urgent. For what is at stake is not simply the question of the "acceptance" of gay and lesbian people in the religious institutions that derive from these traditions, but the very possibility of encountering the one "whose steadfast love endures forever."

Bibliography

Ackerman, Susan. *Warrior, Dancer, Seductress, Queen: Women in Judges and Biblical Israel.* New York: Doubleday, 1998.

Ackroyd, Peter. *The First Book of Samuel.* Cambridge: Cambridge University Press, 1971.

Aelred of Rievaulx. *Mirror of Charity.* Translated by E. Connor. Kalamazoo, MI: Cistercian Publications, 1990.

⸻. *Spiritual Friendship.* Translated by M. Laker. Kalamazoo, MI: Cistercian Publications, 1974.

Bailey, Derrick Sherwin. *Homosexuality and the Western Christian Tradition.* London: Longman, Green, 1955. Reprint, Hamden, CT: Archon Books, 1975.

Bal, Mieke. *Death and Dissymmetry: The Politics of Coherence in the Book of Judges.* Chicago: University of Chicago Press, 1988.

Bamberger, Bernard J. *Leviticus.* Vol. 3 of *The Torah: A Modern Commentary.* New York: Union of American Hebrew Congregations, 1979.

Bird, Phyllis A. "The End of the Male Cult Prostitute." Pages 37–80 in *Congress Volume: Cambridge 1995.* Edited by J. A. Emert. Supplements to Vetus Testamentum 66. Leiden: Brill, 1997.

⸻. "'To Play the Harlot': An Inquiry into an Old Testament Metaphor." Pages 75–94 in *Gender and Difference in Ancient Israel.* Edited by Peggy Day. Minneapolis: Fortress, 1989.

Blenkinsopp, Joseph. *A History of Prophecy in Israel.* Philadelphia: Westminster, 1983.

Bloom, Allan. "The Ladder of Love." In *Plato's "Symposium."* Translated by Seth Benardete. Chicago: University of Chicago Press, 2001.

Boer, Roland. *Knockin' on Heaven's Door: The Bible and Popular Culture.* London: Routledge, 1999.

Boswell, John. *Christianity, Social Tolerance, and Homosexuality.* Chicago: University of Chicago Press, 1980.

Boyarin, Daniel. *Unheroic Conduct: The Rise of Heterosexuality and the Invention of the Jewish Man.* Berkeley: University of California Press, 1997.

Brooten, Bernadette. *Love between Women: Early Christian Responses to Female Homoeroticism.* Chicago: University of Chicago Press, 1996.

Burkert, Walter. *Greek Religion.* Translated by John Raftan. Cambridge: Harvard University Press, 1985.

Bynum, Caroline Walker. *The Resurrection of the Body.* New York: Columbia University Press, 1995.

Cantarella, Eva. *Bisexuality in the Ancient World.* Translated by Cormac Ó. Cuilleanáin. New Haven: Yale University Press, 1992.

Cohen, Martin Samuel. "The Biblical Prohibition of Homosexual Intercourse." *Journal of Homosexuality* 19, no. 4 (1990): 3–20.

Comstock, Gary David. *Gay Theology without Apology.* Cleveland: Pilgrim, 1993.

Derrida, Jacques. "Of an Apocalyptic Tone Newly Adopted in Philosophy." In *Derrida and Negative Theology.* Edited by Harold Coward and Toby Foshay. Albany, NY: SUNY Press, 1992.

Douglas, Mary. *Purity and Danger.* London: Routledge & Kegan Paul, 1966.

Dover, K. J. *Greek Homosexuality.* New York: Vintage, 1978.

Downing, Christine. *Myths and Mysteries of Same-Sex Love.* New York: Continuum/Crossroad, 1989.

Eilberg-Schwartz, Howard. *God's Phallus and Other Problems for Men and Monotheism.* Boston: Beacon, 1994.

Epstein, Julia, and Kristina Straub. *Body Guards: The Cultural Politics of Gender Ambiguity.* London: Routledge, 1991.

Euripides. *Bacchae.* Translated by William Arrowsmith. Vol. 5 of *Euripides.* Edited by David Grene and Richard Lattimore. The Complete Greek Tragedies. Chicago: University of Chicago Press, 1959.

Evans, Linda. *Hard Core: Power, Pleasure, and the "Frenzy of the Visible."* Berkeley: University of California Press, 1989.

Exum, J. Cheryl. *Fragmented Women: Feminist (Sub)versions of Biblical Narratives.* Harrisburg, PA: Trinity Press International, 1993.

Fewell, Danna Nolan, and David Miller Gunn. *Compromising Redemption: Relating Characters in the Book of Ruth.* Louisville: Westminster/John Knox, 1990.

————. *Gender, Power, and Promise.* Nashville: Abingdon, 1993.

Fokkelman, J. P. *The Crossing Fates.* Vol. 2 of *Narrative Art and Poetry in the Books of Samuel.* Assen, Netherlands: Van Gorcum, 1986.

————. *Throne and City.* Vol. 3 of *Narrative Art and Poetry in the Books of Samuel.* Assen, Netherlands: Van Gorcum, 1990.

————. *Vow and Desire.* Vol. 4 of *Narrative Art and Poetry in the Books of Samuel.* Assen, Netherlands: Van Gorcum, 1996.

Fox, Everett. *Give Us a King.* New York: Schocken Books, 1999.

Freud, Sigmund. *Moses and Monotheism.* Translated by K. Jones. New York: Knopf, 1939.

Frymer-Kensky, Tikva. *In the Wake of the Goddess.* New York: Free Press, 1992.

Gide, André. *Saül.* Written, 1893. First published, 1903. In *My Theater.* Translated by Jackson Matthews. New York: Knopf, 1951.

Gray, John. *1 and 2 Kings.* Philadelphia: Westminster, 1963.

Green, Richard. *The "Sissy-Boy Syndrome" and the Development of Homosexuality.* New Haven: Yale University Press, 1984.

Greenberg, David F. *The Construction of Homosexuality.* Chicago: University of Chicago Press, 1988.

Halperin, David J. *Seeking Ezekiel: Text and Psychology.* University Park: Pennsylvania State University Press, 1993.

Halperin, David M. "Heroes and Their Pals." Pages 75–87 in *One Hundred Years of Homosexuality.* New York: Routledge, 1990.

————. *How to Do the History of Homosexuality.* Chicago: University of Chicago Press, 2002.

Henshaw, Richard A. *Female and Male: The Cultic Personnel: The Bible and the Rest of the Middle East.* Allison Park, PA: Pickwick, 1994.

Herdt, Gilbert. *The Sambia: Ritual and Gender in New Guinea.* New York: Holt, Rinehart & Winston, 1987.

————. *Third Sex, Third Gender: Beyond Sexual Dimorphism in Culture and History.* New York: Zone, 1996.

————, ed. *Ritualized Homosexuality in Melanesia.* Berkeley: University of California Press, 1984. Paperback ed., 1993.

Holladay, William A. *A Commentary on the Book of the Prophet Jeremiah.* 2 vols. Edited by Paul D. Hanson. Hermeneia. Philadelphia: Fortress, 1986–89.

Horner, Tom. *Jonathan Loved David.* Philadelphia: Westminster, 1978.

Irigaray, Luce. *An Ethics of Sexual Difference.* Translated by Carolyn Burke and Gillian Gill. Ithaca, NY: Cornell University Press, 1993.

Jennings, Theodore W., Jr. *The Man Jesus Loved: Homoerotic Narratives from the New Testament*. Cleveland: Pilgrim, 2003.

Jordan, Mark D. *The Invention of Sodomy in Christian Theology*. Chicago: University of Chicago Press, 1997.

Kaster, Joseph, ed. *The Literature and Mythology of Ancient Egypt*. London: Penguin, 1968.

Knepper, Jeanne. *Shalom to You* (A Newsletter of Shalom Ministries) 9, no. 2 (February 2001): 1.

Kuefler, Matthew. *The Manly Eunuch: Masculinity, Gender Ambiguity, and Christian Ideology in Late Antiquity*. Chicago: University of Chicago Press, 2001.

Kulick, Don. *Travesti: Sex, Gender, and Culture among Brazilian Transgendered Prostitutes*. Chicago: University of Chicago Press, 1998.

Lemche, Niels Peter. "The Old Testament—A Hellenistic Book?" *Scandinavian Journal of the Old Testament* 7, no. 2 (1993): 163–93.

Leupp, Gary. *Male Colors: The Construction of Homosexuality in Tokugawa Japan*. Berkeley: University of California Press, 1995.

Linafelt, Tod, and T. K. Beal. *Ruth and Esther*. Berit Olam. Edited by D. W. Cotter et al. Collegeville, MN: Liturgical Press, 1999.

Livy. *The History of Rome*. Books 38–39. In *Livy*. Vol. 11. Translated by Evan T. Sage. Loeb Classical Library. Cambridge: Harvard University Press, 1936.

Mann, Thomas. *Joseph and His Brethren*. Translated by H. T. Lowe-Porter. 4 vols. London: M. Secker, 1934–45.

Map, Walter. *De nugis curialium* (Courtiers' Trifles). Edited and translated by M. R. James. Revised by C. Brooke and R. Mynors. Oxford Medieval Texts. Oxford: Clarendon, 1983.

Marion, Jean Luc. *Being Given: Toward a Phenomenology of Givenness*. Translated by Jeffery L. Kosky. Chicago: University of Chicago Press, 2003.

Mays, James Luther. *Hosea: A Commentary*. Philadelphia: Westminster, 1969.

Miller, William T. *Mysterious Encounters at Mamre and Jabbok*. Brown Judaic Studies 50. Chico, CA: Scholars Press, 1984.

Mollenkott, Virginia Ramey. *The Divine Feminine: The Biblical Imagery of God as Feminine*. New York: Crossroad, 1985.

Murray, Stephen O. *Homosexualities*. Chicago: University of Chicago Press, 2000.

Nygren, Anders. *Agape and Eros*. Translated by Philip S. Watson. New York: Harper & Row, 1963.

O'Connor, Kathleen M. *The Confessions of Jeremiah*. Atlanta: Scholars Press, 1988.

Olyan, Saul M. "'And with a Male You Shall Not Lie the Lying Down of a Woman': On the Meaning and Significance of Leviticus 18:22 and 20:13." *Journal of the History of Sexuality* 5, no. 2 (1994): 179–206.

Otter, Monika. *Inventiones: Fiction and Referentiality in Twelfth-Century English Historical Writing.* Chapel Hill: University of North Carolina Press, 1996.

Otto, Walter F. *Dionysus: Myth and Cult.* Translated by R. B. Palmer. Bloomington: Indiana University Press, 1965.

Overholt, Thomas. *Cultural Anthropology and the Old Testament.* Minneapolis: Fortress, 1996.

Pardes, Ilana. "The Book of Ruth: Idyllic Revisionism." Pages 98–117 in *Countertraditions in the Bible: A Feminist Approach.* Cambridge: Harvard University Press, 1992.

Percy, William Armstrong, III. *Pederasty and Pedagogy in Archaic Greece.* Urbana: University of Illinois Press, 1996.

Petersen, William. "On the Study of 'Homosexuality' in Patristic Sources." Pages 283–88 in *Critica, classica, orientalia, ascetica, liturgica.* Edited by E. Livingstone. Studia patristica 20. Leuven: Peeters Press, 1989.

Philo. *The Special Laws.* Translated by F. H. Colson. In vol. 7 of *Philo.* Loeb Classical Library. Cambridge: Harvard University Press, 1958.

Plutarch. *Life of Lycurgus.* In *Plutarch on Sparta.* Translated by Richard J. A. Talbert. Harmondsworth: Penguin, 1988.

———. *Life of Pelopidus.* In *The Lives of the Noble Grecians and Romans.* Translated by John Dryden. Revised by Arthur Hugh Clough. New York: Modern Library, 1932. Reprint, 1992.

Prieur, Annick. *Mema's House, Mexico City: On Transvestites, Queens, and Machos.* Chicago: University of Chicago Press, 1998.

Ringrose, Kathryn M. "Living in the Shadows: Eunuchs and Gender in Byzantium." Pages 85–110 in *Third Sex, Third Gender: Beyond Sexual Dimorphism in Culture and History.* Edited by Gilbert Herdt. New York: Zone Books, 1996.

Rouselle, Aline. *Porneia: On Desire and the Body in Late Antiquity.* Translated by Felicia Pheasant. Oxford: Blackwell, 1988.

Saikaku, Ihara. *The Great Mirror of Male Love.* Translated by Paul G. Schalow. Stanford, CA: Stanford University Press, 1990.

Saslow, James M. *Ganymede in the Renaissance.* New Haven: Yale University Press, 1986.

Schifter, Jacabo. *Macho Love: Sex Behind Bars in Central America.* Binghampton, NY: Haworth Press, 2003.

Sherwood, Yvonne. *The Prostitute and the Prophet: Hosea's Marriage in Literary Theoretical Perspective.* Sheffield, UK: Sheffield University Press, 1996.

Stienstra, Nelly. *YHWH Is the Husband of His People.* Kampen, Netherlands: Kok Pharos, 1993.

Stone, Ken, ed. *Queer Commentary and the Hebrew Bible.* Sheffield, UK: Sheffield Academic Press, 2001.

Suetonius. *The Twelve Caesars.* Translated by Robert Graves and Michael Grant. Penguin Classics. Harmondsworth: Penguin, 1979.

Trible, Phyllis. *God and the Rhetoric of Sexuality.* Philadelphia: Fortress, 1978.

Walls, Neal. *Desire, Discord, and Death: Approaches to Ancient Near Eastern Myth.* Boston: American Schools of Oriental Research, 2001.

Weems, Renita J. *Battered Love: Marriage, Sex, and Violence in the Hebrew Prophets.* Philadelphia: Fortress, 1995.

Wente, Edward Frank, trans. "The Contendings of Horus and Seth." From the Chester Beatty I Papyrus. Pages 108–26 in *The Literature of Ancient Egypt: An Anthology.* Edited by William Kelly Simpson. New Haven: Yale University Press, 1973.

Westenholz, Joan Goodnick. "Tamar, Qedesa, Qadistu, and Sacred Prostitution in Mesopotamia." *Harvard Theological Review* 82, no. 3 (1989): 245–65.

Westermann, Claus. *Genesis 37–50: A Commentary.* Translated by John J. Scullion. Minneapolis: Augsburg, 1986.

Williams, Craig A. *Roman Homosexuality: Ideologies of Masculinity in Classical Antiquity.* Oxford: Oxford University Press, 1999.

Williams, Walter. *The Spirit and the Flesh: Sexual Diversity in American Indian Culture.* Boston: Beacon, 1986.

Wilson, Nancy. *Our Tribe: Queer Folks, God, Jesus, and the Bible.* San Francisco: HarperSanFrancisco, 1995.

Wintermute, Oscar S. "Joseph Son of Jacob." Pages 981–86 in vol. 2 of *Interpreters Dictionary of the Bible.* Ed. G. A. Buttrick. 4 vols. Nashville: Abingdon, 1962.

Wolff, Hans Walter. *The Anthropology of the Old Testament.* Translated by Margaret Kohl. Philadelphia: Fortress, 1974.

Xenophon. *Cyropaedia.* In *The Education of Cyrus.* Translated by Wayne Ambler. Ithaca, NY: Cornell University Press, 2001.

Yee, Gale A. *Poor Banished Children of Eve: Woman as Evil in the Hebrew Bible.* Minneapolis: Fortress, 2003.

———. "She Is Not My Wife and I Am Not Her Husband": A Materialist Analysis of Hosea 1–2." *Biblical Interpretation* 9, no. 4 (2001): 345–83.

Zend-Avesta, The. Part 1, *The Vendidad.* Translated by James Darmetester. In *Sacred Books of the East.* Vol. 4. Edited by F. Max Müller. Oxford: Clarendon, 1880. Reprint, Delhi: Motilal Banarsidass, 1965.

Zlotowitz, Meir, trans. and commentator. *Bereishis/Genesis: A New Translation with a Commentary Anthologized from Talmudic, Midrashic, and Rabbinic Sources.* Overviews by Nosson Scherman. 1st ed. 6 vols. Brooklyn, NY: Mesorah Publications,1977. 2d ed. in 2 vols., 1986.

Index